CROWN
OF THORNS

CROWN
OF THORNS

THE BITTER HISTORY OF A CENTURY'S
HEAVYWEIGHT CHAMPIONSHIP BOXING

NORMAN GILLER AND NEIL DUNCANSON

B🌱XTREE

First published in 1992 by
Boxtree Limited
36 Tavistock Street
London WC2E 7PB

10 9 8 7 6 5 4 3 2 1

Designed and edited by
Anness Publishing Limited
Boundary Row Studios
1 Boundary Row
London SE1 8HP

Colour reproduction in Hong Kong by Dai Nippon Printing Company Limited
Printed and bound in Hong Kong by Dai Nippon Printing Company Limited

A CIP catalogue record for this book is available from the British Library.

ISBN 1 85283 149 9

Editorial Director: Joanna Lorenz
Art Director: Bill Mason
Project Editor: Jennifer Jones

CONTENTS

INTRODUCTION

On September 7, 1892, James J. Corbett defeated John L. Sullivan in twenty-one rounds in the first world heavyweight championship contest in which conventional gloves were worn. *Crown of Thorns* takes an in-depth look at each and every champion in the hundred years since that memorable fight, spotlighting not only their performances but also their personalities.

Television producer Neil Duncanson has thoroughly researched *Crown of Thorns* for four years in preparation for a planned world-wide television series and this accompanying book. He and co-author Norman Giller have talked to each of the surviving old champions, and have dug up many facts and opinions that are not widely known.

And thanks to their privileged association with Mike Tyson's former manager

Bill Cayton, of Big Fights Inc, they have had exclusive access to Bill's unmatchable fight film collection and his impressive photographic library.

For many of the champions featured in *Crown of Thorns*, the winning of the title brought private and public torment that led them into personal nightmares.

JAMES J. CORBETT was hounded after taking the title from the idolized Sullivan. BOB FITZSIMMONS was arrested and charged with manslaughter after one of his sparring partners collapsed and died. JACK JOHNSON's arrogant behaviour in and out of the ring brought a backlash of racial hatred against black Americans, many of whom were lynched in after-fight riots. JAMES J. JEFFRIES saw his fortune wiped out by the Wall Street stock market crash. JACK DEMPSEY had to face taunts of being a coward when he was accused of ducking out of wartime service. MAX SCHMELING fell out with Hitler because he refused to break with his Jewish manager.

JOE LOUIS became hooked on drugs after being brought to his knees by the taxman. EZZARD CHARLES finished up in a wheelchair. SONNY LISTON was found dead in mysterious circumstances. MIKE TYSON, like Jack Johnson before him, was sent to jail after court-case sex scandals.

MUHAMMAD ALI, who ignored warnings about boxing on too long, has a daily battle with ill health. Even GENE TUNNEY, who seemed to have beaten the curse of the champions, was hit by a terrible personal tragedy when his daughter was imprisoned in a hospital for the criminally insane after murdering her husband.

The world heavyweight championship is sport's richest prize. For many of the champions who have won it, the title turned into a crown of thorns.

These are their stories.

CHAPTER ONE

JAMES J CORBETT

GENTLEMAN JIM

You may talk about your champions in
the good old days of yore
   The heroes of the prize ring in savage
mills galore,
   The gallant gladiators who battled
doggedly,
   As brave as jungle lions, and game
right to the core;
   But for splendid speed and science
none of them could compare,
   With him who holds the title now, a
true American,
   Jim Corbett of the Irish breed, the wiz-
ard boxing lad,
   Who took the fighting crown away
from John L. Sullivan!

This is a verse from a ballad they were singing
on the stages of American vaudeville theatres
one hundred years ago, after James J. Corbett
had become the world's first gloved heavyweight champion by knocking out John L.
Sullivan in the twenty-first round in New
Orleans on September 7, 1892. But while the

minstrels were singing his praises, fight fans
across the nation were screaming abuse at him.
Corbett was considered to have perpetrated the
unforgiveable in humiliating the grand old
champion, who was one of the most idolized
sportsmen in American history. Instead of a
championship to celebrate, Corbett had got himself a crown of thorns.

   It was a long time before Corbett began to
receive the universal recognition and respect
that he deserved, but now, with one hundred
years of ring history rolled out before us, there
can no longer be any doubt that James J. Corbett
was one of the all-time greats, a champion who
can comfortably carry the mantle as the father of
modern heavyweight boxing.

   Until the emergence of Corbett, heavyweight boxing was strictly for sluggers, who
fought with their bare fists under the London
Prize Ring Rules. The use of the word 'Rules' is
something of a misnomer, because they hardly
existed: fighters wrestled, mauled, punched,
kicked and gouged in savage, no-holds-barred
battles that could go on for more than one hundred rounds. The rounds ended only when one
of the gladiators went down, so they could last
for as long as ten minutes or as little as ten seconds, with half-a-minute's rest in between each
round. They were 'fights to the finish', and
ended only when one of the contestants was
unable to 'come up to scratch' – which meant
they were too badly beaten to reach the line
drawn or scratched in the middle of the ring. The
matches were so barbaric that boxing was
banned in every American state apart from
Louisiana, and most fights had to be staged at
secret venues out of sight of the police.

   Something needed to be done to restore
respectability and discipline to a sport that had
been considered the noble art in the far-off days
when the likes of Jack Broughton, James Figg
and Daniel Mendoza ruled the rings of England.
The introduction to American boxing of the
Marquess of Queensberry Rules in 1892 could
not have been better timed for James J. Corbett,
or more ill-timed for John L. Sullivan, the last of
the great bare-knuckle fighters, whose career –
including exhition contests – spanned twenty-
seven years from 1878. Suddenly, skill was to
become as big a factor as strength and stamina.

   Sullivan was a product of the 'knock 'em
down, drag 'em out' school of fighting. He was a

John L. Sullivan, the last
of the bare-knuckle
champions.

An artist's drawing of the Sullivan-Corbett fight in New Orleans on September 7, 1892.

huge barrel of a man who was as much a wrestler as boxer, and he would squeeze the resistance out of opponents with bear hugs strong enough to break a man's back. Born on October 15, 1858, in Roxbury, Boston, of Irish stock, Sullivan was a swaggering braggart who could also put action where his mouth was. He was famous for walking unheralded into saloon bars and saying at the top of his voice: 'I'll fight any sonafabitch in the house.' There were never any takers, and he would then win the affection of everybody in the place by slapping a fistful of coins on to the counter and saying: 'The drinks are on John L.'

Known from his youth as the 'Boston Strongboy', Sullivan could lift a full barrel of beer above his head as if it were a paper cup and he would often then drain the barrel dry. He was a larger-than-life-character with a dynamic personality that earned him hero status right across the United States and with people who had never been to a boxing match in their lives.

THE FIGHTING BANK CLERK

James John Corbett, like Sullivan, had Irish parents. There the similarity ends. He was born in San Francisco on September 1, 1866, and was the fourth of ten children raised by Patrick and Katherine Corbett, who had sailed from County

Mayo for the United States in 1854. James was named after an uncle who was a priest back home in Ireland. Patrick and Katherine (a McDonald from Dublin) had hoped that their son would also become a priest, but this dream died when he was expelled from the Sacred Heart College for head-butting one of the college Brothers in the stomach as he attempted to cane the young Corbett.

Like his brother Joe, Corbett's ambition was to become a major league baseball player, but he had to give up his role as a specialist second base when he split the webbing between two fingers on his right hand. He then set his sights on boxing, against the wishes of his father, who insisted he should have a 'decent and proper' job. As the owner of a livery stable and undertaking business, Patrick Corbett had a wide range of contacts and he was able to get his son a job as a messenger boy with the San Francisco branch of the Nevada Bank in 1881.

While working his way up to the position of assistant teller at the bank, Corbett took boxing instruction in the evenings from 'Professor' Walter Watson, a trainer brought over especially from Britain to coach members of the San Francisco Olympic Athletic Club. Watson quickly spotted Corbett's potential and knocked off the raw edges collected during schoolboy neighbourhood scraps. He taught him the art of feinting, the importance of a solid left jab and the advantages of quick, on-the-toes footwork. It was all far removed from the smash-and-grab tactics used by the prize fighters, and Corbett worked hard to perfect each trick and movement and introduced new ones of his own during hours of lonely training in his father's livery stable. Within a matter of months, he was knocking over the best boxers in the club. He became the Olympic Athletic Club middleweight champion and then heavyweight champion, even though he was barely seventeen and weighed less than 170 pounds. He was so far advanced of other boxers in the club that they started to bring in professionals for exhibition matches, and he got the better of all of them.

In what he later described as 'a mad act of youth', Corbett walked out on his bank job in 1884 and ran away to Salt Lake City with his sweetheart, Olive Lake, and another teenage couple. They all lied about their ages to a Justice of the Peace, who married them. Eight years later this marriage would cost Corbett two New York houses and a huge cash payment in a divorce settlement so that he could marry Vera Taylor, who he met in Kansas City while acting on stage in a touring play. Vera was to be his wife for thirty-eight years.

Corbett kept his first bride and himself fed and in lodgings by taking on challenge contests, first under the name of English heavyweight Charlie Mitchell and then as the original Jack Dempsey, a magificent middleweight with whom he had more than held his own during sparring sessions at the Olympic Club. He won each of the contests, but the money soon ran out and when his father finally tracked him down he agreed to return home to a clerical job with the Anglo-Nevada Insurance Company.

THE BATTLE OF THE BARGE

Throughout his amateur career, Corbett had a running feud with a rival from the California Athletic Club called Joe Choynski, who was now a successful professional. Patrick Corbett refused to give permission for his son to box Choynski in a professional club contest, but gave his blessing to him fighting for nothing but his pride in a bout secretly arranged for a barn on a farm ten miles outside San Francisco on May 30, 1889. It was hardly a well-kept secret and thousands of

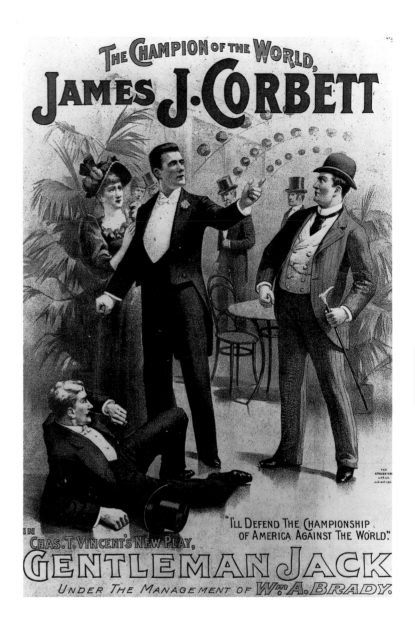

dollars were wagered on the outcome. A wealthy supporter gave Corbett $500 to put on himself to win, but nobody would take the bet.

The two twenty-year-old warriors were into the sixth round of their battle in the barn loft when the local sheriff broke them up, and it was a week later before they could continue the fight – on a barge in the middle of San Francisco Bay. Corbett had broken his right thumb in their abandoned match, and he knew he was going to have to fight a one-handed contest. The bout had been arranged as a 'glove fight', but Choynski arrived on the barge without his gloves. He finally came to the centre of the ring wearing a pair of kidskin riding gloves provided by one of his backers, which had three heavy seams running down across the knuckles.

A poster for the stage play *Gentleman Jack*. Corbett toured with the play in the United States and Britain.

Jim Corbett and his trainers running on Beach 1894 -

An early photograph showing Corbett and his training team taking a brisk walk along a beach in 1894 while preparing for the contest against Peter Courtney.

Early on in the fight Corbett crashed a left jab against Choynski's lowered head and broke two knuckles on his left hand. He was now having to rely on his footwork to get himself out of trouble, and he kept steering his opponent to the corner of the ring where the blinding sun was continually in Choynski's eyes. More by accident than design, Corbett introduced a new punch that had not been seen in the ring before – the left hook. He was unable to land with the full left jab because of the pain, and so he took to throwing his fist on an arc and Choynski had no defence to it as the curving punch continually thudded against the side of his head.

Choynski's nose was soon broken from the attention of the left hooks, and Corbett's face was a mass of red weals where his opponent was landing with his seamed gloves. The vastly experienced cornerman Billy Delaney, who had taken over as Corbett's trainer, kept shouting from the corner: 'Throw the right now, Jim. Let the right go.' Corbett would respond by letting go with a haymaker right with which he would deliberately miss. It was all a subterfuge to stop Choynski realizing Corbett could not use his right hand.

With both fighters showing phenomenal strength and courage, they battled through twenty-eight punishing rounds before Corbett gambled everything on a full-power left hook to Choynski's jaw. He went down as though shot and the ten second count was a formality to end what Billy Delaney described as the fiercest fight

he had ever seen in his life. The two exhausted boxers were carried to a waiting tug to be taken back to shore, and they lay side by side in the cabin, shaking hands with each other and smiling through their bruised lips. It turned a feud into a friendship that would last the rest of their lives, and when Choynski became an instructor at the Pittsburgh Athletic Club Corbett was a regular visitor.

From the tug, both of them were taken to a Turkish bath, where they sat for seven hours with their blistered feet in pails of hot water and their hands encased in ice buckets. Apart from the cuts and bruises, all that the triumphant Corbett had to show for his effort was the $500 that he had been given to bet with, and a new punch, the left hook.

ALL IN THE MIND

A straight, stand-up fighter in the English style, Corbett was a pioneer of scientific boxing as opposed to the old-style, two-handed slugging. He made a study of every opponent, noting their strengths and then working out tactics to nullify them. His objective was to take as few punches as possible while handing out punishment himself, scoring heavily with both hands before dancing just out of range of the counterattack. Corbett also paid close attention to the pyschological side of his sport, and would set out to goad any opponent he thought apprehensive about fighting him. He had a different plan of campaign for every fight, and always tried to impose his will on his opponent. 'Boxing,' he said, 'is as much about being stronger in your mind than your opponent as being physically stronger.'

With slim hands that looked more suited to playing the piano, Corbett was not an imposing man physically. He stood just over 6 foot 1 inch, and rarely weighed much more than 168 pounds (12 stone). On February 18, 1890, he gave 18 pounds and a good hiding to former bare-knuckle title contender Jake Kilrain, of Massachusetts, comfortably outpointing him over six rounds. It was a victory that brought Corbett to national prominence because just eight months earlier Kilrain had given the world champion, John L. Sullivan, his toughest battle.

In May the following year Corbett astonished the boxing world by agreeing to take on Peter Jackson, the black Australian-based West Indian who many rate the greatest fighter never to be allowed to challenge for the world championship (Sullivan had drawn the 'colour line'

with Jackson, saying crudely in what were not enlightened times: 'I don't fight niggers'). Nobody gave Corbett a chance against the exceptionally powerful and talented Jackson, but after sixty fierce rounds most ringsiders thought he was on top. The referee, Hiram Cook, left the ring during the sixtieth round and talked to some gamblers who had backed Jackson, and in the next round he suddenly stopped the action and announced: 'No contest. All bets off.' It went down in the record books as a draw, but Jackson collapsed as he left the ring and it was unlikely that he could have lasted another round.

Corbett was robbed not only of victory but also of much of his purse for the Jackson fight. He had been promised $10,000, but was paid only $2,500. When his supporters heard how he had been short-changed, they organized a testimonial evening five weeks later and invited John L. Sullivan to box an exhibition with their man. Sullivan agreed only on the understanding that they would box in full evening dress. The one concession Sullivan made on the night was to remove his coat before climbing into the ring, which had been set up on the stage

Corbett and Courtney shape up before the start of their contest in front of inventor Thomas Edison's revolutionary Kinetograph. Corbett and Edison later battled in court over the copyright of the film.

Fitzsimmons looks on
as Corbett takes the
count after being
floored by the famous
solar plexus punch, on
St Patrick's Day, 1897.

at San Francisco's Grand Opera House. Corbett took the opportunity to weigh up the world champion as they sparred for four rounds and at the end of the session he announced to his trainer, Billy Delaney: 'I can whip this fellow.'

A CHALLENGE FROM JOHN L

With the money received from the Jackson fight and the testimonial, Corbett set up his brother Harry in a restaurant called Corbett's, which became a popular landmark in San Francisco for many years. Corbett was always generous with his money. With another of his purses, he cleared his father's mortgage on his livery stable business and sent his parents on a holiday back home in Ireland. He was also known to pay for the weddings and funerals of friends.

Corbett was not only a pioneer of the boxing arts, but also the first champion to appreciate the value of being properly marketed. He teamed up with a boyhood pal called William Brady, who had become a successful theatrical producer. Brady got to work creating an image

for Corbett, and took him on a coast-to-coast exhibition tour and offered to pay $100 to anybody who could go four rounds with him. There was never any need to pay the money. Corbett had always been a snappy dresser, but under Brady's influence he became a real dandy and the 'Gentleman Jim' nickname was born.

With his full Irish background, Corbett was a natural talker and Brady started to prepare him for a second career on the stage. He commissioned a boxing play to be written specially for him called *Gentleman Jack*. 'We'll go on tour with this after you've won the world championship,' said Brady. He and Corbett were in a minority of two who thought that Corbett could beat the unbeatable Sullivan.

Corbett was just beginning to despair of ever getting into the ring for real with Sullivan when he was astonished to read a newspaper advertisement in which the champion challenged him! Sullivan named Charlie Mitchell, Frank Slavin and Corbett in the advert, insulting each of them in turn and stating whichever one of them was first to come up with a $10,000 side-stake could have first crack at his title.

'Gentleman' Jim with
his second wife, Vera.

Corbett and Sullivan come face to face again, twenty years after their historic battle.

Corbett, who always moved in social club rather than saloon bar circles, went to his well-heeled supporters and raised the money in a few hours, even though most of his best friends did not consider him in with a ghost of a chance of mastering the old champion. A week before the fight, which was scheduled to be staged at the New Orleans Olympic Club on September 7, 1892, some of his backers lost their confidence, considering him too light, but he satisfied them by scaling a heaviest-ever 197 pounds at a private weigh in. Hidden inside his pockets were lead weights. On the day of the fight he weighed just 178 pounds (12 stone 7 pounds) and was conceding 34 pounds to the champion, who looked as if he was carrying excess baggage around his midriff. It was obvious that he was counting out the challenger before a punch had been thrown.

Although Corbett was dismissed as a 'bombastic bluffer' by Sullivan, he was convinced he could take the title. He said in later years in a revealing interview that underlined his attention to detail: 'I knew Sullivan liked to bulldoze everybody, and I knew he would try bullying me. For a long time before the fight I concentrated day and night on a plan whereby I could dominate Sullivan instead of having him dominate me. I determined to ignore his bullying and to give him a style of boxing that would enrage him to such an extent that he would be practically helpless. I was in no hurry to land a blow, but I was determined that when I did land

it would be a punch of such power and ferocity that it would make Sullivan believe I could hit as well as he could.'

Corbett followed his plan to perfection. For the first two rounds he did not throw a single telling punch as he tantalized and tormented Sullivan with clever side-stepping, slipping and weaving. The champion kept making bull-like charges only to find himself punching the challenger's shadow. The spectators were jeering Corbett's tactics, and as he skipped away from a Sullivan attack he cheekily dropped his hands to his sides and shouted to the ringsiders: 'Just wait a while ... you'll see a fight.'

Midway through the third round Corbett put stage two of his plan into operation. He suddenly stood his ground as Sullivan made one of his rushes and threw his first punch of the fight, a jolting left that broke the champion's nose as it landed flush on target. The champion was almost purple with rage, and the madder he got the more elusive Corbett became. Eight years older than Corbett and out of condition, Sullivan started to puff and blow like a wounded bull as he chased the challenger around the ring, throwing the sort of punches that had crushed previous opponents but which were now hitting thin air. Under London Prize Ring Rules, he would have been able to throw his young tormentor out of the ring after hugging the resistance out of him, but in this 'damn fangled' new gloved era he had to rely purely on punches. He was flat-footed coming out for the twenty-first round and the challenger saw his opportunity to finish the fight. He stopped him in his tracks with a huge left hook and then followed up with a barrage of punches that sent the idolized old champion sinking slowly to the canvas. Apart from the cheers of Corbett's supporters, the crowd was stunned into silence and the count over Sullivan was like a funeral chant. For most Americans the result was unbelieveable, and Corbett suddenly found himself about as popular as the man who shot Jesse James in the back. This extract from a leader article in *The World* the day after the fight was typical of the press coverage that his victory received:

'He (Corbett) has robbed the country of a very striking individual. If he had gone to Switzerland with a shovel and dug away Mont Blanc he could not have hurt the feelings of the Swiss more than he has damaged the feelings of hundreds of thousands of Americans ... It is unquestionably true that he is a very gentlemanly young man and a remarkably gentlemanly fighter, but we do not want gentlemanly fighters. We want a fighter to be nothing at all on this earth but a fighter ... As long as he breathes, this upstart Corbett will not be half the man that Sullivan is. Anybody who knows anything about prize fighting will tell you that there can be nobody fit to follow John L.

Corbett is certainly not that fellow.'

Corbett faced a storm of ridicule and contemptuous indifference from sports followers, but he was intelligent enough to understand the feelings of the public, who loved Sullivan like a favourite son. He shrugged his shoulders, collected his $25,000 purse and his $20,000 side-stake and got on with his acting career. He travelled

Left: Corbett, in later life, as a sportswriter.

the length and breadth of the United States with the play *Gentleman Jack*, and his performances won greater acclaim than his meticulously planned victory over Sullivan.

Below: Corbett in a musical scene from his successful play, *Gentleman Jack*.

Errol Flynn, playing the part of Corbett in the film *Gentleman Jim* (1942), poses in front of a poster advertising a John L. Sullivan stage production.

CHAMPION OF THE WORLD

The public started to give Corbett grudging acceptance when he knocked out the English challenger, Charlie Mitchell, in three rounds in Jacksonville on January 25, 1894. Mitchell made the mistake of getting Corbett riled by keeping him waiting in the ring for an hour and then hitting him with a stream of verbal insults. The man from Birmingham thought his needling tactics would undermine the champion's confidence, but all they did was stoke up the Corbett furnace. He abandoned his usual hit-and-run strategy and went for a knockout right from the start. In the third round Corbett connected so hard with a right to the jaw that he was confidently having his gloves removed before the count was completed. When he came round Mitchell said: 'I got him too damn mad.' After the fight both champion and challenger were arrested for causing a breach of the peace. Three months later a jury selected by the boxers took just 9 minutes to return a verdict of not guilty.

Corbett then took his *Gentleman Jack* play on a tour of Great Britain and got a hero's welcome wherever he appeared. He was treated more like a world champion than at home in the United States, where they were only slowly starting to forgive him for beating Sullivan. The enterprising and imaginative William Brady had a giant, 24-foot wide poster printed that showed Corbett shaking hands with the British Prime Minister, William Gladstone, and surrounded by all the kings and queens of Europe. Underneath was the caption: 'James J. Corbett, Champion of the World, on his triumphal return from Europe.' Brady swamped the major American cities with copies of the poster, giving the impression that Corbett had been mixing in distinguished and royal circles. It gave 'Gentleman Jim' new standing with the public, who were not to know that while in Europe he did not meet a single person featured on the poster.

On September 7, 1894 – two years to the day that he had taken the title from Sullivan – Corbett knocked out Peter Courtney in six rounds of a match organized for the benefit of Thomas Edison's revolutionary Kinetoscope. (The champion later clashed in a bout of legal fisticuffs with Edison over the copyright of the film.) However, despite the introduction of the Marquess of Queensberry Rules, boxing had still not taken on a cloak of respectability, and when Corbett fought Tom 'The Fighting Sailor' Sharkey on June 24, 1896, the San Francisco chief of police stopped the fight in the fourth round and the result was announced as a draw.

FITZSIMMONS TAKES OVER

By the mid-1890s, a new challenger had emerged in the shape of English-born world middleweight champion Bob Fitzsimmons, but after two attempts to promote the fight had been prevented by state laws, Corbett announced his retirement in 1895 and he named Irishman Peter Maher as his successor. Fitzsimmons showed his contempt for this arrogant decision by knocking Maher cold in one round in Langtry, Texas, on February 21, 1896. Corbett had no alternative but to resume his career and he put his title on the line against Fitzsimmons in Carson City on St Patrick's Day, 1897, a sensational contest that is featured in the next chapter (see page 24). Following his fourteenth-round knockout defeat by Fitzsimmons, Corbett split with Brady, who had taken over the management of his former sparring partner James J. Jeffries.

On November 22, 1898, Corbett returned to the ring in New York and lost on a disqualification against Tom Sharkey when one of his second's jumped into the ring in the ninth round to protest about the brawling sailor's rough-house tactics. Corbett decided to base himself in New York, and in 1899 he opened a successful café on Broadway, and appeared in the lead role at the nearby Daly's Theatre in George Bernard Shaw's *Cashel Byron's Profession*, the story of a scientific boxer who masters his slugging rival to become champion. It had been written twenty years before Corbett's scientist-versus-slugger victory over Sullivan.

Corbett kept calling for a return with Fitzsimmons, but Jeffries was given first crack at the title and he was one of his seconds when the 'Fighting Boilermaker' won the championship in 1899. On May 11, 1900, he challenged Jeffries for the title and, ironically, received more praise from the press in defeat than he ever had in victory over Sullivan. For twenty rounds he made Jeffries seem about as mobile as a statue as he boxed rings round him, but then his lack of conditioning began to tell and Corbett was knocked out when he walked into a swinging left in the twenty-third round.

Three months later he was involved in a controversial contest with former world middleweight champion Charles 'Kid' McCoy, who was stopped in the fifth round amid allegations that the fight was fixed. Always a trend setter, Corbett was one of the first sportsmen to have his autobiography published and in *Roar of the Crowd* he states:

> 'This accusation (that the fight was a fake) hurt me more than anything that had ever been said about me or done to me in my life, for I certainly saw no evidence of McCoy's reported efforts to "lay down"; and he fought very hard in the fight. And I knew that I gave to the public the best that was in me. Ever since I started in boxing it had been one of my aims, in addition to making something of myself, to elevate the sport; and I believe I have a host of supporters who will substantiate me in that claim. I had bluffed my opponents sometimes, but it was beyond me ever to descend to fixing a fight.'

A FINAL FLING

At the age of thirty-eight and after three years out of the ring, Corbett had one last fling. He challenged Jeffries for the championship in his home town, San Francisco, on August 14, 1903. Again he gave Jeffries a boxing lesson, but then the strength deserted Corbett's legs and, after having two ribs broken, he could not take the champion's swinging punches to the body. Corbett was knocked out in the tenth round and later announced that he was hanging up his gloves.

It was only in retirement that Corbett at last started to get the appreciation he deserved for having brought science and skill to the boxing ring, and he became an authority on the sport while a regular radio broadcaster and syndicated journalist. In a 1942 biopic on his life, *Gentleman Jim*, he was portrayed by Errol Flynn. It was not the best bit of casting because, unlike Flynn, Corbett was a near-teetotaller and faithful to his second wife for nearly forty years until his death from cancer at Bayside, New York, on February 18, 1933.

More than 2,000 mourners tried to crowd into the 700-capacity church for Corbett's funeral service. 'There were just prizefighters before Corbett,' said former champion Jess Willard. 'He put science into fighting, and was in every sense of the word a gentleman.'

'Gentleman' Jim, still a dandy at the age of sixty-three.

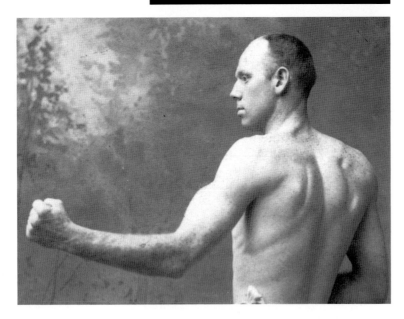

CHAPTER TWO

BOB FITZSIMMONS

THE FRECKLED FREAK

The inhabitants of the picturesque Cornish village of Helston got up a petition in the winter of 1870 to try to persuade their blacksmith, James Fitzsimmons, to change his mind about emigrating. But he said that he wanted better opportunities for his children, and a lot of tears were shed as he and his wife, Jane, the village nurse, set off with their family for a new life in far-off New Zealand. Making the long sea journey with them was their eight-year-old son, Robert, who would one day create history as the first British-born heavyweight champion of the world.

The Fitzsimmons family went first to Christchurch before moving on to the South Canterbury fishing port of Timaru, which had become such a favourite settling place for Cornish immigrants that it was known as 'tin town'. It was here that young Bob started work helping his father and older brother in their blacksmith's forge; he developed an immense, heavily-muscled upper body that looked out of place on his spindly, freckled legs, and his unusual appearance would become something of a trademark in the years to come.

THUNDER DOWN UNDER

Most record books give the birthdate of Fitzsimmons as June 4, 1862, but boxing buff Derek O'Dell has traced his birth certificate, which clearly gives May 26, 1862, as the date. 'Fitz' started fighting for fun at the age of fifteen. He was then introduced to the skills of boxing by Jem 'The Gypsy' Mace, a master of the bare-knuckle boxing arts from Norwich in Britain, who sailed to New Zealand to tour the country giving lessons and exhibitions. Fitzsimmons won two open competitions that Mace organized, and he was so impressed by the boy's natural ability and punching power that he encouraged him to consider becoming a prize fighter.

Mace was grooming a Maori heavyweight called Herbert Slade (who was later knocked out by John L. Sullivan), and decided to test him against Fitzsimmons, who was 42 pounds lighter than Slade. When Mace stopped the bout in the second round to save the outgunned Slade from an embarrassing hiding, the head-strong, eighteen-year-old Fitzsimmons lost his temper and challenged the old master to fight him instead. Mace, then the reigning bare-knuckle champion of the world, was all set to accept the rash challenge until bystanders calmed him down and pointed out that he could not possibly fight such an inexperienced boy.

Even when he was just a welterweight, Fitzsimmons was knocking out heavyweights, and after winning the New Zealand amateur championship, he set off for Australia at the beginning of 1890 to spread his thunder down under as a professional pugilist. He had no money for the passage, and so smuggled himself aboard the schooner *Botany Bay* and arrived in Sydney as a stowaway.

'Fitz' had been fighting with his bare fists to London Prize Ring Rules in New Zealand, but switched to gloved boxing under Queensberry Rules in Australia, where, in between working as a blacksmith, he began to build a reputation for himself as an accomplished box-fighter. So much so that his supporters found it hard to believe when he was knocked out in four rounds by Jem Hall in Sydney on February 12, 1890. Fitzsimmons later claimed that he had taken a dive to help pull off a gambling coup, which gave him sufficient money to sail to the United States without having to stow away again.

Fitzsimmons demonstrates his old blacksmith skills, helped by his sparring partner Bob Armstrong. This picture was taken in 1893 when 'Fitz' was preparing for a non-title fight with Jem Hall. Fitzsimmons alleged he threw their first fight together, but he avenged the defeat with a fourth-round knockout victory.

The Americans found it difficult to take him seriously when he arrived in California at the age of twenty-eight to continue his career. With his small head virtually bald apart from a bright red fringe over his ears and his knock-kneed stance, he just did not look like a fighter. The Californian Athletic Club insisted on him having a trial before they would consider putting him on one of their shows. They matched him in the gymnasium with one of their outstanding middleweights, Frank Allen. Fitzsimmons knocked him out in under two minutes, and his final right landed with such force that Allen did a somersault and broke a wrist as he landed on the canvas.

The officials of the Club were sufficiently impressed to pair him just twelve days later with Billy McCarthy, an Australian who was rated the second best middleweight in the world.

McCarthy made the grave error of getting Fitzsimmons mad by calling him a 'bald-headed kangaroo.' 'Fitz' floored him in the first minute and battered him to a standstill in five rounds. 'I guess I got the kangaroo hopping mad,' joker McCarthy said later.

There were still a lot of people too ready to laugh at his appearance, but he silenced the cynics by knocking out Jack 'the Nonpareil' Dempsey to win the world middleweight title in thirteen rounds on January 14, 1891. 'Fitz' won every round against the fighter many Americans considered the supreme ring master (William Harrison Dempsey took his name when he launched his career as a heavyweight). The champion was floored fourteen times before his seconds threw in the sponge.

During the next two years 'Fitz' saw off all the leading middleweights before setting his

The outdoor ring at Carson City, Nevada, with Fitzsimmons (the boxer on the left) and Corbett (on the right) meeting to battle it out for the world heavyweight title.

sights on the heavyweight championship. On June 17, 1894, he was giving James Corbett's old rival Joe Choynski a hiding when police stopped the contest in the fifth round.

Fitzsimmons had his final fight as a middleweight on September 26, 1894, when he defended his world title by knocking out Dan Creedon in two rounds, and he then started issuing challenges to Corbett. In the meantime, Fitzsimmons married Rose Julian, his second wife and the sister of his manager, Martin Julian, who promptly married Fitzsimmons's first wife! 'Fitz' then applied for United States citizenship, which made the Americans less twitchy about the possibility of losing the world heavyweight crown to a foreigner.

A TRAGIC DEATH

Fitzsimmons was just becoming accepted as something more than a freak fighter when he found himself on the front pages of all the newspapers for the wrong reasons. He had been arrested and charged with manslaughter in the first degree, after an opponent died during an exhibition contest in the Opera House at Syracuse on November 19, 1894. If he was found guilty, it would mean a twenty-year jail sentence. The dead boxer, Con Riordan, had been drinking heavily before the bout and had literally staggered on to the stage to take his turn in the ring with Fitzsimmons. They had been sparring for about a minute when 'Fitz' landed a light right to the side of Riordan's jaw. He collapsed to the floor with the spectators hissing and booing and shouting 'fake'. Riordan was helped from the ring and died in hospital six hours later.

Fitzsimmons was immediately arrested, and he cried in court the next day when charged with manslaughter in the first degree. He was granted bail of $10,000. 'Fitz' broke down as he told the court: 'He was my friend. I would not have killed him for $100,000.'

Later he told reporters: 'Do you suppose I would have hit my sparring partner with any sort of force in an exhibition match? I knew that Con had been drinking heavily, but did not realize he was in such a bad condition. Invariably when I sparred with him he would turn blue around the mouth and it was a sign for me to let up.

'As God is my judge, I never struck him hard. I noticed after the first exchange of blows that he was not right. The blow I delivered that caused the trouble was just a light slap. He fell down and then rose and staggered around the stage before falling headlong. I thought he was faking, and was thoroughly disgusted because spectators in the house were hissing me. I have never been hissed before.

'I began to comprehend a few minutes later that there was something wrong with Con, and I was horrified to discover he was still unconscious. I attributed this to his drunken condition, thinking he would soon revive from the stupor. I have known Con for eight years, and he was always a hard drinker. Being in poor condition I presume he had developed some sort of heart problem that brought on the disaster. It makes my blood run cold to think that they would try to lay that poor man's death at my door.'

It took seven months before Fitzsimmons was brought to trial. During the wait he paid for Riordan's funeral out of his own pocket after the deceased's family had failed to claim the body. The trial lasted nine days and the jury acquitted the world middleweight champion after hearing the defence make out a strong medical case that Riordan had died from apoplexy and not from the effects of the punch on the jaw. Fitzsimmons's supporters let off fireworks in celebration as the verdict was announced.

Four months after his aquittal, Fitzsimmons was arrested again, this time on his way to Hot Springs to challenge Corbett for the world heavyweight title. The Governor of Arkansas ruled that he was breaking state laws in attempting to fight. Corbett called Fitzsimmons a dunderhead for getting himself caught and announced that he was retiring, and he took the unorthodox step of naming Irish heavyweight Peter Maher as his successor as world champion.

This announcement did not go down well with Fitzsimmons, who had knocked out Maher in twelve rounds in 1892. They agreed to a rematch for a $10,000 purse, but when they arrived at the site for the fight in Langtry, Texas, they found a posse of Texas Rangers waiting with orders to stop them fighting. However, Judge Roy Bean, a friend of the promoter and a fight fan, and the most famous law enforcer in Texas, came up with a novel solution to save the contest. While all the fighters' connections

adjourned to the Jersey Lily saloon – owned by Judge Roy Bean – a team of hired hands erected a ring just across the border in Mexico. The boxers, the fight officials and more than two hundred supporters then walked over a pontoon bridge that had been thrown across the Rio Grande. Bat Masterson, the marshal of Dodge City and a boxing fanatic, stood at the entrance to the tent with six-shooters drawn to discourage any would-be troublemakers.

The fight lasted just over a minute. Fitzsimmons sidestepped a left lead from Maher and threw a right counter that landed flush on the jaw and stretched the Irishman out on the canvas. It was the only contest on the bill. Never in sporting history has so much trouble been taken for such little action.

There was more action after the fight, this time involving a stampede by the spectators. Fitzsimmons's manager, Martin Julian, was standing in the centre of the ring making a

Corbett parries an attack by Fitzsimmons during their world title fight in 1897.

Fitzsimmons (right) throws a long right to set up his whirlwind first-round victory over Peter Maher in a make-shift ring just across the border in Mexico on February 21, 1896.

referee's decision was final. Who was going to argue with Wyatt Earp and his gun?

THE SOLAR PLEXUS PUNCH

On March 17, 1897, James J. Corbett came out of retirement to defend his title against Fitzsimmons at Carson City, Nevada. It was the fourth time that promoters had tried to get the two of them together in the same ring.

At thirty-five, Fitzsimmons was four years older than the champion, who arrogantly dismissed his challenger as 'an over-rated nobody'. Corbett's total confidence in his ability to win seemed justified in the first six rounds of the fight as he gave Fitzsimmons a boxing lesson, threading a procession of jabs through his guard and flooring him for a count of nine with a slashing left hook in the sixth. According to who you believe, Fitzsimmons was conceding 20 pounds in weight (his version) or 8 pounds (Corbett's version). Whatever the weight difference, 'Fitz' looked outpowered and in terrible trouble. But from the seventh round on, he switched his attack to the body and the champion suddenly started to run out of strength and stamina. At the end of the thirteenth round, Fitzsimmons was so confident of scoring an upset victory that he told his wife, Rose (sitting by his corner in the role of adviser), to bet everything she could on him ending the fight in the fourteenth.

As Fitzsimmons went out for the start of the fourteenth, Rose shouted: 'Hit him in the slats, Bob'. This referred to the rib area, and early in the round 'Fitz' followed her advice. He switched his stance to southpaw, feinted with a right to the chin and then threw a straight left that corkscrewed deep into Corbett's stomach just below the diaphragm and knocked the breath out of him. Corbett sank slowly to the canvas and took the count on his knees. The ringside doctor told reporters: 'The punch landed in the solar plexus and took Corbett's breath away.' Fitzsimmons had invented what became known as the solar plexus punch.

Four months after he had won the title, an imaginative attempt to get Fitzsimmons to box six rounds with the old war horse John L. Sullivan in Ambrose Park, Brooklyn, was stopped by the police, who stepped between the two boxers as they climbed into the ring. So that

speech about the plans for 'Fitz' to be a fighting champion when there was a crashing sound from the direction of the Rio Grande. A rushing current was threatening to sweep the pontoon bridge away, and Fitzsimmons led the mad scramble back across the bridge to Texas. There has never been a fight night quite like it.

Fitzsimmons – variously nicknamed 'Ruby Robert', 'Freckled Bob' and the 'Lanky Cornishman' – seemed unable to avoid controversy. On December 2 that same year he was disqualified against Tom Sharkey in the eighth round in San Francisco. He had knocked Sharkey down and out with a perfectly fair body punch, but the referee – none other than Marshal Wyatt Earp – ruled that it was low. There was a riot among ringside gamblers and as Fitzsimmons rushed towards the referee to protest the decision Earp drew his six-shooter and ordered him out of the ring. Manager Julian went to court to contest the decision, but the judge ruled that the

the crowd of several thousand did not go away without seeing any action, 'Fitz' wrestled for ten minutes with his friend Greco-Roman champion Ernest Roeber.

Fitzsimmons then went on the road with a touring vaudeville show, which was not the best way to prepare for boxing at world championship level. He was not in the peak of condition when he lost the title to James J. Jeffries in his first defence at Coney Island on June 9, 1899, breaking the knuckles on both his hands against the granite-hard challenger, who outweighed him by 64 pounds. He was knocked out in the eleventh round, and caved in to defeat in the eighth round in a return match in San Francisco on July 25, 1902.

Sixteen months later, at the age of forty-one, Fitzsimmons became the first boxer to win

Fitzsimmons, a creaking veteran of forty-seven, ran out of steam against Australian Bill Lang in Sydney in 1909 and was stopped in the twelfth.

Fitzsimmons in 1910,
looking prosperous
before all his money
ran out.

three world titles at different weights when he outpointed George Gardner to take the newly introduced light-heavyweight championship. He lost it two years later in 1905 to 'Philadelphia' Jack O'Brien.

THE METHUSELLAH OF BOXING

The crown of thorns? Fitzsimmons managed to go through a small fortune, being parted from much of his money by three wives. He was desperately depressed by the death of his second wife, Rose, but then just a few months later, in 1903, 'Fitz' shocked his family by marrying eighteen-year-old Julia Gifford after a whirlwind romance. She moved in with him and his three children on a 47-acre farm in Dunellen, New Jersey. They broke up after eight years and Julia, who became an actress and singer, told the press: 'It was like living with two people. He could be wonderfully kind and considerate and very humorous, but when the whisky got to him he was evil and frightening. It got to the stage when his drinking got so out of control that I could not live with him anymore. We could have had a wonderful life together if it had not been for the whisky.'

Fitzsimmons was very bitter in his last years because he felt he had been cheated out of much of his money. His biggest purse should have been $40,000 for a return match with Jem Hall, who beat him in an allegedly fixed fight on February 12, 1890. He knocked out Hall in four rounds in New Orleans in 1893, but saw less than half of his promised purse.

On July 17, 1907, nineteen months after losing the world light-heavyweight title, he was knocked out in two rounds in Philadelphia by a fighter they were all dodging – Jack Johnson. In a desperate bid to scrape some money together he had four more contests before finally hanging up his gloves at the age of fifty-two – the Methusellah of boxing.

A year after his final fight he got married again, this time to a French woman who was fanatically dedicated to evangelism, and she got Fitzsimmons interested in the work of the church and the word of the Lord. He continued to appear in vaudeville, and after shows he used to try to preach to autograph hunters. It was while appearing on a drafty stage in his adopted home town of Chicago that he caught double pneumonia from which Fitzsimmons died on October 22, 1917.

There was an undignified scene as he lay in his coffin. His son Robert Jr. arrived from a hunting holiday too late to see his father before he died, and then he had a blazing row with Mrs Fitzsimmons in front of several eyewitnesses. He stormed out of the house where his father was laying and told waiting journalists: 'I will not be attending my father's funeral. I don't care to have anything more to do with his burial, or with his widow. I'm going to finish my deer hunt. I'm not welcome here. I have disagreed with my father's widow about his personal effects, most of which cannot be found. It's a mystery to me where all his money and prizes have disappeared to. Then I wanted to carry out my father's wish and have him cremated, but she has made up her mind to have things done her way. As the law is on her side, I'm going to beat it and forget.

'I have a lock of my dad's hair in my pocket, the return end of a round trip railroad ticket in my wallet, and a deer waiting for my gun. I'm off.'

Mrs Fitzsimmons said: 'I am so distressed by this. There are no diamonds or hidden riches that young Bob talks about. Everything has been pawned or sold. My husband was not always provident but he meant all right. He was a good, God-fearing husband but he left me with nothing.

'His one fear in his last years was that he did not want to have a pauper's funeral like so many former boxers. I have saved enough for him to have a decent burial.'

Fitzsimmons was carried to his final resting place at Graceland cemetary in Chicago by six former boxers. The fourth Mrs Fitzsimmons was the only member of his family at the funeral.

His old rival James J. Jeffries said from his ranch in California: 'Bob was a great old general. I can speak of him only in the best of terms. We were together here on my ranch only a couple of months ago chewing over the good old days. He was one of my best friends and I am deeply sorry that he has gone.'

'Honest' John Kelly, one of the prominent referees of the time, sent a telegram that read: WE HAVE LOST THE GREATEST MAN THE PROFESSION OF BOXING HAS EVER KNOWN. MY DEEPEST SYMPATHY.

CHAPTER THREE

JAMES J JEFFRIES

THE FIGHTING BOILERMAKER

If only Jim Jeffries had followed his first instinct and turned a deaf ear to the calls for an American 'white hope' he would have gone down in the history books as the first world heavyweight champion to retire undefeated. Instead, he allowed himself to be talked into carrying the heavy expectancy of white America into a doomed comeback contest for his old world title, which had passed into the hands of the widely despised black champion, Jack Johnson. As a result, Jeffries took a dreadful beating, which no doubt accounted for his health problems later in life.

Until his defeat by Johnson, Jeffries was considered the supreme champion, who was renowned more for his strength than his skill. One of his nicknames, the 'Californian Grizzly Bear', was well earned. Before challenging Bob Fitzsimmons for the title in only his thirteenth fight in 1899, he walked into the champion's dressing-room, pretending that he wanted to wish him luck. When Fitzsimmons reached out to shake his hand, Jeffries grabbed him in a bear hug and squeezed with all his might. It was his

way of letting old Bob know that he could not match his enormous strength.

An hour earlier his manager, William Brady, who had steered Corbett to the title, had called 'Fitz' into the challenger's dressing-room on the pretext that he wanted to discuss the rules. Brady had persuaded 'Fitz' to give Jeffries a crack at the championship, stressing that it would be a pushover because his man was fat and flabby. When Fitzsimmons walked into the dressing-room the first thing he saw was the 6-foot 2.5-tall Jeffries draped naked on a leather couch, looking as if he had been sculpted by Michelangelo. Jeffries' conniving manager said later: 'Bob's nerve went from that moment. He was expecting an easy fight against an out-of-condition novice, and here he found his challenger looking like a Greek god. We had deliberately kept them apart at the weigh in so that Bob could not see that Jeffries had whipped himself into the best shape of his life.'

Proving that it is as much pyschology as punches that win fights, Jeffries went on to batter Fitzsimmons to defeat in eleven rounds; yet he lost money, because he laid out $5,000 on Fitzsimmons to retain his title so that he would have some consolation if he was beaten.

THE CROUCHING CHAMPION

Born in Carroll, Ohio, on April 15, 1875, James Jackson Jeffries was the son of a Methodist preacher, who took his wife and ten children to California when Jeffries was seven. His father, who was from an English-Scottish background, was a pacificist who frowned on violence and found it hard to come to terms with his son's love of wrestling and fighting when he was a schoolboy. It was his mother who explained where Jeffries' aggression came from: 'My maternal Grandpa Boyer was renowned as one of the strongest men in old Schuylkill Valley. He was a righteous Christian, but when roused to wrath he was a real mean man with a wagon-master's tongue and brandished fists.'

Jeffries was followed into professional boxing by a younger brother, Jack, who was a useful heavyweight, but any hopes he had of making it a family double in the title stakes disappeared in 1902 when he was demolished in five rounds by – wait for it – Jack Johnson.

Jeffries left school at sixteen and started work at the Lacey Manufacturing Company, a boiler-making factory near Los Angeles, so when he started boxing professionally he was nick-named the 'Fighting Boilermaker'. After he had won a handful of fights, he was spotted by Harry Corbett, brother of the then world champion, James, who recommended him as a sparring partner. Jeffries joined the Corbett camp at Carson City and picked up a lot of tips to go with his bruises while being punched around the ring by the much more mobile and experienced heavyweight champion.

Trained early in his career by former world middleweight champion Tommy Ryan – famous for his ring skills – Jeffries was taught to fight out of a crouch and his tucked-up style made him a difficult man to pin with any telling punches. The 'Jeffries crouch' was copied by many fighters of his era, but few could match his success with it. William Brady took careful notice of how he handled himself in the sparring sessions with Corbett, and after splitting with 'Gentleman Jim' took over as manager of Jeffries. Billy Delaney, another former member of the Corbett camp, became his trainer.

Their only problem with the easy-going Jeffries was getting him motivated for fights. He lacked real 'killer' instinct and to try to get him worked up they used to invent insults that they pretended his opponents were making about him. Brady realized he was a championship prospect when, in only his sixth and seventh fights in 1897, he boxed twenty-round draws with two highly rated title contenders: Gus Ruhlin and Joe Choynski, the fighter who gave James J. Corbett so much trouble in their memorable 'battle of the barge' in 1889.

After his title-winning triumph against the unsuspecting Fitzsimmons on June 9, 1899 (see page 25), he scored a points victory in a 25-rounds war with 'Sailor' Tom Sharkey on Coney Island five months later. He then had the courage and the character to come from behind against James J. Corbett, whom he knocked out in the twenty-third round on Coney Island on May 11, 1900, after being given a boxing lesson by the old 'Science Master'.

Brady was struggling to find challengers for Jeffries after he had won return matches with Gus Ruhlin (retired fifth), Fitzsimmons (knocked out in the eighth) and Corbett

(knocked out in the tenth). Then, in a disgraceful mismatch in San Francisco on August 26, 1904, Jeffries knocked out Jack Munroe, a Canadian miner and former footballer, in two rounds. The only reason Munroe had got the fight was because, in a meaningless exhibition bout during the champion's nationwide tour of the theatres, he had briefly knocked Jeffries off his feet.

Munroe left the ring with chants of 'coward' ringing in his ears because he had shown little stomach for the fight. Eleven years later he won Canada's highest military honour for his heroism during fighting in the trenches in the

James J. Jeffries, the 'Fighting Boilermaker'.

29

Jeffries (second from right) takes a break from preparations for the 1899 challenge against Fitzsimmons to pose for a photograph with his training team. His manager Bill Brady is seated at the front, and the challenger's brother, Jack, is on the extreme left.

First World War. Ignoring his own wounds, he dragged a crippled officer to safety while chopping down enemy soldiers with his favourite weapon, a woodsman's axe.

A CRAZY COMEBACK

Jeffries realized the public would not put up with any more unequal matches, and he announced his retirement after winning twenty and drawing two of his twenty-two professional contests. It was widely reported at the time that he then named Marvin Hart as his successor as world champion, but in an interview more than forty years later he said that this was the work of a promoter, who did not seek his permission.

Six years into his retirement, however, Jeffries allowed himself to be talked into making an ill-advised comeback for a showdown with Jack Johnson, who was hated by the many white American fans who were unable to come to terms with a black man holding the championship. Tex Rickard, a silver-tongued young promoter, gave the most convincing argument of all for Jeffries to climb back through the ropes when he offered a record purse of $101,000, with 60 per cent for the winner and 40 per cent for the loser.

Jeffries' father said that he would never talk to his son again if he fought Johnson. This brought the taunt from Johnson: 'He just don't want to see his son beaten up. I've already seen off Jack Jeffries. Now let me get to work on his big brother.'

The fight was at first scheduled for San Francisco, and Rickard spent $50,000 erecting an open-air arena and sold $300,000 worth of tickets, but then a month before the event the Governor of California suddenly announced that it could not take place in his state. He gave no official reason, but it was understood that he was concerned at the racial undertones.

It seemed that racial tension was being deliberately stirred up when the venue was switched to Reno, Nevada, on Independence Day 1910. James J. Corbett, brought in by Rickard to help publicize the fight, was widely quoted as saying: 'The black boy has a wide yellow stripe running down his back, and Jeff is going to expose it. The time has come for the title to come back into white hands where it belongs'.

Jeffries, as they say in the American fight game, 'shoulda stood in bed.' At thirty-five, he was no longer a magnificent physical specimen and scaled 227 pounds compared to the 206 pounds he weighed when he first took the title from Fitzsimmons. He had grown fat making personal appearances and touring the country with a theatrical group.

With a blind foolishness that he was to regret later, Jeffries decided to prepare without the help of his former trainer Billy Delaney, who responded by joining the Johnson camp, where he found the champion locked in a bitter feud with his manager, George Little. They had fallen out over a hand of poker, and their differences reached boiling point just three weeks before the fight when Little walked out on Johnson. He astonished the boxing reporters by announcing that he was putting all his money on Jeffries to win. 'I know better than anybody the way Johnson's mind works,' he said. 'He's going to lay down for Jeffries.'

Sam Langford, the 'Boston Tar Baby', who would almost certainly have been world heavyweight champion but for the colour bar, arrived in Reno to challenge the winner. He, too, started to spread the story that Johnson was going to lay down. 'He daren't beat the white man,' he said. 'The fight is fixed.'

Johnson had been a hot betting favourite, but the odds moved in favour of Jeffries as the rumours persisted that the two boxers had agreed on a victory for the challenger. The promoter, Rickard, dismissed the stories as nonsense, and said that to make sure there was no funny business both boxers had agreed that he himself would referee the fight.

Jeffries was trained by his old opponent Joe Choynski, and he vowed before the fight: 'I will bring the championship back to white America where it belongs.' But for once he could not provide the action to go with his words. He was outclassed by Johnson, who battered him to a standstill in fifteen rounds. Jeffries' seconds jumped into the ring to save the old champion from being counted out after he had been knocked to the canvas three times.

There was a horrifying sequel to the contest, when whites went on the rampage in the Deep South after hearing the result and nine blacks were killed in bloody riots.

Although Jeffries had been beaten fairly and squarely, his supporters refused to accept this and they were only too ready to believe a widely published story that claimed he had been doped. This was in fact a theory that had been put to him by a newspaperman, and Jeffries went along with it because it helped ease his public humiliation. Ghostwritten newspaper and magazine articles attributed to Jeffries appeared in which he confirmed that he thought he had been poisoned by a drink slipped to him before the fight. But honesty was always one of Jeffries' endearing virtues, and in later years he backed away from the story. 'I can't be sure I was doped,' he said. 'The simple truth is I should have stayed retired.'

Johnson countered the Jeffries doping claim by revealing that before the fight he had employed tasters to try every drink before he took a drop. 'One drink that was offered to me made one of my handlers sick for days afterwards,' he said. However, as boxers were picking up fistfuls of dollars from newspapers and magazines for their stories, many of the so-called

Referee George Siler separates Jeffries (left) and 'Sailor' Tom Sharkey during their bruising title fight on Coney Island on November 3, 1899. Jeffries, a winner on points over twenty-five rounds, described Sharkey as one of the toughest men he ever fought.

Johnson looks on casually as Jeffries takes a count shortly before their 1910 championship fight was stopped in the fifteenth round.

facts should be treated with a degree of scepticism. The one certain fact is that Johnson gave Jeffries the biggest hiding of his life in front of a 15,760 crowd shoehorned into a wooden-framed arena erected in Reno. The great John L. Sullivan, who drew the colour line throughout his career, was among the spectators. He was big enough to shake Johnson's hand immediately after the fight and told him: 'The best man won.' As well as confirming Johnson as an outstanding world champion, the fight launched the dazzling promotional career of Tex Rickard, who had greater moments to come.

CRUSHED BY WALL STREET

Jeffries – or 'Big Jeff' as he was known to his friends – returned to the small alfalfa farm he had bought for himself in Burbank, California, and to comfortable retirement. He had money in the bank, an interest in a saloon and more than $300,000 safely invested in stocks and shares. Or so he thought. Virtually every penny he had was wiped out in the Wall Street Crash of 1929, and he was forced to declare bankruptcy.

He turned to boxing as a way back to solvency, coaching amateurs and professionals and converting a barn on his farm into a gymnasium and boxing arena. Jeffries promoted amateur

shows at the barn for fifteen years before he was forced to close down in 1947 when the authorities of the city of Burbank denied him a permit because of fire hazards. Jeffries responded by handing the barn over to his local church so that they could use it as a Sunday school.

A light went out in the old champion's life when Frieda, his wife and companion of thirty-seven years, was knocked down and killed while crossing a street in 1941. Those closest to him said that he was never quite the same man after this tragedy. Five years later he suffered a stroke that left him paralysed down one side. But for all his adversity, he never lost his good humour and his easy-going manner that made him such a gentle giant away from the ring.

Jeffries liked nothing better than to talk boxing, and some of his comments in interviews that he gave in his final years make as much sense today as they did then. 'The trouble with today's fighters,' he said, ' is that they don't condition themselves properly. They run three, four miles on the road and they think that's it, I must be fit. Then they wonder why they run out of steam in contests. I would think nothing of running twelve miles a day.

'I think more of today's boxers should consider the crouch style that served me so well. I adopted it after working out in the gymnasium as a young professional with a Los Angeles businessman called Johnny Brink, who was a very useful boxer. During one session he nearly tore my liver out with a body blow from close range. It was after that I worked on the crouch style. It makes you a more difficult target, and you can get more leverage into your punches.

'The best fighter I've seen since I retired is without any doubt Jack Dempsey. He could knock anybody flat with a single punch, and he had lots of heart. Gene Tunney was a good boxer, but I think Corbett or Fitzsimmons would have beaten him in quick time. I haven't seen Joe Louis in the flesh, but he is obviously a class fighter. But I'm sure Johnson would have beaten him. He was such a good defensive boxer that he would not have taken any of those paralysing punches with which Louis knocks over his opponents.

'The best fighter never to have won the championship was 'Sailor' Tom Sharkey. He gave me a helluva scrap in my first title defence. It was hammer and tongs for twenty-five rounds. I cracked two of his ribs but that didn't stop him coming at me like a wild tiger. I remember my trainer Tommy Ryan giving me a swig of champagne before the start of the twenty-fifth round. It got my motor going and I did enough to win the round and the fight. Both Sharkey and I carried the bruises of that battle for a long time. We also had singed hair where the lights they were using to make a movie of the fight were so strong that they burned us. We were almost roasted alive!'

Jeffries was asked if he had any regrets. 'Just one. I should never have let myself be talked into coming back against Johnson. Too much rust had collected since my retirement. Nobody will know the pressure I was under in that fight. I felt as if I had every white American on my back. I would like to have met Johnson at my peak. I'm not saying I would have beaten him, but you would have seen a completely different fight.'

When Jeffries died at the age of seventy-seven, following a heart attack at his Burbank home on March 3, 1953, the boxing world mourned the passing of one of its great heavyweight champions.

'Jim Jeffries was more than a friend to me,' said Jack Dempsey. 'He was my idol. When I was a kid he was the man I wanted to be. I was privileged to get to know him well, and I always

found him a modest man who had a lot of time for other people. Boxing and the world is a poorer place without him.'

Jimmy McLarnin, former world welterweight champion, said: 'As far as I'm concerned he was the greatest fighter of all time. He had unbelievable strength and a lot more skill than people gave him credit for. He could take an opponent's head off with a left jab.'

One of Jeffries's closest friends, attorney Oscar Lawler, delivered a moving eulogy at his burial service in Burbank, where a dozen motorcyle police flanked the funeral procession on its way to the Inglewood Park Cemetary.

'To you, Jim,' said Lawler, 'the bully was an anathema. You were courageous without bravado ... To those around you you were always generous and kindly, and in sports you were honest and square, incapable of dissembling. You were privileged to walk and talk with presidents and kings, yet you remained unaffected to your old friends. You, Jim, were a man among men ... Big Jeff, you fought the good fight with all of your might and you go to your resting place leaving behind people who are richer for having known and loved you.'

Jeffries left most of his estate to a niece who had looked after him following the tragic death of his wife, and to a Mrs Mary Roberts – whom Jim and his wife had looked on as a daughter – he left $5,000. The value of the estate was listed as 'in excess of $10,000'. The old champ had not left a fortune, but he did leave a lot of rich memories.

Jeffries with his wife, Frieda, shortly before she was tragically knocked down and killed in a road accident in 1941. The old champion never recovered from his loss.

CHAPTER FOUR

MARVIN HART

THE PUNCHING PLUMBER

More than fifty years before the 'Louisville Lip', Cassius Clay, came chatter-boxing on to the world stage there was another heavyweight champion who was launched from Louisville in Kentucky – Marvin Hart, the 'Punching Plumber'. Of all the world heavyweight title holders, he has made least impact on the public consciousness, mainly because his was something of a paper crown; but if only for the fact that he was once given a points verdict over the mighty Jack Johnson – 'given' being the operative word – he merits his place in this centenary parade of world heavyweight champions.

Hart became world champion in dubious circumstances. When James J. Jeffries retired undefeated in 1905 the title became vacant. There were two contenders who stood out: Jack Johnson and Sam Langford, but both were ruled out by the boxing establishment because they were black. (There was no sport that could quite match boxing for exposing the cancer of bigotry.)

On May 28, 1905, Hart met Johnson in a non-championship contest over twenty rounds and was adjudged to have won on points. One ringside boxing reporter summed up the surprising result memorably with the line: 'Hart could only have got the decision owing to the fact that in the excitement the referee pointed to the wrong man.'

There had already been behind-the-scenes shenanigans to manoeuvre Hart into a fight for the vacant world title against Jack Root, the former light-heavyweight champion. A defeat by Johnson would have wrecked these plans. Johnson said later: 'Everytime I landed more than two punches in succession the referee would find an excuse to stop the action. Any fair-minded person knows who won that fight. I guess the referee must have been colour blind. All he could see was white.'

Hart was being advised by former world middleweight champion Tommy Ryan, who used to train Jeffries and had the ear of the retired champion. He helped to convince Jeffries that he should lend his name to a plan to hand his title over to the winner of the Hart-Root showdown at Reno on July 5, 1905.

In later years Jeffries insisted that it was all arranged behind his back by the promoters, but nevertheless he lent credibility to the charade by agreeing to referee the fight.

A crowd of less than 7,000 gathered to see the 6-foot tall, 190-pounds Hart stop the out-gunned Root in twelve rounds. While the boxing world was under-whelmed by his claim that he was the new champion, on his return to Louisville back home in Kentucky they greeted him like a hero. A brass band turned out to meet him at the station, and they played 'My Old Kentucky Home' as he walked along the platform through a mass of cheering supporters, who had come from all over Kentucky to greet their champion.

A FIGHTER BY ACCIDENT

Hart was born, grew up and died in the farming community of Fern Creek near Louisville. The son of a family with roots deep in Germany, he was born on September 16, 1876, and attended grade schools in Louisville before learning his trade as a plumber.

Hart was a noted scrapper at school, but he became a prize fighter by accident. He acted as a second for a friend in a grudge fight, and

realized that he could have beaten both of the fighters without breaking sweat. It encouraged him to start training in an old barn on a farm in Fern Creek. He fixed up a punchbag, and spent hours training himself and learning from textbooks how to throw punches correctly. Then a Louisville café owner called John Seitz heard about him and offered to become his manager.

His first real fight was against a local bruiser called 'Big Bill' Schiller, whose ring exploits had until then frightened off all opposition. Hart, who was now twenty-three and settled into his job as a plumber, volunteered to fight him and knocked him out in seven rounds in Louisville on December 12, 1899. Schiller insisted that it was a fluke victory and demanded a return match. This time Hart knocked him out in four rounds.

Above: Hart (centre) poses for a photograph with his trainer and sparring partners while preparing for his 1907 fight against Mike Schreck, who twice beat him in non-title contests.

Right: Hart on his way to a controversial twenty-rounds points decision against Jack Johnson in 1905. 'In the excitement, the referee pointed to the wrong man,' was how one cynical ringside reporter recorded it.

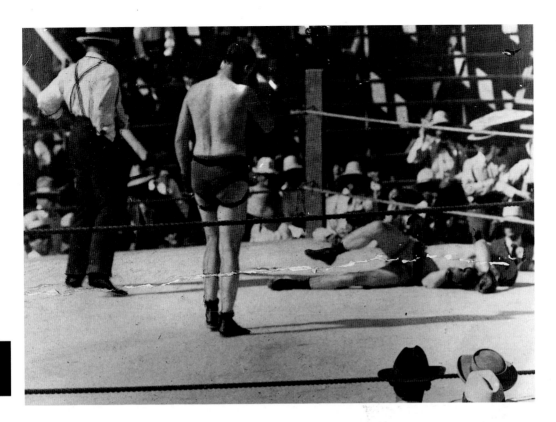

Hart wins his 'paper crown' by knocking out Jack Root in the twelfth round in 1905.

Hart went on to win seventeen of his first eighteen contests, which were all staged in Louisville. He became a local celebrity, and when he married Florence Ziegler in September, 1902, so many people crowded into the Beulah Presbyterian Church at Fern Creek that the main wooden beam cracked with such a noise that it sounded like a gun going off.

Hart's impressive ring record brought him to the attention of Tommy Ryan, who persuaded him to start fighting outside Kentucky. Hart had fallen out with his original manager, John Seitz, because Hart had refused to follow Seitz's advice to go on a coast-to-coast exhibition tour with former champions James J. Corbett and Bob Fitzsimmons.

'Marvin has become too difficult to handle,' said Seitz. 'He will not listen to advice and will suffer the consequences.'

With careful matchmaking, Hart was quickly elevated to a high ranking position and his so-called victory over Johnson in 1905 clinched his place as the number one contender for the vacant championship. Three years earlier he had been outpointed over six rounds by Jack Root in Chicago, and this performance earned Root his title chance, even though at 171 pounds he was hardly of heavyweight build. They met to decide the championship in Reno, Nevada, on July 3, 1905. Root was the more accomplished ring technician, and it looked as if he might spring a surprise when he floored the man from Kentucky in the seventh round; but he eventually found Hart's power too much for him, and he was knocked out in the twelfth round of what proved to be the last but one fight of his long and eventful career.

JUST ONE DEFENCE

Hart slipped quickly from the world stage when he lost his title on points in his first defence against Canadian Tommy Burns in Los Angeles on February 23, 1906. Again, James J. Jeffries, the ex-champion, was the referee. Many years later, a reporter seeking background facts on Hart went to his birthplace at Fern Creek in Jefferson County, Kentucky, and was told by an old-timer: 'Marvin Hart? Yes, I remember him well. He put the plumbing in our house in 1927 and we've not had a bit of trouble with it since. He was a wonderful plumber.'

Hart achieved enough in the ring to be remembered more for his punching than his plumbing. He lost only nine of his forty-seven contests before retiring to a red-shuttered cottage on a small farm in Fern Creek, where he combined the farming life with plumbing. Hart also became a prominent referee in both wrestling and boxing rings.

He was an affable man who used to laugh a lot when questioned about his boxing career. 'All the championship earned me was ten thousand dollars,' he said. 'I guess I was born twenty years too soon.'

Hart was bitter only about his defeat by Tommy Burns. 'He just didn't let me fight,' he said. 'He was an awkward cuss who kept tying me up. I've never been so frustrated as in that fight. I know I was the better man, but what can you do if your opponent keeps holding you and pushing you off balance. Burns will claim they were clever tactics, but only one of us went there to fight.'

Hart complained of feeling unwell after supervising a bout in Louisville just before Christmas in 1930. His doctor diagnosed liver and blood pressure problems, and he was confined to bed in his Fern Creek home where he died on September 17, 1931 – the day after his fifty-fifth birthday.

Hart was buried in Resthaven cemetary just a short distance from where he was born in Fern Creek. The inscription on his headstone

A portrait photograph taken shortly before Hart's death in 1931.

reads: 'A friend of countless hundreds; a clean fighter whose example will continue to inspire coming generations.'

He was no 'Louisville Lip', but Hart achieved enough in the boxing ring to be remembered with respect.

37

The final resting place of Marvin Hart and his wife, Florence, at the Resthaven Cemetary near his birthplace in Fern Creek, Kentucky.

CHAPTER FIVE

TOMMY BURNS

THE CANNY CANADIAN

Tommy Burns left Canada in 1900 with fury in his fists and returned fifty-five years later with love in his heart. As he set foot back in his homeland he handed out visiting cards which read: 'Reverend Thomas Burns, Demonstrator of Universal Love.'

Of all the boxers featured in this centenary cavalcade of champions none is more remarkable than Burns. At just 5 foot 7 inches tall, he was the shortest heavyweight champion of them all. He was also the shrewdest, and one of the few to manage himself. Yet in later life he turned against the sport that had brought him fame and fortune.

'Boxing is vicious and full of hatred,' he said after becoming an ordained minister on Christmas Day, 1948. 'My only purpose in life now is to spread universal love and to help the sick and the suffering.' Burns certainly found out just how vicious and hateful boxing could be during a career in which he was continually matched against men who were bigger but rarely better than him. He may have been short on inches, but he was never short of courage.

A RACING NAME

Burns had an extraordinary life. He was the twelfth of thirteen children born to Frenchman Frederick Brusso and his German wife, Sofia, in a log cabin farmhouse near Hanover in Ontario, Canada, on June 17, 1881. He was christened Noah Brusso, but took the name Tommy Burns from a racing jockey friend so that his mother would not find out that he had gone against her wishes and taken up boxing as a career. He also felt that Burns was a name that would go down well with the public in an era when Irish-raised boxers dominated in nearly every division.

As Noah Brusso, he was well known in Ontario for his ability on the lacrosse field and the ice hockey rink. He showed little interest in boxing until the day he innocently got involved in a fight with a burly second mate on board a Lake Erie passenger boat on which he was working. He was surprised at the ease with which he knocked down his much bigger opponent, and as a result he decided to start studying the finer points of boxing.

When he was nineteen, he left Canada in search of adventure and jumped ship at Detroit and joined the Detroit Athletic Club, where he started to work out in the gymnasium. One of his clubmates, Jack Cowan, invited him to watch him box on a show in Delray. As he reached the ring apron, Cowan turned and waved to Noah and his friends in the crowd. Then he vaulted over the top rope and twisted his ankle on landing. Noah was persuaded to take his place and knocked out his opponent, Fred Thornton, in five rounds. He was amazed to be paid $20 for winning. His amateur status had gone in one hit.

Noah Brusso became Tommy Burns and over the following five years he toured the United States taking on and generally beating all comers. When he returned to Detroit in 1904 he landed in jail after knocking out his opponent Ben O'Grady in three rounds. O'Grady was rushed unconscious to hospital and Burns was held in a police cell for four days on an assault charge until his opponent came out of his coma.

He lost only three of his thirty-eight fights on his way to challenging the pretender to the throne, Marvin Hart, for the undisputed world championship. In an unrecorded contest that took place in Alaska, Burns tangled in an exhibition match with one 'Klondike' Mike Mahoney, a giant famous for his enormous strength (he once carried a piano on his back across the Chilcoot Pass). They fought lumberjack style, which meant the use of feet as well as fists, and Burns was reported to have more than held his own.

After snatching the championship from Hart with a comfortable twenty-rounds points victory in an untidy title fight in Los Angeles on February 23, 1906, Burns celebrated by taking on two opponents on the same night in San Diego. He knocked each of them cold in one round. To substantiate his claim to the title, Burns stopped 'Fireman' Jim Flynn in fifteen rounds and was then held to a draw over twenty rounds by 'Philadelphia' Jack O'Brien. In the return in Los Angeles six months later Burns won a clear points victory.

The Americans were unhappy to see the championship in the hands of a foreigner, even if he did come from the same continent, and Burns decided he would cash in on the title by becoming the first truly international champion. He set sail for Europe, ignoring allegations that he was running away from the title claims of the dreaded Jack Johnson.

The 'Galveston Giant' trailed Burns around the world throwing out challenges, but the 'Canny Canadian' kept one step ahead of him as he successfully defended the world title eleven times in his own version of a 'bum-of-the-month' campaign.

For such a short man, Burns had an extraordinarily long reach and he used to draw in opponents as if he was a spider luring a fly and then knocked them senseless with carefully pinpointed counter punches to the most vulnerable points of the head and body. He revealed his tactical secrets in an excellent coaching manual, *Scientific Boxing and Self Defence*, which was published while Burns was in London in 1908. None of his opponents could have read the book, because they all folded under his powerful two-fisted attacks.

Burns had a finger in the promotion of most of his fights, and his sharp business brain amazed the British boxing fraternity when he made two defences in London. At one stage in his early career he was swindled out of his purse, and he swore it would never happen again. He decided to manage himself and used to insist on receiving his money before throwing a punch in anger.

When he fought the British champion, Gunner Moir, at the aristocratic National Sporting Club on December 2, 1907, he demanded that his £3,000 purse be paid to him in notes in the ring before the fight. The money was counted out in front of him, and then he handed it over to his second before getting on with the business of beating Moir.

The seventh Marquis of Queensberry could not believe the man's impudence. He later

Burns shows off his world heavyweight championship belt.

The publicists decided to give Burns (second right) a debonair image, but he managed to make this staged contract exchange seem like a scene from a gangster movie.

pion of the world sitting in the box office. He waited until all the tickets had been sold and then put half the takings in a bag, locked it up in his dressing-room under the eye of a 'minder', and then climbed into the ring to knock out Palmer in four rounds.

SHOWDOWN IN SYDNEY

Burns went on to be part-promoter of easy defences in Dublin and Paris before sailing for Australia, with Johnson in pursuit. To drum up interest in the inevitable showdown with Johnson, Burns made two defences in nine days against over-matched Australian challengers.

On Boxing day 1908, at a specially built stadium at Rushcutter's Bay in Sydney, Burns put his championship on the line against Johnson on Boxing Day 1908 in the first black versus white world heavyweight title fight. He collected what was then an enormous purse of $30,000, but he had to earn every cent as the giant Johnson – just over 5 inches taller and 24 pounds heavier – hammered him around the ring. The promoter, Hugh McIntosh, acted as referee, and did little to stop the challenger from beating up the champion in a humiliating manner. Johnson toyed with Burns and hit him with a stream of insulting words as well as injurious punches before police jumped into the ring and stopped the savagery in the fourteenth round.

'I badly underestimated Johnson's boxing skill,' Burns said after his battering. 'My plan was to move rapidly around the ring, boxing carefully at all times. But I made the mistake of tearing into him, and his greater strength and punching power told. Johnson was saying some nasty things to me in the ring. He kept calling me Mr Tammy, and ridiculed me whenever he made me miss with his clever defence. I'm not complaining about his tactics. I've used my tongue on many occasions to get an opponent riled. I had a good run with the championship and never ducked a challenge or drew the colour line, and I was a true world champion in that I went to the countries of my opponents rather than making them cross the Atlantic. I know there are people in America who consider me a "cheese" champion, but I beat every white American worth considering before going on my travels.'

observed: 'Burns was prepared to tell anyone who would listen that he was in a class by himself. As champion he was arrogance itself, and during the preliminaries leading up to his fight with Gunner Moir his attitude was so offensive that it was understandable that for once the National Sporting Club members permitted partisanship to sway them. It was not so much a case of plumping for Moir as it was a devout hope that the braggart and mannerless visitor should be taught a salutary lesson.'

It was Burns who gave a lesson in how to pick up easy money. Before the fight he had put on a false moustache and glasses and had slipped into one of Moir's training sessions to size up his opponent. He was so confident of beating him that he put £10,000 on himself to win at even money.

His arrogant, confident manner was an act to give himself a psychological advantage over opponents, and he often used a wicked tongue to undermine the confidence of any boxer he thought was in any way apprehensive.

Two months after flattening Moir in the tenth round he declined a purse for defending against Geordie Jack Palmer at the Wonderland stadium in London's East End. Instead, he chose to take 50 per cent of the gate money. Spectators arriving to buy their tickets on the day of the fight were amazed to find the cham-

After losing the title, Burns tried his hand as a boxing promoter, but this ended in disaster when he staged a show in Calgary in 1913. In the top-line contest a punch from Arthur Pelky snapped Luther McCarty's spinal cord and he died on the canvas. There was such an outcry against boxing that Burns was forced to abandon his promotional plans.

He had five more contests and then he made a one-fight comeback at the age of thirty-nine against British champion Joe Beckett, who stopped the veteran in seven rounds at the Royal Albert Hall in 1920. Burns was part promoter and paid himself a handsome purse of £4000.

Burns invested his money in pubs in Britain and in a speakeasy in New York, but after being stricken with arthritis in 1935, this extraordinary man 'got religion' and started preaching against his old sport. 'To become a successful boxer you must have hate in your heart,' he said. 'The Good Lord has told me that this is wrong. We should love our fellow man.'

His crippling arthritis eased and he insisted that it was his new-found faith that had helped heal him. He and his wife had one child and they settled down in Coalinga, California, where he was ordained as a minister in 1948.

When Burns died of a heart attack at the age of seventy-four while on a preaching visit to Vancouver on May 10, 1955, boxing lost one of its most remarkable characters. In sixty fights he was beaten only five times, and Johnson was the only fighter to stop him before his ill-advised comeback against Beckett. He rarely weighed above the light-heavyweight limit, and had to concede height and weight advantages in nearly every fight he ever had. Yet when he looked back on his career, all he felt was shame. 'We were not put on this earth to hurt each other,' he said. 'Love of God is our only chance of salvation.'

The Reverend Thomas Burns, demonstrator of love, lay in an unmarked grave in Ocean View cemetary in Burnaby until hockey star 'Cyclone' Taylor, who had played lacrosse against the young Noah Brusso, started a fund to raise a monument to one of Canada's most famous sons. Looking back over a century of world heavyweight title fights, Burns must be given the credit he deserves as one of the most astute champions of all time.

Four of the best: Tommy Burns, James J. Corbett, James J. Jeffries and John L. Sullivan, brought together by promoter Tex Rickard for a publicity photograph before the Johnson-Jeffries title fight in 1910.

CHAPTER SIX

JACK JOHNSON

THE GALVESTON GIANT

To understand Jack Johnson – the man, his moods and his motives – it is important to understand the world into which he was born. Slavery had been abolished in America only fifteen years before his birth and he grew up in an environment in which the black man was expected to know his place in a white man's world. The trouble with Johnson was that he really did know his place. It was right up there at the top of the heavyweight boxing heap, and when he got there he found not just a crown of thorns, but a tide of white hatred that brought shame to a so-called civilized world.

It has to be said that Johnson hardly helped himself by his arrogant, even preposterous behaviour in and out of the ring. He taunted and insulted opponents verbally while punishing them physically with devastating punching combinations, and at the peak of his earning powers he led what can only be described as a life of sin and debauchery.

It would be possible to write three books on Jack Johnson, each of them projecting a completely different person. He embroidered so

many stories about his life in return for desperately needed cash in his later years that the true facts have become lost in a fog of half truths and downright lies.

What is clear is that he was without dispute one of the greatest of this first century of gloved heavyweight champions. It took him ten frustrating years to reach the status of number one challenger for the world title in an era when the colour of a boxer's skin rather than his ability dictated matters, and for at least five years Johnson was the best heavyweight fighter on earth; but it cannot be overstated that he was handicapped disgracefully by blind bigotry. In the pages of old, yellowing fight-page reports, for example, he is variously described as 'coon,' 'nigger', 'sambo', 'black gorilla', 'jungle swinger' and 'the uppity-nigger', giving some idea of the poisonous prejudice he had to face throughout his career.

THE RUNAWAY REBEL

The third of five children born to a school caretaker in the south coast Mexican Gulf town of Galveston, Texas, on March 31, 1878, John Arthur Johnson was known to his family and friends by his middle name. His father, a part-time preacher and former bare-knuckle fighter, was a strict disciplinarian and was he was furious when he discovered that his son, encouraged by Lucy, one of Johnson's three sisters, had given a street hiding to a local bully who had been pestering both of them. It was his first fight and his first victory.

By the age of twelve, Johnson had taken to running away from home. He stowed on board a New York-bound ship, but he was discovered and forced to pay his way by working in the galley. After bumming his way around New York's infamous 'drop-out district' called The Bowery, he moved on to Boston and got a job exercising horses in racing stables. He was only there a matter of weeks when he was thrown by a horse and broke his right leg. From hospital, he was sent home to Galveston and, not yet fourteen years old, he got a job working in the docks.

It was while he was working in the docks that he started scrapping, and he became known locally as 'Li'l Artha'. He left home again in his

BURNS - JOHNSON CONTEST. Sydney Dec 1908. 12. Kerry Copyright

late teens and began riding box-cars to find action. To make money he took part in degrading 'battle royals' – pitched battles in which the ring was packed with black fighters, with the last one standing declared the winner. They were staged for the amusement of the all-white audience, and bets were struck as to which fighters would last longest. Johnson was invariably the only one upright at the finish of the undignified scrambles.

It was this grounding that helped him develop some of the finest defensive skills ever seen, and he became a master at picking off punches with open gloves and then throwing cutting counters. His right uppercut was a speciality punch, which he used to deliver at close quarters, bringing it up from below his waist. He was like a skilled swordsman in the way that he feinted, parried and countered. The one time when his ability could not save him was when he was jumped by a gang of Irish-Americans, who beat him up in the street after he had expressed the opinion that James J. Corbett was a better fighter than John L. Sullivan. 'I carried the bruises of that attack for weeks,' he remembered in his retirement years. 'But it didn't make me change my mind. Corbett was a master boxer, while Sullivan was just a slugger.'

Johnson, who had grown to just over 6 foot and had a magnificently proportioned physique, returned to Galveston at the turn of the century to see his home wrecked by a terrifying hurricane. It swept across the Gulf of Mexico, claiming more than 6,000 lives in its wake. He worked to help his family – particularly his

Johnson, smiling and fully in control, allows Tommy Burns to take a breather before continuing the punishment in their world title fight in Sydney on Boxing Day 1908. The referee is promoter Hugh McIntosh.

mother, Tiny, whom he worshipped – get back on their feet, and then returned to boxing on February 25, 1901, after having had only one fight in the previous year. His comeback contest was in Galveston against the vastly experienced Jewish battler from California, Joe Choynski, and Johnson was down from a body blow in the third round when Texas Rangers invaded the ring and arrested both the boxers for violating state laws. They were released after spending three weeks in jail, an experience that was to become commonplace for Johnson. During their jail-yard breaks, Choynski showed Johnson a lot of the tricks of the trade, which he had picked up during his long fighting career.

Johnson proceeded to prove himself the best of the black heavyweights over the next ten years, beating all of his main rivals, including Sam Langford, Sam McVey, Joe Jeannette and 'Denver' Ed Martin. All this time he was carefully avoided by the top white heavyweights, and he had to chase Tommy Burns, the reigning world heavyweight champion, halfway around the world before finally catching up with him and relieving him of the title in Australia (see page 40). On his way down under, Johnson stopped off in London where he was given a royal welcome before disdainfully dismissing two outclassed opponents, Al McNamara and Ben Taylor, in Plymouth in the summer of 1908.

A DESPISED CHAMPION

Johnson's victory over Burns on Boxing Day 1908, coupled with his arrogant manner and controversial lifestyle – and, sadly, the colour of his skin – made him one of the most despised figures in the United States and on his return from Australia a massive hunt was launched for a 'white hope' who could dethrone him.

World middleweight champion Stanley Ketchel, the 'Michigan Assassin', was persuaded to try his luck at Colma, California, on October 16, 1909. The two boxers struck a private agreement that Ketchel would be allowed to go the distance for the benefit of the movie cameras, because a short-lived fight would not have sold in the cinemas. But Ketchel forgot the deal and briefly (and unwisely) floored Johnson with a sneak punch in the twelfth round. Seconds later Ketchel had two of his teeth embedded in

Above: The famous picture that gave support to Johnson's claim that he had thrown the fight against Willard in 1915. It looks as if he is shielding his eyes from the Cuban sun, but the Big Fights Inc film of the contest clearly shows that Johnson was knocked out by a tremendous right-hand punch.

Opposite: Johnson and his wife, Lucille, arrive at Folkestone, Britain, in 1913, after he had jumped bail in the United States.

Johnson's right glove after being knocked cold. Johnson hit him so hard that the champion fell over as he landed his devastating final punch.

Then James J. Jeffries was wheeled out of retirement at Reno, Nevada, on July 4, 1910, only to be pounded to a fifteenth-round defeat. Johnson dared to climb into the ring despite having received threatening letters, promising that he would be shot by a spectator if he was unwise enough to beat the old champion. He was so in command against Jeffries that at one stage during the contest he leaned back over the ropes and started dictating his description of the fight to ringside reporters! There were no shots fired at Johnson, but the outcome of the contest had tragic consequences in the Deep South. Riots flared as news of the fight result became known and nine blacks were murdered by lynch mobs.

TROUBLE WITH WOMEN

Johnson shed managers like old socks – he had eight in all during his career, several of whom ripped him off and cost him thousands of dollars. But Johnson didn't seem to care and spent money as if he had a bottomless pit of funds. A flamboyant figure, he decorated himself with diamonds, had his teeth capped with gold ('...because I want to give my opponents a golden smile as I beat them,' he explained), and bought a different flashy car almost every week; Johnson also surrounded himself with dubious hangers-on, including hordes of white prostitutes. The many women in Johnson's life managed to cause him more grief and pain than any opponent in the ring.

His first wife, a black girl called Mary Austin, walked out on him because of his womanizing. He then had a long affair with another black girl, Clara Kerr, and was devastated when she ran off with his best friend, taking all his possessions with her. (Ten years later, however, he paid the defence costs when she was charged with murdering her brother.) Johnson, who went on a year-long drinking and gambling binge after Kerr left him, later said that the experiences with Mary Austin and Clara Kerr had made him vow that in future he would become romantically involved with only white women because he considered them more reliable.

It was a statement that landed like a stick of dynamite in white households right across America, where mixed marriages were considered sinful. And there were many black people who objected to Johnson's comments.

For several years he lived with a New York Irish girl, Hattie McLay, an association that he broke when she became a helpless alcoholic. He then took up with Belle Schreiber, a white Milwaukee prostitute. She stayed with him in a San Francisco hotel when he went to fight Ketchel, who was even more renowned than Johnson for his weakness for the ladies. Hattie McLay booked into the same hotel and, often in a drunken condition, continually waylaid Johnson and Schreiber, hurling insults at the top of her voice. To avoid the scorned McLay, Johnson took to leaving his hotel room through a window and then lowering himself to the ground down a thick rope, one end of which was tied to the bedstead. It was not the best way to prepare for a world championship defence.

After breaking up with Belle Schreiber, Johnson married white divorcée Etta Duryea in Pittsburgh in 1909. Etta, who was from an affluent and respectable Brooklyn family, suffered from deep depressions and one night she took one of Johnson's revolvers and shot herself dead in their bedroom over the club-restaurant – the

Cabaret de Champions – that he had opened in Chicago. She and Johnson had recently returned from a trip to Europe during which he had hoped to fight the then British champion, 'Bombardier' Billy Wells, at Earls Court in London in 1911. The contest was cancelled, however, on the orders of the Home Secretary after a petition presented by the Reverend F. B. Meyer pointed to the effect a black man's victory over a white British boxer would have on the colonies. It was not only in the United States that they were colour conscious.

Johnson closed down his club in 1912, having sunk a fortune into it and amid unproven stories that the Cabaret de Champions had been used for wild orgies and 'a dangerous mixing of the races.' Many people believed the stories – not because of the weight of evidence, but because of their loathing of Johnson – and extremists started to demand that something should be done about curbing the world champion's behaviour.

To replenish his depleted finances, Johnson travelled to New Mexico to defend his title against 'Fireman' Jim Flynn on July 4, 1912. Flynn, who told promoter Jack Curley that he could shoot him if he lost, was completely outclassed and resorted to foul tactics. By the ninth round the chief of police had seen enough and ordered the bout stopped; Flynn looked as if he had been hit by a hammer.

A PRISON SENTENCE

While he was still mourning the death of his wife, Johnson was introduced to Lucille Cameron, a white eighteen-year-old schoolgirl from Minnesota, who was studying in Chicago. She became his business secretary – or so it was claimed – and when her mother heard the news she informed the police that her daughter had been abducted.

The accusation was just what the white establishment had been waiting for and Johnson was arrested and charged with abduction under the Mann Act, the name given to the White Slave Traffic Act. At his trial the prosecution alleged that he was running an inter-state prostitution ring, and that Cameron was powerless under his Svengalian influence. When Cameron was called to give evidence she caused gasps in the court-

room by admitting that she had been a prostitute, but insisted that this owed nothing to the influence of Johnson.

The world champion was discharged, but white America was appalled at the evidence that had been presented by the prosecution, even though much of it seemed to be the figment of wild imagination and given by witnesses plainly blinded by racial hatred.

The Bureau of Investigation – which later became the FBI – started to dig as deeply as possible into Johnson's background. They came up with Belle Schreiber, who admitted working as a prostitute while with Johnson. The champion was rearrested under the Mann Act, and Schreiber became the prosecution's star witness. Meanwhile, Johnson had caused further outrage in white America by marrying Lucille Cameron.

When he was summoned to appear before the grand jury on eleven charges, ranging from unlawful sexual intercourse, the transportation of a white woman for immoral purposes and crimes against nature, the Governor of South Carolina summed up the feelings of millions of white Americans when he said, 'If we cannot

The big gun of boxing behind bars in 1921.

protect our white women from black fiends like Johnson, where is our boasted civilisation?'

An all-white, all-male jury returned a verdict of 'guilty as charged', and Johnson was fined $1,000 and sentenced to a year and a day in prison. Given two weeks to appeal, Johnson jumped bail and escaped across the border into Canada. He claimed at the time that he had got away disguised as a member of a touring baseball team, but later he admitted that border guards had taken a bribe to look the other way while he skipped the country.

Johnson and his bride sailed to Europe from Canada in 1913, and during a headline-hitting self-exile he made a good living touring theatres giving boxing exhibitions and performing as an entertainer. On his travels he visited Paris, London, Brussels, Berlin, Vienna, Budapest, Bucharest and Moscow, where he mixed with pre-revolution society, including Rasputin. He also fitted in three fights in Paris, knocking out a wrestler, Andre Spoul in two rounds on November 28, 1913, and then just twenty-one days later drawing over ten rounds in the first all-black world heavyweight title fight against fellow-American 'Battling' Jim

Johnson gives himself up in 1921 as he crosses the border from Mexico into the United States, ready to serve his prison sentence.

Johnson (left) gave exhibitions and trained while serving his time in Leavenworth Prison, Kansas.

Johnson. The champion broke his left wrist in the second round and did most of his hitting by leading with his right. Then, on June 27, 1914, he outpointed white American Frank Moran over twenty rounds. An American publicist working on the promotion disputed the financial contract for the fight and the purses for both boxers were frozen in a French bank.

CONTROVERSY UNDER THE SUN

While Johnson was waiting for the courts to resolve the dispute over payment for the Moran fight the first World War broke out, and plans for a fight with Sam Langford in London were cancelled. Johnson, still based in Paris, was just beginning to worry about demands that he should join the French Army when promoter Jack Curley approached him with an interesting proposal. America had a new 'white hope' in the shape of giant cowboy Jess Willard, and Curley wanted to organize a championship contest in Mexico, where revolutionary Pancho Villa had offered to put up the purse money.

With Mexico in turmoil, Johnson feared that he would either be killed or handed over to the American authorities, so he asked Curley to come up with a different venue. They agreed on Cuba, and Johnson and Willard met under a scorching Caribbean sun on the Oriental Park Race Track at Marianao ten miles outside Havana on April 5, 1915. Willard looked clumsy and lumbering compared to the smooth-as-silk Johnson in the first half of a fight scheduled for forty-five rounds, but he was never far adrift on points as he worked behind a long left jab against the 37-year-old champion, who was clearly trying to conserve energy in the boiling-pot conditions.

After twenty gruelling rounds, Johnson's speed was down to slow motion, and although he was just edging the fight he was looking close to exhaustion. It was as the contest reached the halfway stage after an hour and a half of hard duelling that Willard started to enjoy his first moments of real supremacy. In the twenty-sixth round he feinted with a left to the body and then swung a long, jolting overarm right to the jaw and Johnson sank to the canvas like a huge liner

At the age of forty-eight, Johnson married his fourth wife, Irene Pineau, who brought some order to his disorganized life.

going down at sea. He took the count on his back, which saw the end of Johnson's controversial six-year reign.

Ever since the fight, the still photograph featured in this chapter showing Johnson apparently shielding his eyes from the Havana sun as the referee counts over him has been used to prove that he had taken a dive. But the finish as shown on Bill Cayton's Big Fights Inc film of the fight clearly reveals Johnson is knocked over by a mighty whack, after which he lies prostrate, out to the world. Johnson is caught by a photographer's finger on a flash button at the moment he hit the deck with his arms crossed over his face.

This picture was to give the 'Galveston Giant' unexpected evidence to support his claim that he had deliberately thrown the fight in return for a $50,000 bonus (which he did not receive) and the promise that the American authorities would allow him back home without making him serve his prison sentence. He made the statement to the late Nat Fleischer, the highly respected founder of *The Ring* magazine, on

Johnson was prepared to try anything for money after his retirement, and in 1936 made his operatic debut in *Aida*.

nothing but the truth ... I agreed to let Willard win by a knockout because I had been promised that I would then not be molested any more by the U.S. Government, and that I would be allowed home to see my dear beloved mother ....'

Johnson signed the statement, which was published world-wide, but, despite the emotional language, the truth is more likely that age had caught up with a great champion, whose life style was hardly ideal for somebody competing at the highest level of world championship boxing. In Willard he was up against an opponent he would have danced rings around in his prime, but the challenger's strength in stamina-sapping temperatures of 105°F (40°C) was the key factor.

The ex-champion returned to London in 1915, where he starred in his own revue, *Seconds Out*, in which he sang, danced, boxed and played the fiddle. Always a jazzy dresser, Johnson believed in being theatrical off as well as on stage, and he loved to swagger through the streets wearing a fur-collared cashmere overcoat, a black bowler and carrying a silver-topped cane. In 1916 the British Government, embarrassed by the presence of the 'on-the-run' Johnson when they were waiting for the United States to join them in the war against Germany, ordered him to leave the country. He moved to Spain, where he had four contests, toured the theatres and even took part in a couple of bull fights.

In his autobiography, *Jack Johnson, In the Ring and Out*, Johnson makes the amazing claim that he had worked for the United States Government as a spy while in Spain, reporting on German submarine bases. But this statement seems to be further evidence of his imagination in overdrive, because when he returned to the United States via Mexico in July 1920, he was promptly arrested and made to serve his full prison sentence. It was hardly the way the Government would have treated a man who had passed them valuable wartime information.

When he left Leavenworth jail in July 1921, Johnson had just five dollars to his name, but after following a strict training schedule, he was fitter than he had been for several years. He picked up his boxing career, giving exhibitions and taking the occasional fight. At the age of forty-two he was briefly back in the headlines when he issued a challenge to 'that draft dodger' Jack Dempsey, who chose to draw the colour line. Little had changed in the world of boxing.

January 2, 1916, in return for a fee, and he would happily repeat it for anybody willing to cross his palm with silver. His sworn statement opened with the emotive words: 'This confession of mine is the God's honest, Gospel truth. I swear by the holiness of my Maker and my dear beloved mother, because of whom I consented to face Jess Willard in the ring, that I'm telling the truth and

Johnson carried on fighting until he was past fifty, finally retiring from the ring in 1928 after twice being stopped by opponents whom he would not have allowed within punching distance in his days as heavyweight champion of the world. He continued to appear in exhibition matches into his mid-sixties. Of his 113 listed contests he won seventy-eight, forty-eight of them inside the distance, and he drew another fourteen contests. There were also fourteen bouts that were of the 'no decision' variety in which – because of laws banning anything but exhibition boxing – the decisions were left to ringside reporters. He was rarely judged to have come off second best.

When this picture was taken in 1945, Johnson was as near to contentment as he had ever been in his life. Less than a year later he was killed in a car crash.

DEATH AT THE WHEEL

During his world travels, Johnson had picked up a fair command of French and Spanish and also an exaggerated British accent. Virtually self-educated, he liked to read the classics and could quote Shakespeare and Victor Hugo. Long after his retirement he was still giving boxing exhibitions, and he was an entertaining public speaker. He became a popular attraction at New York's Herbert Museum, where – second on the bill to a flea circus – his hand speed on the punchball brought gasps of astonishment from spectators, most of whom did not realize they were watching one of the greatest boxers that ever lived.

He and his wife, Lucille, divorced in 1924, and he soon married his third white wife, Irene Pineau, who got him organized and brought out the better side of his many-faceted personality.

The one passion he never lost was for fast, flashy cars. During his lifetime he picked up enough speeding tickets to have wallpapered a gymnasium and he miraculously survived three serious car smashes in which his vehicles were a write-off.

On June 10, 1946, he was speeding in a huge roadster along US Highway No 1 in Raleigh, North Carolina, on the way home from a speaking engagement when he lost control of the car coming off a bend and crashed into a telegraph pole. The car overturned and Johnson was thrown out. He died of his injuries at St Agnes Hospital later that day. The young doctor writing out the death certificate took the name from the driving licence and entered it as John Arthur Johnson, but an old hospital porter looked at the familiar face and said: 'That ain't John Johnson. That's Jack Johnson, the greatest heavyweight fighter that ever lived.' He was sixty-eight years old. The poor boy from Galveston who had visited almost every major capital in the world had reached the end of his remarkable journey.

Johnson was buried in a bronze, satin-lined casket at Graceland Cemetary in Chicago, close to the grave of an old opponent, Bob Fitzsimmons. Nobody drew the colour line.

CHAPTER SEVEN

JESS WILLARD

THE POTTAWATOMIE GIANT

Just about everything was taken away from Jess Willard. The glory he should have earned winning the world heavyweight title was tarnished by Jack Johnson's claims that he had thrown the fight. Then his championship was ripped away from him by a two-fisted tornado called Dempsey. Double-dealing managers fleeced him and, years later, his lasting place in the record books as the tallest heavyweight champion of them all was taken away.

It was always believed that at 6 foot 6.25 inches Willard stood tallest of all the champions who had worn the world heavyweight crown. But long after the old champ was dead and buried, the physical education director at Harvard University was able to prove scientifically that Willard was in fact a full inch shorter than the records show.

We should not be too surprised at this revelation. Once the unscrupulous promoters who fed off the fight game in his day realized that in Willard they at last had a genuine 'white hope', they were prepared to stretch any statistic for the sake of a cheap publicity headline. They did not believe in letting facts spoil a good story, and when he was first being touted as the man who could 'bring the championship back to the white race', Willard was described as being 'close to seven feet tall.' If an inch or two added to his height guaranteed column inches in the newspapers, then what the heck! His manager fitted him out with a pair of cowboy boots that had extra high heels, and he was paraded in boxing rings and at exhibitions wearing a huge ten-gallon hat that added to the legend that here, truly, was a giant of a man.

Films and photographs of Willard reveal that he did not have the magnificent physique and well-defined muscles of a Johnson or the powerful rawness of a Dempsey. He tended towards podginess, and his long, heavy legs were not the athletic sort made for skipping around a ring at speed. The descriptive words usually associated with him in the ring were 'lumbering,' 'ponderous' and 'cumbersome'. On the plus side, he had immense strength, and he was a far more accomplished boxer than his critics would have you believe. With an 83-inch reach, he was able to keep opponents away by stabbing out a trombone left lead and the following right could lift a mule off the ground if it landed on target.

COWBOY AND INDIANS

Willard's eventful boxing career did not start until he was twenty-nine years old and he was forty-one when he made his last stand in 1923. His background was a publicity man's dream. He was born on a farm near an Indian reservation in Pottawatomie County, Kansas, on December 29, 1881, and he spent his boyhood days among the Red Indians, riding and hunting with them.

He became a teamster, running his own wagon train and breaking horses for sale to ranchers in Kansas and Oklahoma. His early publicity suggested he had started boxing after knocking out two gunslingers in a saloon bar fight. The truth is that one day, when delivering a horse that he had just broken in, he saw two ranch hands struggling to lift bales of cotton on to a wagon. The bales weighed 500 pounds and Willard lifted one on to the wagon without breaking sweat. 'With strength like that, feller,' one of the ranch hands said, 'you'd make a fortune as a prizefighter.' This was at the time when the search for a 'white hope' was at fever pitch, and the newspapers were full of promises from promoters about the riches that were waiting for the man who could dethrone Johnson.

The casual remark from the ranch hand set Willard thinking, and after discussing it with his wife, Hattie, he visited a gymnasium in Oklahoma City and started working out. He lost his first fight on February 15, 1911, on a tenth-round foul, but seven victories in the next five months convinced a local promoter, Billy McCarney, that here was a genuine prospect. A little clumsy on his feet perhaps, but a prospect. And he was white. McCarney was about to match him with a rising star from Springfield called Joe Cox when a fighter rejoicing in the name of 'The Great Romanos' – a vaudeville strong man – hit town and challenged Cox.

McCarney told 'The Great Romanos' that he would get the fight if he could prove himself better than Willard in a gymnasium trial contest. A couple of big rights from Willard took the legs

away from the travelling man and it was decided that Willard should get the bout with Cox. ('The Great Romanos', who had once gone the distance in a non-title fight with Jack Johnson, left the Midwest and headed for California. He ended up in Hollywood, where he won an Academy Award for Best Actor in *The Informer* in 1935. His real name was Victor McLaglen, the British-born movie star.)

A huge question mark was thrown over Willard when he quit in mid-contest against Cox, suddenly pushing the referee between himself and Cox and then climbing out of the ring. He later said that he had got confused after taking a heavy right to the jaw, and that as he had been warned before the contest not to take the fight he felt he was better off getting out of there. But in boxing circles the word went round that the giant cowboy was 'a quitter.' He would later make nonsense of that slur.

Willard was now a genuinely hungry fighter, having let his wagon business run down while concentrating on boxing. He went to Chicago in 1912 in search of fight purses and

The giant Willard (right) poses for the photographer with Al William before their eight-round non-title fight in Reno, Nevada, on July 4, 1913. Willard won on points to confirm his arrival as the new 'white hope' of boxing.

came under the influence of Charles 'Kid' Cutler, a former heavyweight boxer turned professional wrestler. Cutler showed him the finer points of boxing, and was just getting him established as a possible title contender when Willard was sweet-talked away from him by an impresario called Tom Jones. Cutler swore that one day he would get his revenge for having Willard stolen from under his nose – Willard had been staying in his house with him at the time of his defection – and a couple of years later he got his own back. He walked into a saloon in Chicago where he saw Tom Jones holding court at the bar. Jones was suddenly in need of a large drink when he looked up and saw the massive figure of Cutler descending on him. One right-hand punch spread-eagled him over the bar stools, and when he regained his senses he agreed to pay Cutler $5,000 compensation for having stolen Willard from him.

With Jones banging the publicity drum and Willard knocking over a string of good-quality opponents, the 'Pottawatomie Giant' began to emerge as the brightest of the 'white hopes' while the champion, Johnson, was in exile in Europe. One unwanted headline came when Bull Young, his opponent in a fight in Vernon, California, in 1913, went into a coma and died after Willard had hammered him to defeat in the eleventh round. Willard was arrested on a manslaughter charge and then exonerated, but he lost a lot of appetite for the fight game and Tom Jones had to be at his most persuasive to convince him to battle on in search of the world title.

By the time he got his shot at Johnson on April 5, 1915, in Havana, Willard had acquired an unofficial syndicate of managers who were between them creaming off 75 per cent of his purses, but by his wagon-rolling standards he was still earning a small fortune. He gave the performance of his life against Johnson (see page 48), and was for many years bitter over the way his victory was dismissed as 'an arrangement' to suit Johnson. The public in general believed

(see page 48)

Willard and Johnson greet each other before their title fight in Havana in 1915.

Johnson's statement – made for a cash payment by *The Ring* magazine – that he had thrown the fight and they did not have the benefit of seeing the film of the contest. There was a ban on the movie being shown, and it was more than forty years before it was released for viewing. Bill Cayton's Big Fights Inc film clearly reveals Willard giving a good account of himself throughout the fight, and his final punch against a fast-tiring Johnson was powerful enough to have knocked out any man.

When the film was finally shown, Willard said in his slow, drawling voice: 'I've had to wait a long time but at last people are beginning to believe me when I say that I beat Johnson fair and square. If this was a man throwing a fight why did he wait twenty-six rounds in temperatures over one hundred degrees before he quit? Then he said nothing about taking a dive until he was broke and desperate for money. I was trained good and ready to go the full forty-five rounds if necessary, but Johnson was getting so tired he could hardly hold up his hands. When I met him in New York in 1944 I asked him why he made his false statement. He just shrugged and gave me that gold-toothed smile of his. Jack knew and I knew that he was lying. But the feller was desperate for money, so who could blame him. It just wasn't fair to me, but now I hope the record is straight.'

BACK TO THE RANCH

Willard never really had his heart in boxing after the death of Bull Young, and he was not interested in becoming a fighting champion. He invested the money left by the hangers-on feeding off him in a travelling ranch circus, and included his own riding act on the bill, for he was a better horseman than he was a fighter. It was a short-lived enterprise, however, because the Government, in desperate need for riding stock for the cavalry forces going to Europe for the First World War, bought him out, cutting off a considerable source of income.

Forced by his dwindling finances to defend his title, Willard met Frank Moran, the 'Pittsburgh Dentist', over ten rounds in New York on March 25, 1916. It was a 'no decision' match and the only way Moran could have taken the championship was to have stopped Willard.

Above: Willard in his short-lived silent film career. For him, silence was not golden.

Left: The fighting cowboy from Kansas.

But he was never able to land his pet knockout punch – the 'Mary Ann' – and after ten tedious rounds the newspapers were unanimous in naming the champion a clear winner.

The world championship was put into mothballs and Willard went back to ranching, riding, touring the theatre exhibition circuit and performing in a circus for $1,000 a day. He also

appeared in several silent movies, usually as a cowboy who did not need a stand in when it came to riding stunts. He played the lead role in one film, *The Challenge of Chance*, which opened at the Park Movie House in New York in June, 1919. It might have been better if it had never left the cutting room. The film had been put together so hastily to cash in on Willard's status as world champion that the theatre management had to apologize in advance about the editing. What was supposed to have been a romantic drama became an unintended comedy. Scenes appeared out of sequence and hero Willard is seen thumping a series of black-hatted villains in a storyline that has little or no coherence. In one wild fight scene Willard knocks out a dozen assailants without once being parted from his white ten-gallon hat.

It was fairly obvious that Willard was not going to become a rival to Rudolph Valentino,

and he reluctantly got back into training to shift the 30 pounds he had put on during his lay off. He had been out of real ring action for more than three years when the dynamic promoter Tex Rickard caught his interest with an offer of $100,000 to defend his title against a mauler from Manassa called Jack Dempsey.

A STANDING TARGET

When Willard and Dempsey met to battle it out in an open-air arena at Toledo, Ohio, on July 4, 1919, Willard's only contribution to the contest was that of a human punchbag. The champion came in at an overweight 245 pounds, and he was a standing target for the murderous punches of the 185-pound Dempsey. Willard toppled to the canvas seven times in a sensational first round as Dempsey swarmed all over him. Just before he got into the ring, manager 'Doc' Kearns told Dempsey that he had put the entire $10,000 purse on him to win in the first round at odds of 10-1. Thinking he had won the bet, Dempsey left the ring in triumph as the referee waved it all over, with Willard sitting in a neutral corner minus two front teeth and with a broken jaw and two cracked ribs.

Then, in a farcical about-turn that would have sat neatly in his recent movie flop, Willard discovered there was still more punishment to come. There was so much pandemonium as the champion was chopped down like a rotting tree that the referee did not hear the bell ringing to signal the end of round one. Dempsey was recalled to the ring to finish the demolition. Goodness knows what the 2,000 women in the 20,000 crowd – all sitting together in a fenced-off section – thought of it all.

Willard, dismissed as a quitter at one stage in his career, showed enormous courage as he stood up to Dempsey's battering ram attacks for two more rounds. But the effort had been too much for the gentle cowboy from Kansas and he was unable to get off his stool to start round four. Jack Dempsey was the new heavyweight champion of the world.

It was later suggested that Dempsey's wily manager, 'Doc' Kearns, had soaked his fighter's bandages in plaster of Paris. 'I've got it on good authority that Dempsey's bandages were hardened,' said Willard in his retirement years. 'I am positive it's true. Nobody could hit as hard as he did in that first round. He had fists of iron. Every time he hit me, particularly with his left, it was like a hammer landing on my jaw. It wasn't what I'd call natural power.'

When the allegation was put to Kearns he chuckled and said: 'Naw, come on, would I pull a stroke like that? The truth is I soaked the bandages in cement!'

It was expected that Willard would never fight again, but after four years of retirement in California he wanted to get some money together to open Hollywood's first supermarket. He made a comeback against a rising young heavyweight called Floyd Johnson in New York in 1923 on a show sponsored by Mrs Randolph Hearst's Milk Fund at the Yankee Stadium. He confounded the experts by knocking out Johnson in eleven rounds. Then, at the age of forty-one, he was paid the highest purse of his career –

$125,000 – to fight Luis 'Angel' Firpo in Jersey City on July 12, 1923, with the winner promised a championship match against the dynamic Dempsey. For seven rounds Willard dished out punishment against the South American, but his legs finally let him down and Firpo steamrollered over his exhausted opponent and stopped him in the eighth round.

Willard retired with his wife and two sons – Jess Jr. and Alan – to a comfortable home in California, where he had numerous ups and downs with investments and business ventures. He lived to the grand old age of eighty-six before succumbing to a heart attack, and he died in Pacolma Memorial Lutheran Hospital, Los Angeles, on December 15, 1968. When the final bell rang for him, he was remembered with great warmth by the close-knit boxing community.

'Jess was a man's man and a credit to the fight trade,' said his old foe Jack Dempsey. 'He was a true sportsman.'

A lot may have been taken away from the 'Pottawatomie Giant', but no one was ever able to take away his dignity.

57

Willard's tools of destruction become loving hands as he cuddles his son, Jess Jr.

CHAPTER EIGHT

JACK DEMPSEY

THE MANASSA MAULER

Jack Dempsey rose from barroom brawler and hobo to become one of the most famous and fêted sportsmen in history, yet there was a time when he was very nearly as unwelcome and rejected by the American public as Jack Johnson, and this was without the handicap of what would, in those days of prejudice, have been considered the wrong colour skin. Dempsey was accused of ducking Army service during the First World War, and although a jury cleared him of a charge of draft dodging, the damage to his popularity looked as if it might be permanent.

The man who was to become the first world superstar of the boxing ring and whose fame transcended his sport struggled for acceptance from a large section of the public until the night in 1926 that Gene Tunney punched him almost blind and snatched his world title. Both his eyes swollen and closed, Dempsey said to his cornerman as Tunney was announced as the points winner and new heavyweight champion: 'Lead me out there. I want to shake his hand.'

When he came face to face with his actress wife, Estelle Taylor, after the fight she almost fainted when she saw his bruised features. 'Ginsberg,' she cried, using her pet name for him, 'What happened?'

'Honey,' said the former champion, 'I forgot to duck.'

Newspapermen were witnesses to this touching moment, and when it was reported that Dempsey did not bleat in defeat or try to make any alibis he was transformed into a folk hero whose fame never diminished. Some fifty-five years later President Ronald Reagan used the same line to his wife, Nancy – 'Honey, I forgot to duck' – when a bullet from a would-be assassin hit him.

Reagan, like all Americans, was a Dempsey fan, and when the old champion took the final count on May 31, 1983, at the age of eighty-seven, the President spoke for the nation when he said: 'In the hearts of the people, Jack Dempsey never lost his title. He will always be looked on as "The Champ".'

A SPIRIT OF ADVENTURE

The story of Jack Dempsey's rise from freight-hopping bum to holder of the world's greatest sports prize would have stretched the imagination of a Hollywood scriptwriter. For much of his career and for the rest of his life Dempsey's name was synonymous with Manassa in Colorado, but he hardly knew the place. His nomadic parents just happened to be passing through there on a journey west from Mudfork, West Virginia, when their son William Harrison Dempsey was born on June 24, 1894. Years later it was the more than somewhat gifted 'Guys and Dolls' sportswriter Damon Runyon who dubbed him the 'Manassa Mauler'.

He was known as Harry to his parents, Hyrum and Celia Dempsey. Hyrum Dempsey was a rugged and restless descendent of Irish immigrants and had left his job as a school-teacher to venture west in search of new opportunities for himself and his family. There was a strain of native American Indian blood in both parents, revealed in their son's blue-black hair and high cheekbones.

Dempsey inherited his father's adventurous spirit and when he was sixteen he ran off to find work in mountain mining camps. He first realized the power he carried in his fists when

An early shot of Dempsey before his 1916 fight against Johnny Sudenberg. He won by a knockout in the second round.

knocking out drunks in barroom brawls, and he did not take much persuading to start fighting for much-needed cash under the ring name of 'Kid Blackie'. After working down the mines, he rode the freight cars on trains and slept in hobo hang outs while travelling to fairs, where he would take on opponents of all shapes and sizes. He shined shoes, picked fruit and generally hustled for a living until he decided to become a full-time fighter.

An older brother, Bernie, was fighting as Jack Dempsey – taking the name of the old-time middleweight champion known as Jack 'The Nonpareil' Dempsey. One night in Denver Bernie was injured and asked Harry to substitute for him. He was introduced by the ring announcer as Jack Dempsey. The name stuck.

After a string of unrecorded contests as 'Kid Blackie', Dempsey became managed officially by Jack Price and then John 'The Barber' Reisler, but it was when he joined forces with a dynamic young manager called Jack 'Doc' Kearns that his career really started to get under way. With Kearns doing all the shouting outside the ring and Dempsey beating all the opposition inside the ring (twenty-one opponents falling to him in the first round), they came to the astute attention of promoter Tex Rickard, who was like Barnum and Bailey rolled into one.

CUTTING DOWN THE GIANT

Rickard teamed up with Kearns, and persuaded Jess Willard to come out of hiding and put his title on the line against Dempsey, who, although only just past twenty-four, was already a veteran of more than eighty fights, many of them not to be found in any boxing record book. On Independence Day 1919 Dempsey unleashed one of the most savage attacks ever seen in a boxing ring. He knocked the giant Willard down seven times in the first round, and the renowned *New York Times* sports columnist Red Smith captured Willard's plight memorably when he wrote: 'He did not look in need of a doctor so much as a coroner.'

Believing that the seventh knockdown had finished the fight, Dempsey and Kearns left the ring to celebrate winning the world championship and an audacious $10,000 bet at odds of 10-1 that the challenger would win in the first round. Nobody had heard the bell to signal the end of round one, and it's difficult to imagine whether Dempsey or Willard was more perturbed when he was summoned back to the ring. Dempsey had lost his earlier momentum and it took him two more rounds to finish the destruction of the outgunned cowboy from Kansas.

It was Dempsey who later revealed that he had not received a penny piece for his work, and

Dempsey (second from right) catches up with the news during a break in his training for the championship challenge against Jess Willard. Disabled patients from a local veterans' home were invited to watch his training sessions.

claimed that it was Kearns who had placed the bet. His purse should have been $27,500. So where did the rest of the money go? 'It was eaten up by training expenses and publicity over-heads,' said Kearns, sewing the seeds for what would be a bitter break up of their partnership in later years.

In a ghostwritten autobiography long after Dempsey's retirement, Kearns claimed that the rumours about his soaking Dempsey's bandages in plaster of Paris were true. But this came from a man given to wild exaggeration, and the old champion always swore that his gloves were loaded only with his dynamite-packed fists.

A WAR DODGER ?

The demolition of Willard convinced fight fans that boxing had discovered the most exciting heavyweight champion since the barnstorming days of John L. Sullivan, but the bad odour attached to his draft dodging court case hung heavily over the Dempsey camp. He had claimed exemption from serving in the US Army on the grounds that he was doing essential work in a Philadelphia shipyard. He posed for pictures carrying a riveting gun and wearing overalls – but with patent leather shoes on his feet. Workers at the shipyard who had been served

their call-up papers said they had never seen him do a single shift. A jury exonerated him, but few people really believed his story that he was 'doing his bit' for his country in the shipyard. A lot of mud was thrown at Dempsey in the court-room, including an allegation that he had been living with a prostitute. But what damaged him most of all was the accusation that he had let down his country in a time of need. Being unpa-triotic in the United States at that time was con-sidered unforgiveable. What Dempsey's many detractors wanted to know was that if he was so busy working in the Philadelphia shipyard, how did he manage to squeeze thirty-six professional contests into 1917 and 1918, the two years when so many of his fellow-Americans were fighting a war in Europe? And only three of those fights were in Philadelphia.

When he made his world title defence against Frenchman Georges Carpentier in 1921 public opinion was still heavily against him. Even at this distance the feeling massed against him can be gauged from this quote from *Labour*, an influential American trade union paper:

'Of the 115,000,000 people in the United States at least 114,900,000 would be happy to see Dempsey beaten. The rea-son is clear. When Dempsey stayed out of the war he damned himself for ever. The American people will not forget or

This photograph of Dempsey working as a riveter in a shipbuilding yard was meant to prove that he was doing his bit for his country during the First World War. But workers at the yard revealed that it was a staged picture, and Dempsey had to face a court trial before he was cleared of being a draft dodger.

forgive a slacker, and when the slacker is a professional fighter, his absence from the front line is infuriating and, frankly, sickening. A man who will not stand up and be counted for his country is not fit to hold the heavyweight championship of the world.'

Tex Rickard never missed a trick, and he capitalized on this leg-chopping publicity by drawing attention to the fact that Carpentier was a First World War hero who had been decorated for his bravery on the western front. It was the classic white hat versus black hat confrontation, with the champion reduced to the role of the villain who everybody wanted to see gunned down. It was a masterstroke by a master publicist, and the fight in a wooden arena in Jersey City on July 2, 1921, attracted boxing's first million-dollar gate.

A crowd of 80,183 paid $1,789,238 to witness the showdown, and 'the villain' Dempsey disappointed all those who wanted to see him fall by knocking out the 'Orchid Man' from Paris in the fourth round. There was no disputing the

The 1921 fight that drew the first $1 million gate ends in the fourth round, with a concerned Dempsey helping up his opponent, Georges Carpentier, after he had been counted out.

crowd-pulling power of Dempsey. His all-action style of fighting made him one of the most exciting attractions in sporting history. He fought out of a bobbing, weaving crouch, which made him look shorter than his 6 feet 1 inches. Opponents would tell how he was always humming a barely audible tune as he came hunting them, swinging punches to the rhythm of the song. When asked what tunes he hummed, Dempsey shrugged and said, 'I ain't got no idea. I guess I'm too busy trying to knock my opponent's head off to know what I'm humming.'

Dempsey was 187 pounds of unbridled violence. That is not big by the standards of today's super-heavyweight , but he hit as hard as any heavyweight in history. In a poll conducted by Associated Press in 1950, Dempsey was rated ahead even of Joe Louis as the greatest fighter of the half-century. He had long ago been forgiven for his non-participation in the First World War.

Having broken all records in the fight with Carpentier, Dempsey and Kearns then broke the bank of the city of Shelby in Montana. The bank had been persuaded to put up the townsfolk's money to stage Dempsey's defence against Tommy Gibbons. Dempsey won on points over

The 'battle of the long count' in Chicago in 1927. Gene Tunney is just about to rise after spending fourteen seconds on the canvas. Dempsey stalks from the neutral corner. If he had gone there in the first place, he might have regained the world heavyweight title.

fifteen rounds before sneaking out of town on a train specially hired by manager 'Doc' Kearns for a fast getaway. Kearns had the takings safely tucked into a bag. It took shell-shocked Shelby a generation to recover from the experience and Dempsey was about as popular there as a skunk in a beauty parlour.

His championship clash with Argentinian Luis 'Angel' Firpo in New York on September 14, 1923, has been acclaimed as the most thrilling fight of all time – and it was all over inside two rounds. Firpo was flattened seven times in the opening round, and then somehow found the strength to knock Dempsey through the ropes and out of the ring with a couple of crude swings. The champion was pushed back in by pressmen just before the bell, and he then tamed the 'Wild Bull of the Pampas' by knocking him out in the second round.

BATTLE OF THE LONG COUNT

There was a bitter falling out between Dempsey and Kearns after the Firpo fight, and the champion did not put the title on the line again for three years – avoiding, among others, outstanding black contender Harry Wills.

Dempsey had divorced his first wife, Maxine Gates, a saloon bar piano player, and Kearns disapproved of Dempsey's choice of silent film star Estelle Taylor as his second wife. This, along with wrangles over purse monies, caused an irreparable rift and subsequent legal battles that led to the end of their partnership.

The champion was anchored by worries about lawsuits and domestic problems when he finally returned to the ring to defend the title against Gene Tunney, who was the complete opposite to Dempsey in style. While Dempsey was a rugged, crouching swinger of a two-fisted fighter, Tunney was a smart, upright technician, and he jabbed his way to a convincing ten-rounds points victory. The fight drew a huge crowd of 120,757 to a big horseshoe shaped stadium in Philadelphia on September 23, 1926, and while cheering Tunney's skill, the rain-soaked spectators cheered even louder for Dempsey's courage and determination. He was a bigger hero in defeat than he had ever been in victory.

The return was again over ten rounds, and Tunney retained the title with another points win

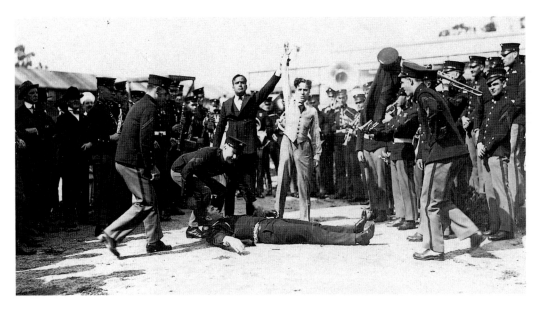

Dempsey played guest roles in several films. Here, he has just been knocked out by Charlie Chaplin, and Douglas Fairbanks Sr. is raising Charlie's hand in victory.

in the famous 'battle of the long count' in Soldiers Field, Chicago, on September 22, 1927. Gracious and gentlemanly outside the ring, Dempsey was like a mad bull inside the roped square. In the seventh round he floored Tunney for the first time in Tunney's career with a seven-punch barrage to the head. Dempsey forgot the new rule about retiring to a neutral corner and five seconds had elapsed before referee Dave Barry managed to usher him away. Only then did he pick up the count, and Tunney had been on the canvas for fourteen seconds before he scrambled up at nine. Dempsey charged in to deliver the knockout, but Tunney was too evasive for him and floored the 'Manassa Mauler' for a brief count in the eighth round as he came rushing after him with fists swinging wildly.

Tunney finished a clear points winner, but Dempsey's followers argued that the champion was saved by the long count. Tunney insisted that he was in command of his senses while on the canvas, and Bill Cayton's Big Fights Inc film of the fight supports his theory that he could and would have got up in time. He was listening intently to the count and would certainly have risen before ten, but it will always be the subject of debate what those extra four seconds meant because there was no doubt that he was badly dazed by the power of Dempsey's punches.

Tunney's victory signalled the end of Dempsey's explosive career, but he kept raking in the money with exhibition matches that drew bigger gates than any of the active heavyweights in the 1930s until the emergence of Joe

Louis. *The Ring Record Book and Boxing Encyclopedia* records that Dempsey was watched by a total of 230,155 spectators in thirty-four exhibition contests and earned a total of $477,260. His official boxing record, which misses out at least thirty contests in the early part of his career, lists eighty-one contests, of which he won forty-nine inside the distance. He was outpointed six times and stopped once when Jim Flynn knocked him out in one round in 1917. Dempsey returned the compliment in a return match a year later. There are also eight draws and six 'no decision' bouts on his record. He defended the world title five times between 1919 and 1926 before the first meeting with Tunney, including winning defences against Billy Miske and Bill Brennan in 1920.

When the United States went to war after the bombing of Pearl Harbour in 1942, Dempsey enlisted in the US Coastguard and was commissioned a Lieutenant Commander. He had finally wiped out the stigma of being a draft dodger in the First World War.

MANHATTAN MADNESS

Like James J. Corbett, John L. Sullivan and Jack Johnson, Dempsey was attracted to the stage. He made many personal appearances in coast-to-coast tours and he featured on Broadway in a play called *The Big Fight*, which had his wife, Estelle Taylor, as the female lead. They then appeared together in a Hollywood movie called

Manhattan Madness, which prompted one rather unimpressed critic to write: 'Can their marriage survive this catastrophe?'

The answer appeared to be 'no'. He divorced Miss Taylor and then married the singer Hannah Williams, with whom he had two daughters – Joan in 1934 and Barbara in 1936. Dempsey divorced Hannah in 1943 and it was 1958 before he married for a fourth time, to the former Deanna Piattelli. He later adopted her daughter from a previous marriage. She took the name Barbara Dempsey and helped him write his absorbing autobiography, *Dempsey*, which was published in 1977.

Dempsey kept close links with boxing as a referee and allowed his name – the best known in the fight game – to be used in several promotions. He was always quick to pass on tips to young hopefuls, and once told a prospect who was seeking his advice: 'Some night, son, you'll catch a punch between the eyes and all of a sudden you'll see three guys in the ring against you. Pick out the one in the middle and hit him as hard as you can, because it's odds on that he's the one who hit you.'

For many years his New York restaurant, Jack Dempsey's, which he co-owned with wealthy racehorse owner Jack Amiel, became the place where big-fight matches were made and where old-timers gathered to remember the days when Dempsey was king. He lived to see New York become a mugger's city, and added some unreported scalps to his record of knockouts.

Late one evening he was sitting at a red light in a cab in midtown Manhattan when two muggers pulled open the two rear doors and demanded money. The old champ later told customers at his restaurant: 'I took care of it. I knocked out one with a right and the other with a left. The last thing a fighter loses is his punch.'

Another stirring tale with which he used to regale customers was of an experience he had while driving through the Colorado mountains when he was a hungry young fighter. He had just earned what was for him a massive purse of $800, which was in a bag held by his old friend Otto Flotto, who was sitting alongside him in the passenger seat. They were followed from the mining camp where he had earned his purse by four men in a car, who forced him to pull over. 'This is a hold-up,' one of them said, flourishing a pistol. The four men took the bag containing the $800 and drove off.

About an hour later Dempsey and Flotto stopped at a small hotel to beg for a coffee. In the dining room they recognized the four hold-up men. Dempsey pounced on them, flattened them one by one, recovered the $800 and then chased them out into the street. 'If you want any more,' snarled Dempsey, 'you can come back, and bring your gun if you want to. But you'd better be prepared to die for my money.' He never saw them again.

It's the stuff of which legends are made. And Jack Dempsey, the 'Manassa Mauler', was a legend in his own fighting time.

Jack Dempsey's restaurant was a favourite meeting place for any fight fans visiting New York. The restaurant's slogan was, 'Love matches are made in heaven, but boxing matches are made at Jack Dempsey's'.

CHAPTER NINE

GENE TUNNEY

THE FIGHTING MARINE

He was a scholar, and a ripe good one;
  Exceeding wise, fair-spoken, and persuading:
  Lofty and sour to them that love'd him not;
  But, to those men that sought him, sweet as summer.

There can be no doubt that Gene Tunney was the only world heavyweight champion to start an address to the scholars of Yale University with this quotation from Shakespeare's *Henry VIII*, with whom he was more familiar than he was with most of his contemporaries. He felt as comfortable lecturing on the written works of the Bard as he did dancing around a boxing ring, winning nearly every one of his contests with 'scientific' skill as opposed to the brute force that swept Jack Dempsey to the world crown.

Tunney was never a champion who appealed to the masses. He was too cold and calculating for the fans fed on the raw meat diet of the dynamic Dempsey. While Dempsey was murderous, Tunney was methodical. He planned every contest like a military campaign and did only what needed to be done to win. Tunney was a no-risk boxer who knew that he could be dull to watch. But he did not care. He was not there to donate his blood but to earn big bucks. To him, boxing was purely a business which he used as a means to an end – the end being a fortune in the bank and unscrambled brains so that he could enjoy his riches in the manner to which he was determined to become accustomed. He retired as undefeated world heavyweight champion after only two defences of the title and with nearly $2 million tucked away and a wealthy heiress on his arm as his new bride.

THE SWEET SCIENCE

A myth was allowed to grow into something approaching fact that because Tunney was so well read he came from a middle-class background with all the privileges that entailed. Many fight fans looked on him as a snob, and the 'man-of-the-people' comedian Will Rogers conveyed what many of them were thinking when he said: 'What we want are prizefighters with more wallop and less Shakespeare.'

Tunney had battled to the top – educating himself on the way – from a starting point in life that was anything-but-privileged. He was born in New York City on May 25, 1898, the son of a longshoreman, who struggled to make ends meet for a family of six. He was christened James Joseph Tunney, but became Gene because of his baby sister's inability to pronounce 'Jim' properly. When he was just three months old, his family moved to an apartment above a grocery store in Greenwich Village, and it was there that he attended state schools until he was sixteen, when he started work as a $5-a-week office boy.

Tunney later said that his family's move to Greenwich Village was the best thing that could have happened to him. An area of New York well known for its artistic community, this was where many poets, artists, authors and musicians congregated while waiting for their work to be acknowledged, and the young Tunney had his mind stimulated listening to them and watching them at work. One day he determined he would become as articulate and as literate as these fascinating people.

To Tunney, boxing was a sweet science. He could never see the sense of taking unnecessary punches, and much of his early work in the gymnasium was dedicated to learning how to avoid punches. He started boxing professionally at the age of eighteen in 1915 and was unbeaten in his first twelve contests before joining the US Marines, winning the US Expeditionary Forces light-heavyweight title in France immediately after the end of the First World War.

A stylist with a rapier-like left jab and a solid right cross, he took the American light-heavyweight crown from 'Battling' Levinsky in 1922. Four months later Harry 'Smash-and-Grab-'em' Greb gave him a terrible hiding which put him on his back in bed for a week. It was the

Tunney at the German front with the Inter-Allied Armies' heavy-weight champion, Bob Martin, at the end of the First World War. Tunney was the services light-heavyweight title holder.

only loss of his career and he proved that he could learn from defeat by getting the better of Greb in four subsequent contests. Greb ('Give me broads before boxing any day') could not have been more different from Tunney if he had tried, and he was as famous as a playboy as he was a fighter. In 1925 in their final fight – each one went the distance – Greb was on the edge of exhaustion, and during the seventh of the ten rounds he pleaded with Tunney as they went into a clinch: 'You've got it won, Gene ... please don't knock me out.'

Tunney replied, 'Stay in close, Harry. I'll carry you.' This was one great warrior laying down his shield to another. The story came from Greb, who rated Tunney not only a gentleman of the ring, but also one of the hardest punchers he ever met, even though he was generally not noted for devastating power.

Tunney was one of the most single-minded sportsmen of his time, and he parted company with a string of managers who did not share his vision. After signing with manager Billy Gibson for the best years of his boxing life, he started having trouble with brittle hands and he used to soak them daily in brine to harden them. He also became a frequent visitor to a Maine lumber camp, where chopping down trees with an axe helped strengthen his hands and develop his upper body.

THE TITLE CAMPAIGN

Tunney launched a carefully mapped out campaign for the heavyweight title by eliminating each of the leading contenders, stopping Georges Carpentier in fifteen rounds in New York on July 24, 1924, and Tommy Gibbons in twelve rounds in New York on June 5, 1925. Dempsey, who had managed to duck outstanding black challenger Harry Wills, could not stall Tunney any longer and they finally met in a rainstorm in Philadelphia on September 23, 1926. The challenger – just half an inch over 6 foot tall and half a pound lighter than the 190-pound Dempsey – boxed cleverly on the retreat to win an undisputed points victory over ten rounds, the maximum allowed under Philadelphia law. The new champion made out a balancing cheque to Tex Rickard for $9,555 and collected in return a cheque for $1 million – the first million-dollar purse paid to a fighter. Tunney had the cheque framed and hung at his home.

Two months after winning the championship Tunney was arrested on the grounds that he had given an unlicensed boxing exhibition at Loew's State Theatre in New York City. The champion was exonerated, and he later sued for false arrest. It was his first experience of what was to become frequent visits to the courtroom.

The world nearly lost its new heavyweight champion on Christmas Day 1926. A devout Roman Catholic, Tunney was walking across a frozen lake in Rockwood on his way to morning Mass when the ice gave way and he tumbled into treacherous water that was 100 feet deep. A group of companions with him formed a human chain and managed to drag him out. 'That was the closest call I ever had,' said the champion. 'If I had been on my own there was no way I could have got out. It was like a nightmare.'

Tunney gave Dempsey a chance for revenge in Chicago on September 22, 1927, and came perilously close to losing the title in the famous 'battle of the long count' (see page 63). It was reported that a betting syndicate were prepared to pay Tunney $1 million to throw the fight, but they were wasting their breath. Tunney was a man of great integrity, and he would never have anything to do with boxing's seamier side.

Golf was Tunney's way of relaxing away from the ring. His partner here is middleweight Mickey 'Toy Bulldog' Walker. A week after this picture was taken in 1924, Tunney knocked out Georges Carpentier in the fifteenth round.

A BOXING SCHOLAR

The two victories over Dempsey had given Tunney the financial independence he had always wanted, and now he was able to travel 'to educate my mind'. He went to London to take up an invitation for a private meeting with the Prince of Wales in St James's Palace, spent a couple of days with George Bernard Shaw, who had become a pen pal, and then crossed over to Paris with his author friend Thornton Wilder to meet F. Scott Fitzgerald and boxing *aficionado* Ernest Hemingway. A sportsman who preferred the company of writers to that of fighters, mixing with these literary heroes gave Tunney a bigger thrill than winning the world heavyweight championship.

When it was suggested that he was becoming a snob, he said: 'If being a snob is about trying to improve my mind and to learn anything I can from reading books and meeting writers and artists then I am happy to own up to being a snob. There are those in boxing who consider me a snob. They don't like my independence and my aloofness. This does not worry me. I have a great affection for people, and I have never knowingly let down the general public.'

In 1926 Tunney gave the following revealing interview to English poet and magazine writer Robert Nichols, which provides a remarkable insight into the way he thought and fought:

'As soon as the first bell rings and I leave my corner every thing in the world vanishes but my opponent and the figure of the referee, rather felt than seen. There we are in the large white ring, space about us. I don't even hear the crowd, and nothing that anybody yells nor what my opponent may say – and some fighters talk a great deal – makes any difference to my concentration. Then I am myself, if you know what I mean.

'First there's my brain, as clear and as hard as crystal. Then there's my body, which translates its prompting into action. Finally, there's something else inside which drives and sustains the whole.

'I fight by intuition directly I am out of my corner, but the intuitions are modified by disciplined thinking and are

A crucial victory for Tunney as Tommy Gibbons takes the count in the twelfth round of their 1925 heavyweight title eliminator.

instantly translated into deeds. The great thing is to have something inside burning brightly and steadily. Once it begins to go you are likely to be shaken, and once you are shaken you lose coordination. You can tell by a fighter's knees when his coordination has gone. They begin to sag. It is always the first telltale sign.

'Fighting – all else being equal – is largely a matter of being focused, absolutely focused on the job in hand. Your mind, your body, they have to be as one.

'You have to control something within you that I can only describe as a sort of inspiration. You can no more fight without it than an author, or so I would imagine, can write without it. A fighter builds up this inspiration for a fight – it is a sort of morale plus something else that I cannot define that is deeply personal to each fighter. The something else is what you reach for and hopefully find when you feel all-in. That's when you call on this inner strength.

'I'll tell you a fight when I called on this more than in any other – in my only defeat by Harry Greb. I was badly cut and lost a quart of blood. Even Harry was pleading with me to quit, and the referee kept asking if I wanted him to stop it. But I called on that inner strength and finished the stipulated fifteen

rounds. My pride demanded that I should not quit.

'After the fight I was lying exhausted on my back in the dressing-room with my two eyes just slits when a little ringside betting man bustled through the door. He came over to where I was lying and was all excited, tears rolling down his face. "You've got it, boy," he said. "You've got it. I'm going to put every

Tunney and Dempsey before their 'battle of the long count' in Chicago on September 22, 1927. It was to be Dempsey's last official fight, and Tunney fought just once more before retiring.

Left: Mayor Jimmy Walker and the Marines turn out to welcome Tunney home to New York City as the new world heavyweight champion in 1926.

Below: Tunney is all smiles before his title defence against New Zealander Tom Heeney in New York in 1928. Perhaps he already knew that this would be his final fight before retiring as undefeated champion.

cent I have on you to one day become heavyweight champion of the world."

'Other people in the dressing room thought he was quite mad. But he had recognised that I had that indefinable quality ... that inner strength ...'

FIGHTING IN THE COURTS

Tunney was not enough of a real fighting man to capture the public imagination, and promoter Tex Rickard dropped more than $150,000 when he made a second title defence against New Zealander Tom Heeney at Yankee Stadium in New York City on July 26, 1928. After stopping Heeney in eleven rounds, Tunney stunned boxing in general and Rickard in particular by announcing his retirement from the ring. He was just thirty, and he wanted to get on with a life away from boxing. It was also to be the flamboyant Rickard's last fight. He died in Florida six months later.

Three months after quitting the ring Tunney quietly slipping off to Rome where he married Polly Lauder, heiress to a wealthy Greenwich businessman. While he and his new bride toured Europe, however, the fury of a woman scorned was breaking loose back home in the States. A divorcée called Katherine King Fogarty filed a $500,000 breach of promise suit, claiming that Tunney had said he would marry

her as soon as she got a divorce. Then her former husband also sued Tunney for allegedly enticing his wife away from him.

The former champion was also hit with a law suit by sports promoter Timothy Mars, who was demanding a share of his ring profits. It was revealed in court that in the three years from his first fight with Dempsey his earnings had totalled $1,715,863 – which was an absolute fortune in those days and not to be sneezed at in this day and age. These revelations did not boost Tunney's popularity with the public. There is such a thing as being too successful.

He won his case against Mars, and Katherine Fogarty and her former husband eventually dropped their charges after long legal battles that caused the former champion great embarrassment. 'I never want to see another courtroom or lawyer's bill,' he said.

DAUGHTER ON MURDER CHARGE

Tunney adopted the lowest profile possible as he started to concentrate on a business career that added to his immense wealth; at one time he held places on twelve company boards. His main interests were in timber, coal, banking and rubber.

In an era when the Charles Lindbergh baby kidnapping caused fear among wealthy parents, Tunney and his wife had to suffer the nightmare of kidnap threats against one of their baby sons, Gene Jr., in 1932. Another son, John, grew up to become a US Congressman, with Jack Dempsey among his supporters helping to 'press the flesh' in election campaigns.

Tunney, the longshoreman's son, became a close friend of presidents. He worked for all of Roosevelt's elections, and after serving as a naval lieutenant commander in charge of recreational activity during the Second World War, he bought a farm in Stamford, Connecticut, where he had a gymnasium and a steam bath to help him keep his weight somewhere close to his final fighting weight of 192 pounds. He also had a luxury summer house in Maine, which he often lent to his friend President John F. Kennedy.

Tunney was fiercely patriotic, and served as a chairman of the Greater New York Anti-Communism Crusade.

The crown of thorns? The old champ was inconsolable in 1970 when his thirty-year-old daughter, Joan, the youngest of his four children, was charged with murdering her husband in the village of Chenies, near Amersham, in Britain where they had set up home just a few months earlier. Joan was found guilty and was committed to Broadmoor, the top-security hospital for the criminally insane.

Tunney could not go to England for the trial because he was convalescing in Arizona accompanied by his wife, following serious spinal surgery. It was said that he never really recovered from the heartache, and he took his sadness with him to his grave when he died at the age of eighty on November 7, 1978.

The thinking man's champion was mourned by a boxing world in which he was considered one of the most skilful of all the heavyweight champions. More important to Tunney, he was without doubt the best read.

'We were as inseparable as Siamese twins,' said 83-year-old Jack Dempsey. 'As long as Gene was alive, I felt we shared a link with that wonderful period of the past. Now I feel all alone.'

71

Tunney and Dempsey, firm friends after their two fights, come together in 1964 to campaign for the re-election of Gene's son, Congressman John Tunney (centre).

CHAPTER TEN

72

MAX SCHMELING

THE BLACK UHLAN

Max Schmeling is the only man in this century of champions to have won the world heavyweight crown while writhing on the canvas. He had been dropped there by a vicious low punch from Jack Sharkey in the fourth round of a 1930 title fight to find a successor to the throne vacated by Gene Tunney. Within seconds of Schmeling sinking to the canvas, his voluble manager, Joe Jacobs, jumped into the ring screaming in protest, and he persuaded the referee, Jim Crowley, to reluctantly disqualify Sharkey after forcing him to consult the two ringside judges.

A distraught Sharkey was close to tears and the disqualification stunned and then angered the near 80,000 crowd at Yankee Stadium in New York. They could not believe that they were seeing Schmeling become the first fighter to take the heavyweight crown away from North America (Bob Fitzsimmons adopted American citizenship), and – worse still – it was going to Germany, where Hitler was just starting to win popularity and power on the back of his anti-Semitic policies.

Opposite: Max Schmeling, the 'Black Uhlan'.

Five years later Schmeling – held up by Hitler as a standard bearer of Aryan superiority – would repay Jacobs for the important part he played in making him world champion by defying a Nazi order to sack his Jewish manager.

INSPIRED BY DEMPSEY

Maxmillian Adolph Otto Siegfried Schmeling was born in Klein Luckaw, Brandenburg, on September 28, 1905. He was taught to box as a young boy by his father, a tax inspector, who was also the first man to knock him out. The story passed down by his mother, Amanda, is that Schmeling arrived home late one evening to be met at the door by his furious father. 'Young Max was astonished when waking up the next morning to find that he was still wearing his clothes,' she said. 'He went out like a light when my husband hit him.'

Immediately after the First World War the Schmeling family moved to the Ruhr, the major industrial area of northwest Germany, and Schmeling joined the St George 1816 sports club, where he became an outstanding footballer and athlete. But it was boxing that became his first love after his father had taken him to the cinema to see newsreel coverage of Jack Dempsey's world championship defence against Frenchman Georges Carpentier in 1921.

'Dempsey became my idol,' said Schmeling in an exclusive interview for *Crown of Thorns* in 1992 when, at the age of eighty-five, he was still remarkably active and with total recall of his eventful career. 'Many people commented on how he and I looked like brothers. I was proud of that because I wanted so much to fight like him. I considered him the greatest fighter then, and to this day it remains my opinion.'

Schmeling started his amateur career with a victory in an open-air contest at the plum market in Wandsbek. He combined his boxing with a job as a salesman in the advertising firm William Wilkens, where he picked up a business acumen that was to serve him well in later years.

After moving to the Rheinland, he got a job on a building site to help develop his strength. Professional boxing, banned in Germany until after the war, was just beginning to flourish and Schmeling started fighting for money on August 2, 1924, when he knocked out

Kurt Czapp in six rounds. He made quick progress despite knockout defeats by British-based heavyweights Larry Gains (1925) and Gypsy Daniels (1928).

Schmeling then won the European light-heavyweight title in Dortmund in 1927 and set sail for New York City the following year after capturing the German heavyweight championship with a fifteen-rounds points victory over Franz Diener in Berlin.

'WE WUZ ROBBED!'

Guided by the cigar-chomping Joe Jacobs, Schmeling launched his career in the United States with five successive victories that were virtual eliminators for the world title left vacant by the retirement of Gene Tunney. Jack Sharkey had removed the other leading contender, Phil Scott, with a controversial victory that ended with the British champion on his knees complaining of being hit low.

Jacobs noted how Sharkey allowed his punches to wander below the belt, and when in the title fight showdown on June 12, 1930, he landed a painful left to Schmeling's groin, his manager was up in the ring shouting 'foul' almost before Schmeling had hit the canvas.

Remembering that night and that fight clearly, Schmeling explained in his interview: 'I was terribly hurt, but also embarrassed. This was not the way I wanted to become champion of the world. In the dressing-room after the fight I announced that I would not accept the title, but the distinguished writer Paul Gallico got hold of me and said that I should not be so foolish. "You won it within the rules," he said. "Now you must defend it with pride." My idol Jack Dempsey, who had become my friend and promoter, also said that I was entitled to keep the championship. So I went home to a hero's welcome in Germany as heavyweight champion of the world. It was a boyhood dream come true.'

A year after winning the championship in such unsatisfactory circumstances, Schmeling proved his ability to the doubting American fight fans by stopping the vastly experienced William 'Young' Stribling – the 'Pride of Georgia' – in the last seconds of a fifteen-round title defence in Cleveland on July 3, 1931. The powerful New York State Athletic Commission had in

History is made in 1930 as Max Schmeling wins the world title on the canvas after Jack Sharkey landed a low blow in the fourth round.

the meantime stripped Schmeling of the title and named Sharkey as their paper champion. To settle all arguments Schmeling was pressed into giving Sharkey a return match in Madison Square Garden's open-air arena on Long Island on June 21, 1932.

The majority of ringside reporters judged that Schmeling had scored a clear points victory in a gruelling battle, but the split decision went to Sharkey, and the Americans got their title back. Joe Jacobs yelled, 'We wuz robbed ... we shoulda stood in bed' – which entered boxing language to be used by future boxers and managers when they felt they were on the wrong end of a bad decision. Jacobs threatened to take his protests to the courtroom, but the verdict was allowed to stand in the record books like an open sore. 'At the very best Jack deserved perhaps a draw,' Schmeling said in his interview sixty years later. 'But I am not in any way bitter.

It was all part of boxing business, and I was so pleased and proud to have been involved in it all. Even now I exchange greetings with Jack. We are the only ones left from that great era. It was much harder to be a fighter then because there were so many outstanding men around. Today you can become a champion after only a handful of fights. They do not have the same iron will and determination. That is not a criticism. It is just a fact of life. It was different all those years ago. So different.'

A PLEA TO HITLER

In 1935 Schmeling was dragged into the political arena from which he always tried to hide. He was involved in a row with the Nazi party over his links with his Jewish manager, Joe Jacobs. The argument had been simmering for years ever since Hitler had come to power in Germany, and it exploded to the surface after Schmeling had fought Steve Hamas in Hamburg on March 10, 1935.

The Nazi newspaper, *Fraenkische Tageszeitung*, made a front-page attack on Jacobs for what it described as 'a despicable insult by a Jew to our Fuehrer'. Jacobs had been pictured during the playing of the German national anthem before the fight giving the Nazi salute while holding a giant Havana cigar in the fingers of his saluting hand. 'Adolf Hitler has been grossly offended,' the editorial screamed, 'and Schmeling should discharge the Jew immediately in the interests of Germanhood.'

Hans von Tschammer, the Imperial Sports Minister and a top-ranking Nazi, followed this with a letter to Schmeling demanding that 'you disassociate yourself from your Jewish connections. The Jew Jacobs has greatly offended our beloved Fuehrer.'

Schmeling decided, rather rashly, to go over von Tschammer's head to Hitler himself to try to iron out the problem. He requested a meeting with the Fuehrer, who invited him to tea along with his film actress wife Anny – the Czechoslovakian-born daughter of an Austrian army officer.

The past suddenly came to life as Schemling gave this graphic account of the meeting at the Imperial Chancellor's private residence at Wilhelmstrasse:

'Hitler played the perfect host – "tea or coffee, madam … tea, how nice, Frau Schmeling, I always drink tea but it mustn't be too strong." Then the Fuehrer asked my wife which cake she would like, and when Anny said "Gugelhopf" (an Austrian cake) Hitler was absolutely delighted. "I have not heard that word for so long," he said with a great sigh of nostalgia. Soon he and Anny were in dialogue about her father's Austrian background and then about the Czechoslovakian city of Prague. "Beautiful old Prague," as Hitler called it.

'I finally managed to get a word in and started to plead for my manager, for whom I had always had only respect. "Certainly Herr Jacobs is Jewish," I said, "but we are not conscious of protestants, catholics, jews or negroes in boxing circles.

Schmeling, his right knee heavily bandaged, takes a right from Werner Vollmer in his comeback fight in Frankfurt on September 28, 1947. Max won in the seventh round.

We are interested only in boxing."

'It was clear from Hitler's stony silence that he did not like this at all, but I insisted that I needed Herr Jacobs and that so much of what I had achieved in the United States was due to him. Hitler said nothing, but his face showed displeasure and he slurped his tea loudly. So I tried again. "Herr Jacobs is efficient, orderly, honest and trustworthy," I continued, feeling very irritated by the Fuehrer's continued silence. "Honesty is surely a German virtue."

'That was too much for Hitler. I had gone too far. He made an angry gesture, stared into space and then suddenly said to Anny: "Gugelhopf – I had

almost forgotten that word. Nice that you reminded me of it." With that he rose and said goodbye, and walked out of the room. Our audience was over.'

Schmeling chose to ignore the letter from von Tschammer, who got his revenge when war broke out by making sure that Schmeling was one of the few of Germany's sports stars to get called up for active service. And Anny found her stage and screen scripts being heavily censored by Goebbels – Gugelhopf or no Gugelhopf. However, this did not stop the Nazis from using Schmeling for propaganda purposes when he returned to the United States in 1936 as an intended victim for the fast-rising Joe Louis, who had been an impressive winner of all his twenty-seven fights. Schmeling was not given a hope of victory, and was thought to be there purely as cannon fodder. But Schmeling, by then a cagey veteran of thirty-one, wrecked Louis's script and $1 million world title plans when he grounded the 'Brown Bomber' with his favourite straight right in the fourth round and finally knocked him out in the twelfth of a sensational contest in New York on June 19, 1936. 'I had seen Joe knock out Paolino Uzcudun in a previous fight,' recalled Schmeling, 'and I noticed that he was open to a right hand over the top of his left lead. When I told reporters that I had spotted a weakness they thought I was just saying it for publicity.'

Joe Louis is on his way down to his first defeat as Schmeling lands the final knockout blow in round twelve of their non-title fight in 1936.

BROWN BOMBER'S REVENGE

After his victory over Louis, Schemling was asked to consider becoming an American citizen. 'I told them that I loved my country,' Schmeling said. 'I was not a Nazi. How could I be when I retained so many Jewish connections in America? But once a German, always a German.'

Schmeling was entitled to a shot at the world title held by James J. Braddock, but he was cheated out of it by behind-the-scenes shenanigans and it was Louis who got to Braddock first and relieved him of the championship. Joe Jacobs and Schmeling were, to put it mildly, upset at being sidetracked. On the date originally agreed for his fight with Braddock, Schmeling went through the routine of a weigh in and turned up in his boxing kit in an empty stadium

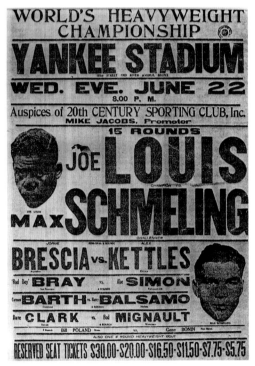

Above: The Nazis organize a huge 'welcome home' parade for Schmeling after his victory over Louis.

Left: The bill poster advertising the return between Louis and Schmeling, this time with the world heavyweight championship at stake.

and the Jewish promoters in the United States were in no mood to put themselves out to help a German battle for the world crown. Schmeling would get his chance, but first he had to wait for Braddock and Louis to settle their argument.

When Schmeling and Louis finally got together again for their title fight on June 22, 1938, racial hatred poisoned the atmosphere because of Hitler's doctrine. The Nazis had been trumpeting that Schmeling was fighting for the white race, and it was an ironic commentary on their racialist nonsense that the 6-foot 1-inch tall Schmeling – nicknamed the 'Black Uhlan' – looked far darker than the *café-au-lait* Louis as they climbed into the Yankee Stadium ring in front of 70,000 screaming fans. 'He looks nearly as dark as that famous Aryan Hitler,' was one memorable aside from the master British sportswriter, Peter Wilson.

The fight lasted just two minutes four seconds, and almost every moment was filled with pain for Schmeling. He spent most of the time either helpless on the ropes or rolling in agony on the canvas. Louis launched more than forty punches and not one of them missed its target. There was a really terrifying moment when Schmeling, half-conscious on the ropes – the top

to try to lay claim to the title and to prove that he had kept to his part of the contract. But this was in the days when Hitler and his Nazi party were getting into their stride with their anti-Semitism,

Right: Schmeling was called up as a paratrooper in the German army at the start of the Second World War.

Below: Schmeling recovering in hospital after his first-round destruction by Louis in 1938. His injuries included broken vertebrae caused when he turned his back on the ropes and took a punch from Louis that made him cry out in agony.

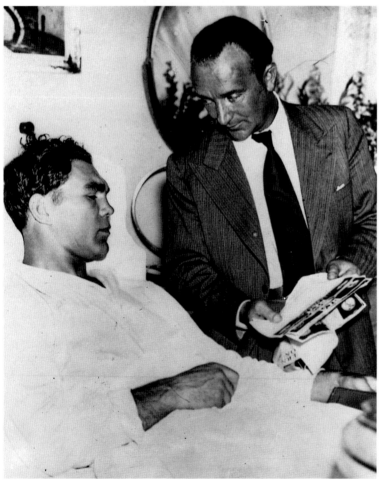

one running under his right armpit and his head lolling over it as if his neck was broken – swivelled round so that his back was facing Louis, who swung a punch that dug into his kidneys. He let out an involuntary scream of pain that could be heard above the yelling fans. It was later discovered that this punch had fractured vertebrae in his back.

As a left hook and right cross to the head sent Schmeling crashing to the canvas for a third time, his friend and trainer Max Machon tossed in the towel. The referee, Arthur Donovan, kicked it aside and waved the fight over. 'I stopped it to save Schmeling from getting killed in there,' Donovan said later.

AWARDED THE IRON CROSS

After spending two weeks in the Polytechnic Hospital in New York, Schmeling returned home to Germany and spent another six weeks recuperating from one of the worst hidings ever handed out in just one round of fighting.

Eleven months after his humiliating defeat by Louis, Schmeling won the European heavyweight championship by knocking out Adolf Heuser in one round in Stuttgart. Then came his call up as a paratrooper, and he was invalided out in 1944 after breaking a leg while making a parachute landing during the Battle of Crete. 'It was my first taste of action and I did not fire a shot,' Schmeling said. 'But I was awarded an Iron Cross first class.' He had been used as a propaganda tool by the Nazis for the last time.

Schmeling's Pommerian estate was wiped out during the war, and he was so broke that he had to make a comeback at the age of forty. He retired after losing the fifth of his comeback fights against Richard Vogt in Berlin on October 31, 1948, and turned his attention to business ventures. And here again he proved himself a champion.

He ran a mink farm, and had interests in poultry and fish ponds. Then in 1957 he landed the lucrative franchise to bottle and distribute Coca-Cola in Germany. More than thirty years later he was still actively running the business – Max Schmeling and Coke – and employed more than five hundred people in two large plants. He made frequent visits to the United States, and his

friendship with Joe Louis stayed strong to the day that Louis died. Schmeling never sought publicity for it, but it can be revealed that he often quietly passed money to the old 'Brown Bomber' to help him over his financial problems, and that Schmeling paid the bill for one of Louis's stays in hospital.

Schmeling had lost his beloved Anny after fifty-four years of marriage, while he himself was a fantastic advertisement for a life in which he had never touched either alcohol or tobacco, even though at one time he owned a tobacco factory. He still avidly followed the sports scene, and even at eighty-five he kept fit by jogging and riding a cycling machine that he had placed in front of a television set at his Hamburg home.

Despite the rise of Boris Becker and Steffi Graf, he was voted Germany's outstanding sports personality of the century. 'If I had my life to live over again,' he told us, 'there is nothing that I would change. It has been a wonderful life. Ja, wunderbar.'

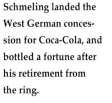

Schmeling landed the West German concession for Coca-Cola, and bottled a fortune after his retirement from the ring.

CHAPTER ELEVEN

JACK SHARKEY

THE BOSTON GOB

Jack Sharkey was without argument the most moody and temperamental of fighters in a century of world heavyweight champions. He was also the most slandered and libelled. Sharkey often became so excited and emotional in the ring that he would be unable to stop himself bursting into tears, and he was cruelly tagged by some as the 'Weeping Warrior'. The treatment he got from the media and public alike was enough to make any man cry.

If anybody knew the secret ingredient that makes one fighter become idolized and another disliked on sight they could bottle it and make a fortune. Sharkey did not have enough charisma to fill a thimble, and he became the boxer the fans loved to hate. He was booed into and out of the ring so many times that he must have thought they were playing his theme music.

Sadly for Sharkey, he will always be remembered as the man who fouled Schmeling, robbed him in the return match, and then lost the world title to Primo Carnera in controversial circumstances on June 29, 1933. Several ringside reporters claimed he was knocked out

by 'a phantom punch', and it has become part of boxing legend that he took a dive against Carnera. However, judging from the Big Fights Inc film of the championship contest, it is clear that the punch that dropped Sharkey face first to the canvas like a corpse in the sixth round was a devastating uppercut that would have lifted a charging bull into the air. Sharkey's manager, Johnny Buckley, complained that Carnera must have had weights in his gloves, but this was later dismissed by cynics as a smokescreen to cover the scandal of what they believed was a fixed fight.

Sharkey had clearly outpointed Carnera over fifteen rounds in a non-title fight in 1931, but in the title bout he boxed tentatively against the giant Italian. His apprehension was understandable. Just four months earlier, on February 10, 1933, he had been working in the corner as chief second to his ex-Navy pal Ernie Schaaf when the unfortunate Schaaf absorbed the punishing blows from Carnera that killed him.

'People don't realize how much they have hurt me by suggesting that I dived against Carnera,' Sharkey said in his retirement years. 'What do these people know? They have never taken a punch in their lives. Carnera knocked me out with as hard a punch as I ever took. There would have been no sense in me throwing the fight. I was enjoying being champion of the world. There was a lot of money to be made defending it. Why would I have given up the most prized possession in the world?'

He added as if he could still hear those boos in his ears: 'I guess some fans just wanted to believe it. A lot of them were always sour on me. Don't ask me why. I always gave my best.'

A CHANGE OF NAME

Sharkey always seemed to find himself the outsider. Born Paul Zukauskus in Binghampton, New York, on October 6, 1902, he was the son of Lithuanian immigrants and had to learn to defend himself early in life when running into Irish, Italian and Jewish gangs. 'There were no Lithuanian gangs that I could join,' he said with a sense of humour that was sometimes considered to be misjudged.

When, for example, he was adjudged to have beaten Schmeling for the world crown in

their return match on June 21, 1932, reporters asked him what the title belt was worth to him. 'At least thirty dollars,' he joked. 'Maybe fifty bucks at a pawn shop.' It was a throwaway statement that did not go down well with a public weaned on the devastation of Dempsey and the dignity of Tunney. The Depression was at its peak, and it was considered almost heresy to mock the value of a championship belt that all fight fans and boxers dreamed of owning.

At eighteen, Paul Zukaukus became restless and unsettled at home and he ran away to sea after first shovelling coal and working the New York bars for his daily bread. He joined the US Navy, and found that the strict discipline aboard the *USS South Carolina* suited him. For the first time in his life he felt as if he really belonged, and he earned the instant respect of his shipmates with his powerful punching and clever footwork in sparring sessions on the deck of the *South Carolina*. After four years at sea, the self-taught fighter decided to try his luck in the professional boxing ring, and in 1924 he took the surname of the old fighting sailor Tom Sharkey

Above: Sharkey and Jack Dempsey (right) spar for an opening in their 1927 title eliminator. Dempsey earned a rematch with Gene Tunney with a controversial seventh-round knockout. He landed the finishing blow while Sharkey was complaining to the referee about his low punches.

Left: Sharkey pictured during training for his 1927 fight against his hero, Jack Dempsey.

After losing his first title fight with Max Schmeling (right) on a foul, Sharkey won the return with a disputed points victory over fifteen rounds in 1932.

and added Jack because it belonged to his ring idol, Jack Dempsey. Little could he have dreamed that just three years later he would be fighting his hero, with the promised prize of a world championship match against Gene Tunney for the winner.

Sharkey, who was just over 6 foot tall and had an impressive 190-pound physique, was highly strung and occasionally eccentric. When he fought Britain's 'Phainting Phil' Scott – the original horizontal heavyweight – in a title eliminator in Miami in 1930 he had to be restrained from climbing out of the ring in tears when it looked as if he was going to be disqualified for yet another of his low blows. He had one leg over the top rope on his way out when the referee came across and held up his hand in victory. The sports fans – who had idolized lions like Jack Dempsey and baseball's Babe Ruth – could not believe that here was a

prizefighter who cried. It made them laugh, and all he got in return for his emotion was their contempt. His sensitivity was seen as a sign of weakness.

CAREFUL WITH MONEY

Sharkey earned his fight with Dempsey by beating the best black fighter around, Harry Wills, who had grown old waiting in vain for a title shot that his ability and his record warranted. Sharkey, an expert boxer who was continually handicapped by fragile hands, was getting the better of exchanges with Wills in Brooklyn on October 12, 1926, when yet again he was involved in a foul incident – this time on the receiving end. The desperately unlucky Wills was disqualified in the thirteenth round, wrecking any hope he had of a title fight.

Right: Happy family man Sharkey with his wife, Dorothy, and three of their four children.

Below: From throwing boxing hooks, Sharkey switched to fishing hooks and became one of America's most successful flycast fishermen.

To try to give Sharkey some sort of image, a publicist played up some of his bolder boasts. One of them – 'I can lick any son-of-a-bitch who walks on shoe leather' – fitted nicely with his ex-seaman's nickname, the 'Boston Gob'. He couldn't lick his old idol Dempsey, however, but he gave him a tough battle before going down to defeat in New York on July 21, 1927. Dempsey threw the rule book out the window when he climbed into the ring for this rehabilitation contest after his first defeat by Tunney. Dempsey kept letting his punches stray below the borderline, and when Sharkey turned to protest to the referee in the seventh round the desperate Dempsey – cut around both eyes – landed a devastating knockout right to the jaw.

Sharkey had six more contests after losing the title to Carnera before being chosen as the sacrifice to Joe Louis, who was looking to re-establish himself following the defeat by Max Schmeling. Sharkey was knocked out in three rounds in New York on August 18, 1936.

He went into retirement with the satisfaction of knowing he was the only man to have fought both Jack Dempsey and Joe Louis. Over the following years with his wife, Dorothy, and his four children, he got even more satisfaction from becoming one of America's foremost fly-cast fishermen. 'I could handle fishing better than boxing,' he said. 'The fish don't hit back!'

Though sometimes reckless with his punches, the old sailor was always careful with his money. He ran a Boston bar called Sharkey's and lived to see the 1990s, and in old age at his home in Epping, New Hampshire, was surrounded by his grown-up children and grandchildren. He was no longer an outsider.

CHAPTER TWELVE

PRIMO CARNERA

THE AMBLING ALP

Primo Carnera rose from circus strongman to heavyweight champion of the world, but for most of his boxing career he was manipulated by ruthless crooks and at one stage he was cruelly abandoned in hospital as a pathetic, penniless wreck. Yet out of the wreckage, the likeable Italian giant managed to salvage some self-respect by making a small fortune in the wrestling ring, and when he died at the age of sixty, he had recovered the dignity stolen from him by the parasites of the boxing world.

It had always been believed that Carnera's boxing record was about as genuine as a counterfeit $10 bill, and his original manager, Frenchman Léon Sée, confessed that more than thirty of his eighty-two fights on the way to the world title were *combat arrangé*. There were many more that Sée believed were fixed by American mobsters, who muscled in on Sée's meal ticket and fed off Carnera like vultures seizing on the carcass of a large, wounded animal.

It was while Carnera was the huge and helpless puppet of gangsters that professional boxing gained an unwelcome but fitting new description. The fight game became known as the fight racket. The mobsters would order opponents when and how to lie down in the path of the 'Ambling Alp' – a nickname memorably created by Broadway's master storyteller Damon Runyon. Carnera, so it was claimed, rarely knew that his victories were choreographed, and there were times when neither boxer in the ring realized that the result was outside their control.

Often it was the referee who was 'under orders', and there was one occasion when a boxer who did not want to go along with the mob's instructions to 'take a dive' was nobbled by his own cornerman. He rubbed a peppery substance into his fighter's eyes between rounds. Even then the boxer tried to fight on, and when his second threw in the towel, he was set upon by ringside gamblers. Another time a manager made the cut on his boxer's eyelid worse by slitting it with a razor blade, forcing the referee to stop the fight in Carnera's favour.

Carnera stood around 6 foot 5.75 inches tall (one official medical report listed him at 6 foot 7.25 inches) and he weighed 260 pounds. With his 20-inch neck and huge shoulders he was an awesome sight to behold. He was always a magnet for spectators and drew massive crowds throughout his career, particularly in New York, where the vast Italian population idolized him. Some fans may have come only to laugh at him, but they came none the less. Money flooded into the box offices, but Carnera saw little of it. Several title-winners in this first century of world heavyweight champions were parted from their money by unscrupulous promoters, but the exploitation of Carnera was of Maxwellian proportions.

THE GENTLE GIANT

It was all too much for the sincere but simple Carnera to comprehend. All he knew was that the world was a kinder place when he was growing up in the ancient northern Italian village of Sequals, close to Venice, where he was born on October 25, 1906. His parents were not oversized people, and it was the talk of the village when Carnera weighed in at a reported 20 pounds at birth. Before he was ten, the boy giant was having to wear hand-me-down clothes that had belonged to his father, a mosaic worker. He gave little time and attention to schoolwork because he hated being teased about his size by other children. There was little aggression in him, and he used to run away rather than stand and fight his tormentors. His boxing career almost finished before it started when he fell off a farm wagon. The huge wooden wheel rolled over one of his legs, crushing it and it affected his mobility for months and helps to explain why he was so heavy-footed in the ring.

Primo – so named because he was the first born – worked as a carpenter's apprentice at the age of thirteen, but decided after a year that he would rather try his luck in France because work was easier to find there immediately after the First World War. He arrived in Le Mans wearing one of his father's suits, his feet cushioned by rope sandals that had been made for him by his grandmother and carrying all his worldly goods in a cardboard box. He tried many labouring jobs before joining a circus as a seventeen-year-old strongman. Carnera's act was billed as 'Juan, the Unconquerable Spaniard', and his speciality was a tug of war in which he out-pulled a heavy motorcar.

Above: Carnera swings and misses against Tommy Loughran, but he landed enough times to win this 1934 title fight on points over fifteen rounds.

Left: Jack Sharkey and challenger Carnera shake hands after signing for their 1933 world title fight.

Early in 1928 he was spotted by a retired French heavyweight boxer, Paul Journeé, as he wrestled in the circus ring. Journeé saw Carnera's potential as a fighter, and offered to give him boxing lessons. He then introduced him to Léon Sée, and the diminutive boxing manager and entrepreneur immediately realized Carnera's novelty value. Just by his size alone, he knew Carnera would be an attraction.

Sée was careful to ensure that Carnera's lack of boxing ability was not exposed by simply selecting cooperative opponents who would lie

Referee Arthur
Donovan sends Max
Baer to a neutral corner
as Carnera makes one
of eleven visits to the
canvas during their
chaotic 1934 champi-
onship contest.

down when necessary. Within a year the Carnera boxing act – for that's what it was – was on the road and, with the publicists exaggerating his already impressive physical statistics, he packed in the crowds as he travelled through Milan, Berlin, Leipzig, San Sebastian, Marseille, Dieppe and London.

Carnera beat Young Stribling at the Royal Albert Hall on November 18, 1929, when the American was disqualified for landing a low blow in the fourth round. Three weeks later they met again in Paris, but this time Carnera suffered his first defeat when he was thrown out for hitting Stribling on the back of the head when his back was turned. Manager Sée later claimed that both contests with Stribling were *combat arrangé*.

Inevitably, the next stop for the Carnera road show was the United States. He immediately attracted attention with his size, and in a barnstorming four-month tour he stopped sixteen opponents – the majority of them of the 'cooperative' kind. While he was picking up a lot of boxing tricks, Carnera was not doing so well picking up the lingo. Asked by a reporter in California what he thought of Los Angeles, he replied: 'Los Angeles? I knocka hima outta in two rounds.' He improved his English by spending hours in the cinema watching movies. His favourite stars

were British actors Leslie Howard and Ronald Colman, and he tried to copy their accents.

During a return trip to London he was able to try out his accent on the Prince of Wales, a keen follower of boxing who asked to meet the man they were calling 'Da Preem'. He also met British-based Canadian ringmaster Larry Gains, and was outfoxed and lost on points at the Royal Albert Hall on May 30, 1932. And it was in London that he met a Soho waitress called Emilia Tersini, and he lost his heart to her. He proposed marriage, but later changed his mind – dithering that cost him £4,200 in a breach of promise case. Unfortunately for Emilia, all Carnera's money disappeared into the pockets of the hangers-on who clung to him like leeches, and it was years before she saw any of it.

MANSLAUGHTER CHARGE

Carnera was handled in America by two managers, Louis Soresi and 'Good Time' Walter Friedman, who were closely associated with New York racketeer Bill Duffy and an English-born contract killer called Owney Madden. Friedman admitted to reporters in later years: 'Yeah, a lotta Primo's fights were what you might call mischievous. But his title fight with

Jack Sharkey, that was on the level. He could box better than a lotta people realized, and when he connected properly with that right of his it was curtains for whoever was on the receiving end.'

To clinch his title fight with Sharkey, Carnera needed to beat Ernie Schaaf, who was part-managed by Sharkey, at Madison Square Garden on February 10, 1933. Schaaf, known as the 'Tiger of the Sea', was jeered throughout the contest for fighting like a man in a sleepwalk and the obvious conclusion was that he had agreed to lose. Carnera, who had developed a solid left-jab and a jolting though telegraphed follow-through right, handed out heavy punishment against an opponent noted for his strength.

In the thirteenth round a flurry of punches sent a distressed-looking Schaaf collapsing to the canvas. He was carried unconscious from the ring and never came out of his coma. He died in hospital five days later. The distraught Carnera, a gentle giant whose aggression in the ring was totally out of character, was preparing himself for a court appearance on a charge of manslaughter when an autopsy revealed that Schaaf had gone into the ring suffering brain damage from a previous fight against Max Baer.

Carnera cried on the transatlantic telephone when his weeping mother rang to ask if it was true that he had killed an opponent. He was considering giving up boxing until Ernie Schaaf's German mother told him: 'Please don't blame yourself, my son. It was not your fault that my boy died. It was an accident. It could have happened to you, and then it would have been your own mother who would be crying.'

There was a nationwide debate about the dangers of boxing, and the New York State Athletic Commission responded by announcing that Carnera should not only be banned from fighting Sharkey, but that he should in future be allowed to box only men of his own enormous stature – 'super-dreadnoughts'.

Yet the moment Carnera had been exonerated, negotiations were clinched for Sharkey to defend his title. Just four months after the death of Schaaf, Carnera, now expertly trained by a former top-ranking featherweight, Billy Defoe, landed the sixth-round right uppercut against Sharkey that made him the heavyweight champion of the world. Out of his promised purse and ancillaries of $10,000, Carnera pocketed just $200. But all that mattered to the gentle giant was that he was the *campione del mundo*.

'My congratulations,' cabled Benito Mussolini. 'Fascist Italy and its sports-loving people are proud that a Blackshirt has become boxing champion of the world.' Carnera went on to feature in an exhibition tour that raked in $20,000 for his managers, and included a demeaning sparring session with a kangaroo in the programme. He then earned – but never saw – $25,000 for an appearance in the 1933 film

Ex-champion Primo Carnera receives treatment to the ankle he damaged during one of his early knockdowns against Max Baer.

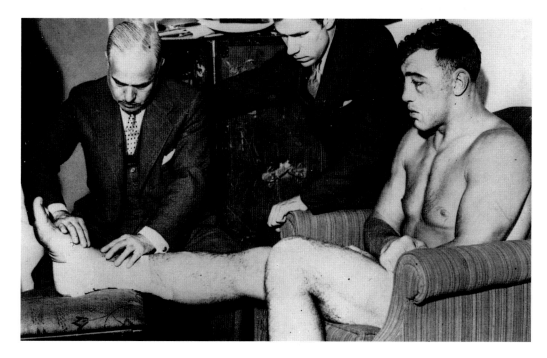

The Prizefighter and the Lady in which he boxed a draw with Max Baer, with Jack Dempsey in the role of referee. The result was scripted, so it was nothing new for the Carnera camp. Then Carnera returned home to a hero's welcome, and in Rome on October 22, 1933, he retained the championship by outpointing the veteran 'Bull of the Pyrenees' Paolino Uzcudun over fifteen rounds. Mussolini's Fascists, who until his title victory had dismissed Carnera as a freak, now jumped on the bandwagon and persuaded him to parade around Rome in their Blackshirt uniform, and got him to agree to pledge his purse for the Uzcudun defence to the Party. Carnera was honoured with a place in the famous Mille Miglia car race as co-driver to Italian ace Tazio Nuvolari. This stunt ended when the car broke down under the weight of the man mountain from Sequals.

THE CHOPPING BLOCK

The mobsters controlling him were determined to cash in on the championship while they could, and on Carnera's return to the United States they picked out former world light-heavyweight champion Tommy Loughran as an ideal challenger in Miami on March 1, 1934. Loughran, in boxing parlance, could not break eggs, and it was well known that he was having problems with fallen arches. Carnera revealed at a press conference that one of his tactics would be to stamp on Loughran's feet with his huge size fifteen boxing boots. 'With the size of his feet,' said joker Loughran, 'Carnera could be the greatest grape treader in history.' The challenger's manager, Joe Smith, complained to the boxing commission about Carnera's threat, and they ruled: 'It is up to fighters to protect their feet just as they do their jaws.' Loughran came up with a ploy of his own. He smothered his hair with an evil-smelling grease to dissuade the champion from hanging around at close quarters.

Carnera was happy to keep the fight at long range against a clever but outpowered opponent, and he jabbed and stomped his way to a fifteen-rounds points victory. This set up a second title defence against Max Baer that was to bring him humiliation and make him a laughing stock throughout the nation (see page 95). Carnera was made to look a clown of a champion: he was bludgeoned to the canvas ten times – and went down without a punch once – before the referee rescued him in the eleventh round. Carnera showed immense courage, particularly as it was later revealed that he had torn ligaments in an ankle while taking one of three counts in the first round. But he was inconsolable when the referee, Arthur Donovan, who had let Baer get away with a procession of foul blows, stopped the fight, and in the funereal dressing-room the gentle giant broke down and cried uncontrollably.

Carnera's hangers-on disappeared like thieves in the night after he had been tossed as a chopping block into the path of the rising contender, Joe Louis, who blasted him out in three rounds in New York on June 25, 1935. An attempt

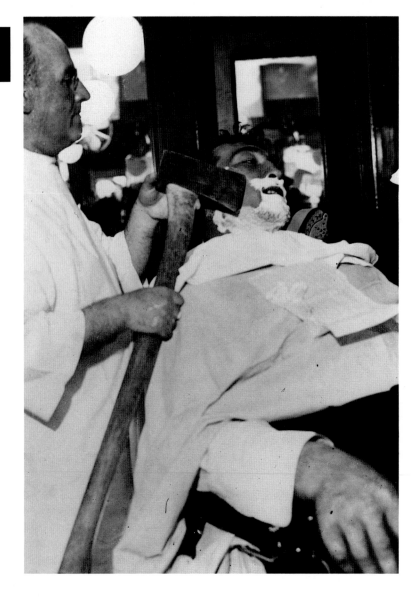

Anything for a headline. Carnera faces the axe in a publicity picture to help sell fight tickets.

89

by Carnera to suggest that he had been drugged during the fight by a doctored sponge brought the retort from Louis: 'I guess he must mean the knockout drops I had in my gloves.' Members of the Italian Boxing Commission investigated the matter and later reported that they could find no grounds for Carnera's complaints.

A PROPAGANDA TOOL

Barely a year after he had won the world heavyweight title – the richest prize in sport – Carnera was not only an ex-champion but also flat broke. At his bankruptcy hearing in 1935 he made a comment that changed public ridicule to sympathy: 'I don't never pay attention to money and those things. Now I no gotta dough. Everybody, that's all they want from me – dough, dough, dough. I no gotta dough.'

At least somebody wanted him – the Italian Fascists. When he returned home to Sequals for a holiday with his parents in the summer of 1935 he was called up for army service. As usual, Carnera found himself being used – this time as a propaganda tool for Mussolini, whose army had just 'bravely' invaded Abyssinia. Carnera served only two weeks in the

army, during which time he gave two exhibitions to raise money for the Italian Red Cross before being allowed to return to the United States to pick up his boxing career.

In a desperate bid to get some money together, he had eight more fights following the battering from Louis. After the second of two stoppages by Leroy Haynes on May 27, 1936, he was taken to hospital concussed and semi-paralysed. He lay in the hospital on the New York waterfront alone and penniless. The New York State Athletic Commission announced that they were suspending him, and when he was discharged from hospital he begged enough money to get home to Italy. 'I just wanna be home with my mamma,' he said.

Carnera then allowed himself to be talked into taking a fight in Paris in 1937 following a visit to London, where he was arrested for non-payment of tax from his previous visit in 1932. He moved on to France, where he was outpointed over ten rounds by the French Army champion Albert Di Meglio, and just a month later, on December 13, 1937, he was stopped in two rounds by Josef Zupan in Budapest. The Fascist press in Italy could not bring themselves to report a morale-lowering defeat, and announced that Carnera had won by a knockout in the second

In his second career as a wrestler, the 'Ambling Alp' was much happier because he knew the ground rules.

Carnera with his wife, Pina, behind the counter of their Californian liquor store that – so legend has it – he tried to drink dry.

round. Meanwhile, Carnera had collapsed suffering from a kidney haemorrhage, and was rushed to hospital where doctors told him that he would be risking his life if he fought again. Returning to Italy, he had his damaged kidney removed.

Once back on his feet, Carnera joined a travelling vaudeville show in which he performed a rope-skipping routine surrounded by a troupe of dancing girls. He was whistled and jeered off the stage in Milan.

Carnera got some order into his messed-up life in 1939 by marrying a 24-year-old Italian-based Yugoslav girl, Pina Kovacic, the intelligent daughter of a local mayor. She presented him with a son, Umberto, and a daughter, Jean Marie, on whom he doted.

Only Carnera could have got himself into the complicated situation which faced him when all the European countries were put on a war footing. He had become a French citizen early in his boxing career, and he was posted as a deserter by the French Army. But as he was in Italy and under the thumb of Mussolini, he elected to join the Italian Army. Tommy Loughran would have enjoyed the irony when he failed the medical test because of flat feet.

Legend has it that Carnera then regained hero status with many Italians when he flattened half a dozen off-duty German soldiers after they had insulted his wife. He was arrested by the Gestapo, and released after questioning without them discovering that he had joined the Italian anti-fascist partisans.

THE WRESTLING HERO

Life was much kinder to Carnera after the war. He tried one comeback fight at the age of thirty-nine in Milan on November 21, 1945, and was stopped in seven rounds by Luigi Musina. 'I had wanted to change my mind about going through with the contest,' he said later, 'but a spectator pulled a gun and forced me to get into the ring.' It could only happen to Carnera.

After failing to impress in two exhibition contests with Musina, he switched to wrestling in 1946 and became massively popular both in Europe and the United States in a sport in which *combat arrangé* is the accepted way of things. Crowds flocked to see the 'Ambling Alp' touching the peaks again, and he got enough money together to open a successful liquor store in Westwood, California, where he and his wife became citizens of the United States. He was justifiably proud of his son, Umberto, who became a US naval officer before returning to university to pass his exams as a doctor of medicine.

Carnera thought he was going to hit a golden jackpot in the courtroom in 1956 when Budd Schulberg's explosive novel about heavyweight boxing, *The Harder They Fall*, was released as a film starring Rod Steiger and Humphrey Bogart in his final screen appearance, with former heavyweight champion Max Baer playing a fighter who causes brain damage to an opponent. Carnera sued for $1,500,000, claiming that it was a thinly disguised account of his career and that this invasion of privacy had led to ridicule because of the way the main character – a heavyweight boxer left punch-drunk and poverty-stricken – was presented. But all Carnera got for his trouble was a legal fee and another defeat. The judge ruled that anybody who became a celebrity or public figure waived the right of privacy and did not regain it by changing profession.

Before taking on Hollywood in court, Carnera had tried his hand at film acting. You can hardly miss him in his walk-on roles in *Mighty Joe Young* (1949), *Casanova's Big Night* (1954), *Prince Valiant* (1954) and *On the Waterfront* (1954). In the 1955 British film *A Kid for Two Farthings*, Carnera gives a suprisingly good performance as a 'heavy' who is a villain in and out of the wrestling ring. He handles his dialogue extremely well and had clearly come a long way from the man who a little over twenty years before had thought Los Angeles was a boxer, and when helping to publicize the film he gave interviews in Italian, Spanish, French and English.

Hollywood closed its doors to Carnera after he had made his court challenge, and he returned to wrestling and a world tour that took him to Australia, Singapore, Japan, Britain, India and to most of the major European cities. And this time he was not accompanied by crooks with their hands in his pockets. His wrestling opponents included old boxing rivals Max Baer and Larry Gains, whom he 'beat' in London on the same day that his British back taxes debt was cleared. Jack Dempsey and Joe Louis refereed some of his contests and joined in mock battles. Carnera was winding up his sporting career the way he had started it – with prearranged duels.

In 1967, aged sixty, Carnera – who it was said did his best to drink dry his liquor store – became seriously ill with cirrhosis of the liver. He requested that he should be taken home to die. In his village of Sequals they staged a rose festival in his honour, but he died without being able to acknowledge the warmth and love of the hundreds of people who had turned out to see 'Da Preem'. The date of his death – June 29, 1967 – was exactly thirty-four years to the day that he took the world title from Jack Sharkey with that explosive right uppercut. Thousands turned out to pay their last respects at his funeral, and the mile-long procession was led by Italy's dual world boxing champion Nino Benvenuti, carrying the one possession that the parasites failed to get their hands on: Carnera's diamond-encrusted world championship belt.

The mobsters had robbed Carnera and left him broken and abandoned, but they couldn't keep him down. By the final count, Primo had proved himself quite a champ.

Carnera returns home to Italy in 1967 for his final days.

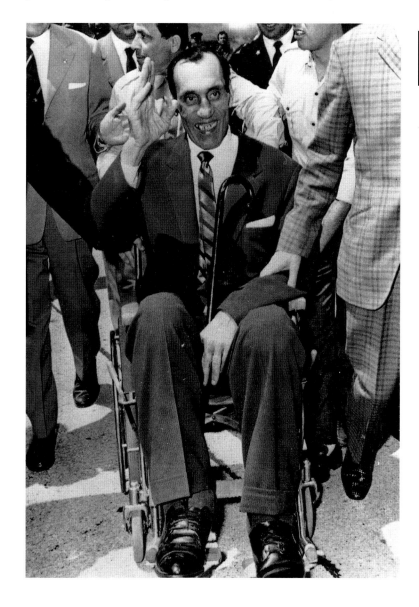

CHAPTER THIRTEEN

MAX BAER

THE LIVERMORE LARRUPER

Maxmillian Adalbert Baer was one of the most magnificent physical specimens to climb into a boxing ring during the first half of this century of world champions. Close to 6 foot 3 inches tall, he had such wide shoulders that he instinctively went through a doorway sideways. His waist was as slim as any of the model girls who were always clinging to his arm, and he could fell a steer or kill a man with his blockbusting right-hand punch. He did both in his day. Baer was endowed with all the attributes needed to become one of the greatest of all the world champions, apart from one thing – he behaved as if he was as mad as a March hare.

It might seem disrespectful to hang such a description on a man capable enough to win the world heavyweight title, but Baer was quite happy to own up to being something of a wise-cracking nutcase, and once said of himself: 'I've got a million-dollar body and a ten cent brain.'

Baer found it impossible to take himself or boxing seriously, and literally clowned his way to the world title. Throughout his crazy championship contest with Primo Carnera he was laughing and joking like a vaudeville comedian. No wonder he was variously known as 'Madcap Maxie' and the 'Magnificent Screwball'.

The eccentricities of 'Mad Max' lapped over into his private life. Acting like the last playboy of the Western world, he went through a fortune while getting engaged to a procession of leggy chorus girls, actresses and beauty queens. One marriage, to movie actress Dorothy Dunbar, in 1932, lasted a year, and the predictions were that his second marriage, to Washington beauty Mary Ellen Sullivan while he was world champion in 1935, would be just as short-lived. However, Mary not only presented him with two sons and a daughter, but they were still happily together when he died of a heart attack twenty-four years later.

He admitted having no money sense, and at one time during his career had signed away 110 per cent of his boxing earnings to a string of managers with whom he had signed contracts. Baer had to battle through a labyrinth of lawsuits before Ancil 'Pop' Hoffman emerged as his sole manager. 'I was spending money faster than I was earning it until Pop got hold of me,' Baer said after his retirement. 'Thank goodness he made me put $200,000 into annuities when I was at my peak. It meant I never had to worry about where my next meal was coming from when I hung up my gloves.'

AN EXPLOSIVE PUNCHER

Baer was born in Omaha, Nebraska, on February 11, 1909, of German-Scots-Jewish extraction. While he was still a child, his family moved to Livermore, California, where his father became a successful butcher and cattle breeder. Baer started helping out in his father's meat factory when he was just thirteen, and it was by carrying heavy slabs of meat that he developed enormous upper body strength.

It was a right-hand punch thrown during a brawl with a train driver whose flagon of wine he had stolen for a joke that woke Baer up to his punching power. He was just eighteen, and as he watched the railwayman collapse from the weight of his punch he realized he could make a fortune with his fists.

Baer bought a punch bag and boxing gloves and set up a small gymnasium on his

Max Baer, the
'Livermore Larruper'.

'Last one up's a cissy!' jokes Baer as he and Primo Carnera tumble together to the canvas during their 1934 championship contest.

father's ranch, next door to the slaughterhouse where he had the job of killing the cattle. He knew, however, that he would have to leave Livermore if he wanted to succeed in launching his career, and so in 1928 he took a job in a factory in Oakland where he was coached by former Californian light-heavyweight title prospect Ray Pelkey.

Billed as the 'Livermore Larruper', Baer – who had an ego that could fill a room – turned professional in 1929, and his explosive punching and eccentric behaviour in and out of the ring quickly made him one of California's top box-office draws. He was rocketing into national prominence when in his twenty-seventh fight his opponent, Frank Campbell, died of head injuries after being stopped in five rounds. Baer had to be talked into continuing his career and lost four of his next six contests.

He had developed boxing skill to go with his God-given power, and victories over King Levinsky, Paolino Uzcudun, Johnny Risko, Tom Heeney and Ernie Schaaf lifted him into title contention. Then Schaaf died following his next fight with Primo Carnera in 1933, and the coroner declared that his fatal brain damage had

been inflicted in his contest against Baer six months earlier.

It was all too depressing for Baer, who decided to throw himself into enjoying his life. He was driven everywhere in a chauffeured limousine, and was always accompanied by a bevy of beautiful girls who he called 'my social secretaries.' He had only one fight in 1933, stopping former champion Max Schmeling in ten rounds in a title eliminator promoted by Jack Dempsey. The Nazis were just beginning to spread their anti-Semitic poison in Germany, and Baer – a Star of David on his trunks – was in no mood for joking as he tore into Schmeling like a man possessed. He used every dirty trick in the book and was warned seven times for foul tactics before clubbing the German to defeat.

Baer cashed in on his growing popularity by taking a starring role in the 1933 Hollywood movie *The Prizefighter and the Lady* in which Myrna Loy played the Lady. In a fight scene Baer was seen boxing with Primo Carnera; Jack Dempsey appeared as the referee. Baer later said that it was during this scripted contest that he noticed that world heavyweight champion Carnera was open to a right cross.

His challenge for Carnera's championship at the Long Island Bowl on June 14, 1934, was one of the whackiest fights in the history of heavyweight boxing. Baer climbed into the ring wearing the same dressing-gown that he had worn in the film. It had Steve Morgan – the name of his character in the movie – in large letters on the back. He joked with ringsiders and winked at the row of pretty girls who had come to cheer him on. Baer had one plan, and that was to hurl his right across Carnera's long left lead at every opportunity. It was a simple tactic, but it brought him the championship. Every time Baer tagged the Italian giant with a right to the jaw it caused an avalanche in the 'Ambling Alp's head and he came tumbling down to the canvas. In the second round, Carnera was reeling drunkenly around the ring and twice pulled Baer down with him. The second time Baer said, 'Last one up's a cissy!'

Later in the fight Baer feinted to throw a right and Carnera, handicapped by torn ligaments in his right ankle, went down without taking a punch. Baer almost fell over with laughter. The referee, Arthur Donovan, whose handling of the fight seemed biased towards Baer, finally called a halt with Carnera staggering around after his eleventh visit to the canvas.

Before the fight New York boxing commissioner Bill Brown visited Baer's training camp

and he saw him clowning with sparring partners, blowing kisses to the dozens of girls crowded round the ring, and showing off the latest craze for rhumba dancing. Brown was disgusted and told Baer: 'You're a bum.'

Above: In all, Baer had Carnera down eleven times before referee Arthur Donovan stopped the fight in the eleventh round to give 'Mad Max' the heavyweight championship of the world in 1934.

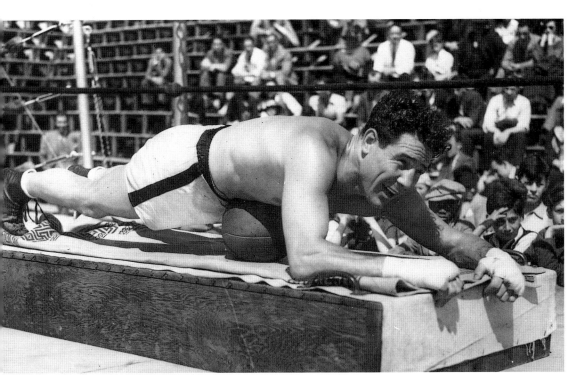

Left: Whether training or fighting, Baer usually found something to laugh about.

Baer burst out laughing, and replied: 'I think ham would be more fitting, but let's see what you think after the fight.'

As he was announced as the champion, Baer leant over the ropes and said to Brown: 'Well, what have you gotta say now?'

'You're still a bum,' he said. He then added after a pause: 'Carnera's a bigger bum.'

FEARS OF A CLOWN

Just one year less a day later in the same Long Island ring Baer amazingly lost the championship in his first defence against 10-1 underdog Jimmy Braddock (see page 100). Baer did not take Braddock's challenge seriously and in the build-up to the bout spent much of his time entertaining on stage and radio and enjoying himself in nightclubs. 'I just clowned the title away,' he said later. 'Then I nearly caught cold in the dressing-room after the fight, it was so empty. Where had everybody gone? Where were all my so-called friends? What a difference a year made.'

After losing the title Baer was tossed to Joe Louis, and for the first time in his life he froze with fear. 'I guess I knew something bad was about to happen to me,' he said. He refused to leave his dressing-room for the fight until Jack Dempsey, working as his second, snarled: 'Look, you either get in that ring or I'll beat you to a pulp right here and now.' Baer hardly threw a punch as he backed away from Louis, who bombed him to defeat in four one-sided rounds. He announced his retirement, but nine months later launched a comeback campaign that included a defeat and a victory against Welsh ringmaster Tommy Farr.

There were suspicions about Baer's heart for battle after his display against Louis, but he silenced the doubters with a brave show against 'Two Ton' Tony Galento, a tough brawler infamous for his 'I'll moider da bum' boasts. Galento butted, gouged, hit to the kidneys and below the belt, but Baer refused to give ground and he forced Galento to quit after eight bloody rounds in Jersey City on July 2, 1940.

Baer's hopes for a crack at the championship now held by Louis ended in New York's Madison Square Garden on April 4, 1941, when he was stopped in eight rounds by Lou Nova. It was left to his older, bigger brother Buddy Baer to try to salvage family honour against the 'Brown Bomber', but Louis hammered him to defeat in two title defences.

After briefly serving in the US Army, Baer was discharged because of an old training injury. He became a radio disc jockey and a public relations director, and toured the theatres as one half of a double act with 'Slapsie' Maxie Rosenbloom, another great boxing entertainer of the thirties. Baer and brother Buddy both appeared in dozens of Hollywood movies in walk-on parts. He did not live to see his son, Max Jr., become a hit on television as Jethro Clampitt in *The Beverley Hill Billies*. Baer suffered a heart attack while shaving at the Hollywood Roosevelt Hotel on November 21, 1959. Just a few days earlier he had refereed the Zora Folley-Alonzo Johnson fight, and after giving his decision waved to the fans and then vaulted out of the ring over the top rope. What a way to go.

When he collapsed at the hotel, a bellboy asked if he wanted to see the house doctor. 'I'd rather see a people doctor,' said Baer. They were his last words. In true spirit, he left us laughing.

Right: There was a brutal side to the clowning Baer, as he proved in his 1940 eighth-round victory over 'Two Ton' Tony Galento.

Left: Still laughing and joking (and now smoking) in middle-age. Baer died of a heart attack a year after this photograph was taken.

CHAPTER FOURTEEN

FROM HELL'S KITCHEN

The son of Irish parents who had lived in Lancashire in Britain before emigrating to the United States, Braddock was born in New York City's tough west side area known as Hell's Kitchen on June 7, 1906 (although historian Nat Fleischer always insisted it was six months earlier on December 6, 1905). He became the central character in a West Side story that was to cause an earthquaking shock in the boxing world. 'I came from a fighting family,' he revealed as reporters scrambled to find out just who the world had as the new heavyweight champion. 'My dad used to hang around the boxing booths in the old country and answer any challenges that were made. He picked up quite a few shillings that way. His brother, my Uncle Jim, was an even better scrapper, and was rated one of the best no-holds-barred fighters in the whole of Ireland. I was named after him, so I guess I was born to be a fighter.'

When he was still a youngster, Braddock's family – he had four brothers and two sisters – moved across the Hudson River and settled in New Jersey. He put together an impressive amateur record while working in a printing works before turning professional as a middleweight at the age of twenty. His amateurish tactics were given a professional polish by the coaching of Joe Jeanette in his gymnasium in Hoboken, where Braddock attracted a lot of attention in sparring sessions with prominent Brooklyn welterweight Harry Galfund.

Braddock, standing 6 foot 2 inches tall and with a cultured style of boxing, was managed by Joe Beigel – known professionally as Joe Gould. It was Gould who manoeuvred Braddock into a fight for Tommy Loughran's light-heavyweight world title in only his fourth year as a professional, but his career went into a sharp decline after his points defeat over fifteen rounds in New York on July 18, 1929.

He became something of a stepping stone for up-and-coming prospects, and when he could not get fights or find work as a longshoreman he was forced to join the degrading Depression breadline queues to support his wife, Mae, and their two sons and a daughter. After he had become the world champion he quietly repaid every cent of the $17 a week relief money he had been receiving while on the dole.

JAMES J BRADDOCK

THE CINDERELLA MAN

Much to his own astonishment, James J. Braddock emerged as the most unlikely champion of this centenary parade. Just a year before he took the title from the playboy puncher, Max Baer, he was apparently finished as a fighter, and was labouring on the Hoboken waterfront trying to earn daily bread for his wife and three children. On the night that Baer won the championship by beating Carnera, 29-year-old Braddock was called out of retirement as a sacrifice on the undercard for hot contender Corn Griffin. The sacrificial lamb turned into a rampant lion.

Griffin floored Braddock in the first round, but as he came looking for the kill in the second he was knocked cold by the punch of a lifetime from the dock worker who was supposed to be there only in a walk-on role. A year and a day later Braddock, who followed his sensational win over Griffin with victories against rated fighters John Henry Lewis and Art Lasky, conquered Baer in one of the biggest upsets in boxing history. Suddenly, the disbelieving world had a champion who had won only forty-six of his previous eighty-three contests.

The story of the title fight is captured in this one photograph – Baer hitting and missing. Braddock kept pecking away with his cultured left jab to earn a clear-cut points victory and the heavyweight crown on June 13, 1935.

AN EXPENSIVE MISTAKE

Braddock, who boxed mainly as a middle- and light-heavyweight, had failed in a bid for the 175 pounds title in 1929 when he was outpointed over fifteen rounds by Tommy Loughran. He lost his appetite and his ambition, and in his next thirty contests he was beaten nineteen times. It was hardly the stuff of which world heavyweight title challengers are made, but Baer's handlers were searching for an easy defence and, on paper, they looked no easier than Braddock.

Braddock, who had the appearance more of an old-time friendly Irish cop on the beat than a prizefighter, was a neat, orthodox boxer, but he lacked the punching power to make a real impact in the heavyweight division – that is until he got his chance against Baer, who believed along with the rest of the boxing world that he had been selected as 'strictly an opponent'.

Baer treated Braddock with a contempt that was to prove suicidal and expensive. 'Here I am folks,' he would say with a broad grin. 'You're lookin' at the guy who blew a million dollars.' During the build-up to the fight, he spent more time on the stage and in nightclubs than in the gymnasium, and he was not in anything like the best of condition for his first defence of the championship that he had laughingly won from Carnera. In the meantime,

Braddock whipped himself into the best shape of his life. 'I was determined not to make a fool of myself,' he said later. 'It was obvious from what I was reading in the papers that Max was not taking me seriously, but I was not going to let him have a laugh at my expense. I decided that I would set a fast pace that would really test him.'

He adopted smart hit-and-run tactics, and stole the title from Baer with snapping left jabs and jolting rights that stopped the big-hitting champion in his tracks every time he set himself to try to land his own feared right. For once in his life, Baer could not see the funny side of things as Braddock continually made him miss with clever footwork and then pummelled him with stinging and accurate counter punches. His

Braddock did have rare moments of success against Joe Louis as this picture proves. But Louis recovered from taking this right-hand punch to knock out Braddock in the eighth round in 1937.

lack of condition showed from the middle rounds when he started puffing and panting like an overworked horse. The challenger was taking him for a ride.

Braddock had been a strong puncher early in his career, but he broke bones in both hands in a fight with Abe Feldman in Mount Vernon, New York, on September 25, 1933, and he announced his retirement that lasted until he got the call to fight Corn Griffin on the Carnera-Baer bill. It triggered the extraordinary rags-to-riches story for Braddock, who after his clear points victory over Baer was dubbed the 'Cinderella Man', because he had arrived late for the brawl.

A DEAL WITH LOUIS

Braddock, paid $17 a week on welfare, was earning at a rate of more like $17 a minute when for two years after winning the title he went on a personal appearances and exhibition tour while Max Schmeling and Joe Louis screamed out for the chance to challenge him.

He should have met former champion Schmeling in his first defence, but he was bribed into putting his title on the line against Louis by being secretly guaranteed 10 per cent of his challenger's future purses as title-holder if the championship changed hands. It was as smart a piece of business as any boxer ever did.

Despite dropping the 'Brown Bomber' for a brief count in the first round, Braddock was no match for his young challenger, who blasted him to a knockout defeat in eight rounds in Chicago on June 22, 1937, to start the greatest reign of any champion in the history of boxing.

Braddock had one more fight – a points win over British heavyweight hero Tommy Farr in New York on January 10, 1938 – and then retired for good. He had won only fifty-one of his eighty-five professional contests, but the one victory that really mattered – against Baer – brought him boxing immortality.

Braddock's income, boosted by regular payments from the Louis camp, was wisely invested and he became a prosperous businessman. He teamed up with his old mánager, Joe Gould, in the management of a stable of fighters, and often gave exhibitions and appeared in the ring in the role of referee.

The 'Cinderella Man', who died in North Bergen, New Jersey, on November 29, 1974, aged sixty-eight, finished up having a ball.

Battered Braddock goes home after his defeat by Louis to count his dollars. The 'Cinderella Man' has had his ball.

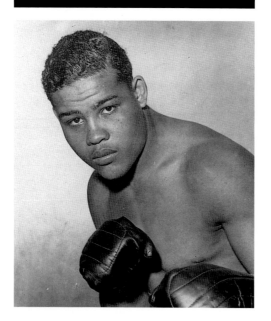

CHAPTER FIFTEEN

JOE LOUIS

THE BROWN BOMBER

Joe Louis would have an army of supporters in any argument as to who has been the greatest in this first century of gloved world heavyweight champions, but there was one opponent he could never beat: the taxman. Poor old Joe fought on long after was good for his health in a bid to clear back taxes, and his plodding performances clouded the memory of some of the most devastating displays ever witnessed in a boxing ring.

At his peak, Louis took on and beat all-comers. They called it his 'bum-of-the-month' campaign when he was knocking over challengers for his championship at intervals of just a few weeks. But towards the end of what had been a glorious career, he was fighting not because he wanted to but because he had to, and it should weigh on the consciences of a lot of people that this exceptional athlete was allowed to continue boxing when it was clear that his reflexes had gone and that he was in danger of serious injury.

Perhaps the greatest victory for Louis was that he earned new respect for the American black man. He suffered his few defeats with dignity, and was the model of modesty in his many famous victories. Everybody loved Louis. There have been extremists who argue that he put back the march to complete freedom of black people in America with his servility, but it has to be remembered that when he became champion in 1937 he had to carry the legacy of hatred left over by Jack Johnson's reign of arrogance.

His early mentors, joint managers Julian Black and John Roxborough, had grown up in the Johnson era and they had suffered the backlash that had resulted from the champion's outrageous behaviour. They were in a small minority of black managers, and they continually stressed to Louis that he should set an example of how a champion should behave in and out of the ring. An even tighter reign was put on Louis by his trainer, Jack Blackburn, a former top-flight lightweight fighter who had a paranoia about Johnson. In an interview during a visit to London after his retirement Louis recalled that when Blackburn first took him under his wing he told him: 'You know, boy, the heavyweight division is no place for a Negro, all because of that no-good Jack Johnson. The white man don't want to see the title in black hands ever again. You have to really be something special to get anywhere, 'cos they're not going to want you to beat up on them white boys. No sir. You've got some hope if you make up your mind you ain't gonna be another Johnson. The white man hasn't

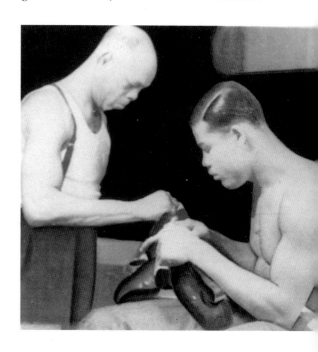

forgot that fool nigger with his white women, acting like he owned the world. You try behaving like him and you'll be wasting your time and mine. Whatever you do, when you beat a white man don't smile. Johnson used to really gloat, and it caused all sorts of trouble for the rest of us black people.'

What the slim, scar-faced trainer kept locked away in his memory was that he and Johnson once had a war in a gymnasium during what was supposed to have been a friendly sparring session. They had been sworn enemies ever since, and the sore between them never healed. It flared up again after Blackburn was released from jail after serving five years on a murder charge. His friends in boxing put together a testimonial to raise funds for him, and it was reported back to Blackburn when Johnson refused to chip in and made some less-than-complimentary remarks about a man who was not exactly your average guy. (Blackburn, who was known to pack a gun, used to wear his boots two sizes too big so that he could keep his money tucked away at the front. It was a form of banking that never quite caught on.)

Johnson even tried to get Blackburn removed as Louis's trainer. He told John Roxborough that he was the only man fit to train Louis. The manager's reply, overheard by reporters, must have dug deep into Johnson like a punch to the solar plexus: 'It's pointless me trying to tell you anything about loyalty. You're a

no-good nigger who gives black people a bad name, and you're not welcome in this camp anymore.' From then on Johnson rarely had a good word to say about Louis, and many people put it down to the fact that he was jealous of Louis's success and his popularity.

Louis was also lucky, he had the media on his side. His insatiable appetite for women was rarely reported, and he managed to keep secret the fact that during his climb to the championship a beautiful high-society white woman used to buy him a new limousine every Christmas in return for the sort of favours that Louis was more than happy to provide. His reputation could have been torn to pieces if the affair had got into the newspapers. But after the cards dealt to Louis at birth he deserved every one of the hidden aces that came his way.

A HUMBLE BEGINNING

It would have taken a Charles Dickens at his most morbid to dream up a more humble start in life than that experienced by Louis, who was born Joseph Louis Barrow in a ramshackle cabin in the cotton fields of Lafayette, Alabama, on May 13, 1914. He was the seventh child of Monroe and Lily Barrow, whose parents had been slaves on a plantation owned by their wealthy white master, James Barrow. Lily's mother was a full-blooded Cherokee Indian, and Louis's father was from

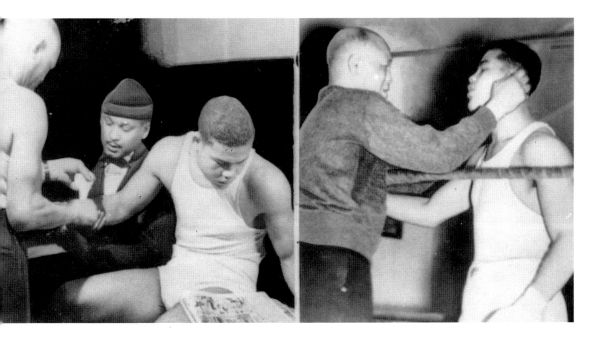

Rare shots of Louis being prepared for a training workout by 'Chappie' Blackburn.

Sweet, savage revenge. Louis on the brink of his first-round victory over Max Schmeling in New York in 1938.

Negro-white stock. Louis was still a baby when his father was carted off to a 'Hospital for the Negro Insane', and Louis grew up in abject poverty. The family's only income was the money his mother and older brothers and sisters could scrape together by picking cotton.

When it was reported that Monroe Barrow had died – nobody ever got definite proof – Louis's mother married widower Patrick Brooks, a poor sharecropper struggling to bring up eight children of his own. So there were now seventeen mouths to feed, and this was the poverty-line environment that was to shape the future heavyweight champion of the world. Little wonder that young Louis had a terrible stutter until a schoolteacher found the time to help him learn to speak properly.

Louis, who could barely read and write, was twelve when his family moved to Detroit. His mother wanted him to learn to play the violin, but he used to skip lessons to study the art of boxing at a local gymnasium. He certainly never fiddled around in the ring, although his boxing debut should have been enough to turn him off the sport for life. His mother cried when he came home from his first amateur contest with a bashed-in face after being dropped seven times. But Louis had found in the boxing ring a place where for the first time in his life he had an

identity of his own and where he felt in control of his own destiny. He had natural punching power that nobody could have taught him, and he developed lightning-fast punch combinations during which his fists were a blur of action. His publicists claimed that his favourite trick was catching flies as they buzzed by – that's how quick his reactions were.

It was soon obvious that Louis was the best prospect in town, and he was on his way to prove just that at a local championship show when he was pounced on by a posse of policemen and arrested on a charge of murdering his wife. By the time the police realized they had been hoaxed and that Louis was not even married the championships were over. The theory was that Louis had been 'fingered' by bookmakers who did not want to pay out on the wagers being laid on Louis to win the title.

Despite the fears of his devout Baptist mother, Louis gave up a job working on the conveyor belt at a Henry Ford factory to concentrate on professional boxing after winning a coveted Golden Gloves light-heavyweight title at the age of nineteen. He moved to Chicago to launch one of the greatest boxing careers of all time with a first-round knockout of a highly regarded local heavyweight called Jack Kracken on July 4, 1934. Although to most onlookers it looked a pulverizing performance, his demanding train-er, 'Chappie' Blackburn – he and Louis called each other Chappie – was less than impressed. 'You didn't have your usual hand speed in there tonight, Chappie,' he said to Louis. 'What have you been up to?'

Under interrogation, Louis confessed that he had scoffed a dozen bananas on the afternoon of the fight, and from then on he was put on a strict diet aimed at helping to build the perfect fighting machine – a target that was met within a year of Louis turning professional.

It was not long before Louis was a magnet for the mobsters who ruled many of the leading fighters in the thirties, but Louis stayed loyal to his managers, John Roxborough and Julian Black, despite threats of what would happen to him if he did not break with the black partners. The two managers were also under heavy pres-sure to give up at least part of their prized prop-erty. Much later in life these threats played on Louis's mind and he developed a paranoia that

'hit men' were out to get him. But in the peak days of his career he was the most devastating hit man of them all.

The one white man who was allowed to hold sway with Louis was the promoter Mike Jacobs, who opened doors for Louis that would have remained shut to Roxborough and Black. As Louis started to sweep all opponents out of his path he was suddenly into big money, and he cel-ebrated by buying his mother a house and a chicken ranch. He also paid for a sister to go to teaching college and quietly paid back the wel-fare money his family had collected when they first moved to Detroit. 'It made me feel I was my own man,' said Louis in his slow, shorthand way of communicating during which he rarely uttered a sentence of more than half-a-dozen words.

Louis had a string of unpublicized romances – a euphemism for what would today be described as sexual encounters – before marry-ing his first wife, the beautiful Marva Trotter, on September 24, 1935. He had courted her slowly

Louis goes to war ... as a physical training instructor and in a pub-lic relations capacity for the US Army in 1943.

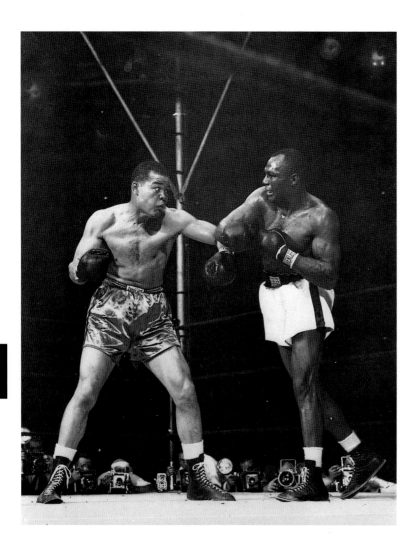

Walcott was ahead on points in his return fight with Joe Louis in New York in 1948 until the old 'Brown Bomber' dug into his memory to find a vintage knockout punch combination in the eleventh round.

It is hardly a secret that there have been several sexual athletes among the heavyweight champions. Most people would expect the shortlist to be topped by perhaps Mike Tyson or Jack Johnson, with Max Baer or Muhammad Ali challenging them. What will come as a surprise is that Louis, who managed to go through his career with a Mr Clean image, rivals any of them as a lover man.

'I could never resist a pretty girl with a sparkle in her eyes,' he said in his retirement years, chuckling at suddenly uncorked memories. 'And there were lots of those girls coming on strong, you'd better believe it!' He had a ball, so to speak, in Hollywood, where he cashed in on his popularity after the victory against Baer by co-starring with Edna Mae Harris in the 1937 film *Spirit of Youth*. Louis was to acting what Einstein was to ladies' hairdressing, but he enjoyed himself in the film capital – particularly, he revealed, with the Norwegian ice skating star, Sonja Henie.

Louis usually managed to confine his sexual conquests to periods outside his training schedule, but the one time he broke his rule was before fighting Max Schmeling at Yankee Stadium on June 19, 1936. So many girls flocked to his training camp that at one stage his trainer, 'Chappie' Blackburn, took to beating them off with a stick, but Louis – then a headstrong twenty-two year old – later confessed that he managed to sneak away with one of his fancies. He failed to give Schmeling the respect he deserved, and paid the price for a relaxed preparation during which he spent as much time on the golf course as in the gymnasium.

Jewish organizations called for a boycott of the contest, because they claimed that Schmeling represented Nazi Germany. This unwanted publicity coupled with rain storms cut the attendance to half the anticipated 80,000, and there was a rougher storm waiting for Louis in the ring. Schmeling gave him a fearful beating, hardly missing him with his bomb of a right hand. Louis's mother was at the ringside to watch him fight for the first time. She was taken out of the stadium in tears halfway through a contest in which Louis looked sluggish and completely outpowered. In the twelfth round Schmeling landed his right more than thirty times, and

and then married at haste, tying the knot on the evening of his biggest test to date against former world champion Max Baer. Louis and Marva were married by the Reverend Walter Trotter – Marva's brother – in a New York City apartment at 7.45 p.m., and at 8.00 p.m. Louis left for Yankee Stadium where he gave what he always described as the finest display of his life. Mrs Louis was at the ringside to see her husband of less than two hours destroy a strangely subdued Baer in four rounds. 'I never liked Baer much,' Louis said in retirement. 'He had too big an ego and said nasty things about my race. I never missed a shot against him before knocking him out in the fourth. Baer was scared to death of me. I enjoyed shuttin' his big mouth, but it didn't stop him making a lot of insulting remarks after the fight. But I did all my talking with these.' He held up his 12-inch fists – 'my six-shooters' – that stopped fifty-four of his seventy-one opponents inside the distance.

Louis finally slumped to the canvas and rolled over on his face as, for the only time in his career, he took the ten second count. There were riots in the streets of Harlem when the result was announced. Louis was idolized and his fans were convinced that he must have either taken a dive or been nobbled. Neither theory was true. Louis had just not got himself right for the fight either in body or spirit and Schmeling had, as he kept telling everybody before the fight, discovered the one weakness in the Louis armoury: he was open to a right over his left lead.

The lethal Louis left hook disposes of Tami Mauriello in the first round in New York on September 18, 1946.

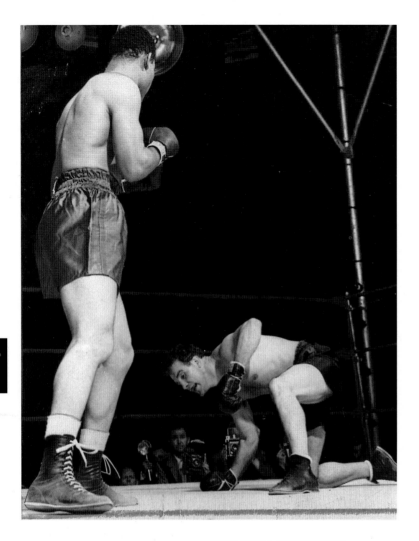

Billy Conn goes down on his way to an eighth-round knockout defeat in his return fight with Louis in New York in 1946.

THE NEW CHAMPION

After Louis's defeat at the hands of Schmeling, 'Chappie' Blackburn took Louis back into the gymnasium, got him to faithfully promise that in future he would give total concentration to his training and then he set about mending the flaw in his defence. Louis was re-established as a championship contender just two months later with a crushing third-round knockout victory over former title-holder Jack Sharkey in New York on August 18, 1936. He crowded in three more victories that year as a behind-the-scenes battle raged as to who could get the new champion, James J. Braddock, into the ring for a title defence. By rights it should, of course, have been Schmeling. But the American boxing establishment would rather the title were in black American hands than risk it going out of the country to, of all places, Hitler's Germany. Schmeling signed to fight for his old title, but

was then sidetracked and it was Louis who got the shot at Braddock in Chicago on June 22, 1937, knocking him out in the eighth round to become world heavyweight champion. In Harlem, Detroit and Chicago thousands of Louis's black fans held all-night street parties in celebration.

Almost lost among the hundreds of congratulatory telegrams that Louis received the next day was a cable from a mental institution in Alabama. It gave him the stunning news that his father – reported dead nearly twenty years earlier – was still alive. He was mentally deranged, and Louis could not bring himself to go to see him, but he paid all his medical bills and took care of the funeral arrangements when the father he had never known was officially reported dead the following year.

Louis had one of his closest calls of all as champion in his very first defence when Welsh lionheart Tommy Farr took him the full fifteen rounds before dropping a narrow points decision in New York on August 30, 1937. 'Man, that Farr had some balls,' Louis said after the fight. 'Everytime I thought I had him he would come back at me like a bulldog. They can be real proud of him back home.'

After bombing out Nathan Mann (three rounds) and Harry Thomas (five rounds), Louis wiped out the memory of his only defeat when he destroyed Max Schmeling in one round in New York a year to the day after becoming champion (see page 77).

With money flooding in, Louis was spending as if there was no tomorrow. He sponsored the 'Brown Bomber' Softball Team (he was more than $50,000 out of pocket when it folded), bought wardrobes full of clothes for his wife and himself, and he was the easiest of touches for a sob story and gave away thousands of dollars to black 'brothers' who had hit hard times. When one of his sisters went off the rails and became an alcoholic, he paid for her to receive medical treatment. Louis also sank much of his money into business ventures that seemed to boost the bank balances of a lot of people apart from himself. One by one the businesses fell apart. Little did he know it, but he was sowing the seeds for the problems that were to ruin him in later life. He had no head for figures, and claimed that he got bad advice from an accountant who told him not to pay the IRS, because he would be able to work out a special deal for him. Instead of saving the money, Louis squandered it – with the help of spongers and sharp businessmen.

In his fourth title defence, Louis met former world light-heavyweight champion John Henry Lewis in the first all-black world heavyweight championship contest since Jack Johnson's battle with Jim Johnson in Paris in 1913. Lewis was rated one of the finest defensive boxers of all time, but he was no match for Louis, who knocked him out in the first round in New York on January 25, 1939.

Jack Roper was next up for slaughter, and he was knocked out in the first round on April 17, 1939. When Roper was asked what had gone wrong with his pre-fight plans of ending the Louis reign he said: 'Well it was like this, I zigged when I shoulda zagged.'

THE DEBTS GROW

When the United States entered the Second World War, Louis donated the entire purses for two of his defences to the US Navy and US Army Relief Funds. For this generosity alone, many people in the United States felt that the IRS should have shown him some compassion when they were continually hounding him in his retirement, but they kept at him like bloodsuckers.

Louis continued to enjoy the company of beautiful women, and he counted the singer Lena Horne and 'Sweater Girl' actress Lana Turner among his 'closest' companions. Marva, Louis's long-suffering and now pregnant wife, found a letter from Horne to her husband and threatened to divorce him, but he talked her out of it on the understanding that he would stop his 'womanizing' and that he would soon give up boxing and concentrate on being a husband and a father. But that was like asking a gambling alcoholic to give up both betting and boozing at one go. Marva gave birth to a baby daughter in 1943 while Louis was serving in the US Army as a physical training instructor and in a public relations capacity. They named their daughter Jacqueline in memory of Louis's former trainer Jack 'Chappie' Blackburn, who had died of pneumonia in 1942. Soon after the devastating news of 'Chappie''s death came another blow for the champion when his manager and friend, John Roxborough, was sent to jail for running an illegal numbers racket in Detroit.

Louis's world was crumbling around him. He was beginning to feel cornered, and his tax debts were growing into huge unconquerable mountains. Louis searched around for an escape valve and while in Hollywood making an Army propaganda film he came across Lena Horne again. They had a passionate fling which ended – according to Louis in his 1978 autobiography, *My Life* – with a violent argument. Louis returned to the arms of Marva and their new daughter.

Back on Army duty he was sitting in a services bus station at Camp Sibert in Alabama with his lifelong friend 'Sugar' Ray Robinson (known to Louis by his real name of Walker Smith) when an M.P. came along and arrested them for refusing to move to the coloured section of the bus station seats. All charges were dropped when the Army realized the scorching-hot publicity any disciplinary action would attract at a time when black as well as white Americans were laying down their lives for their country, but it was an incident that left lasting mental scars on two of the world's finest boxing champions.

The colour bar hit Louis again in, of all places, Salisbury in Britain. He was giving an exhibition tour of Europe as part of his US Army public relations work in the last year of the war and visted a theatre in Salisbury with a group of black soldiers. They went to sit in the stalls only to be ushered to a 'special' section. Louis called the manager, who told him he was acting on orders from the US Army. Louis's complaint went right to the top in Washington, and all 'colour' restrictions in European theatres and cinemas were lifted.

Against Marva's wishes, Louis decided to continue his boxing career after the war, and she took that as a sign that their marriage was over and – to Louis's lasting heartache – Marva divorced him. It cost him a small fortune in a settlement, and his debts were piled higher and higher. He had to fight on to try to force a way out of the money maze in which he had lost himself. To try to help pay the alimony, he named Marva as his manager so that she would get 25 per cent of his purses. He also still had the recently paroled John Roxborough as a manager on his payroll, and he signed with yet another manager, Marshall Miles, after falling out with Julian Black, following a row over a loan. With the IRS vultures counting themselves in, Louis was weighed down with percentage takers.

For a couple of years Louis looked almost as good as in his pre-war peak period. He had been a great champion – perhaps the greatest – for a dozen years, chalking up a record twenty-five successful defences, including two memorable fights with ex-light-heavyweight champion Billy Conn. Louis came from behind to beat Conn in the thirteenth round of their first encounter on June 18, 1941, and he won the return in the eighth round five years and a day later. Then he had another return engagement – this time with Marva. They remarried and a second child came along, a son who was christened Joe Louis Barrow Jr., although he was affectionately known as 'Punchie'.

After winning two battles with Jersey Joe Walcott – the first on a split points decision and the second on an eleventh-round knockout – Louis announced his retirement from the ring in March 1949. The 'Brown Bomber' was grounding himself as undefeated champion: he knew he had lost the power and timing that set him apart from ordinary fighters. He elected Walcott and Ezzard Charles to fight for the vacant crown, a championship contest that was not universally recognized. Louis was at the ringside in Chicago to see Charles win an uninspiring fight on points. The date was June 22, 1949 – twelve years to the day that Louis had first become champion.

THE TRAGIC COMEBACK

Sadly, Louis's story does not end there. A string of business ventures collapsed on him, and to raise desperately needed money he was reduced to endorsing cigarettes, even though up to that moment in time he had never smoked in his life. His tax troubles were so pressing that – after divorce from Marva for a second time in 1949 – he was forced into making a comeback. At the age of thirty-six and looking bloated at 218 pounds, a plodding Louis failed in a bid to regain the title from skilful points-winner Ezzard Charles in New York on September 27, 1950. The fight with Charles was his twenty-seventh and last for the world championship, and the only one in which he finished a loser. Twenty-three of his title fight victories came inside the distance. Only Tommy Farr, Arturo Godoy and Walcott stayed the full course, and both Godoy and Walcott were knocked out in return fights.

Though a shuffling shadow of his former self, he had eight more contests and was then allowed to climb into the ring against a rising young bull of a heavyweight called Rocky Marciano in New York on October 26, 1951. The fight produced one of the saddest sights in sporting history, Louis being pounded through the ropes and stopped in eight one-sided rounds. 'I couldn't bring myself to count Louis out, so I stopped the fight,' said referee Ruby Goldstein, capturing the supreme status that Louis had in boxing.

The IRS became ridiculously petty in their chase for the taxes owed by Louis, even snatching the $660 that his mother left him in her will. Then, really scraping the barrel, they claimed the annuities that he had put aside for his children. But he managed to put a light back into his life on Christmas Day, 1955, when he married a longtime friend, Rose Morgan, who ran a chain of hairdressing salons. Louis had too much pride to live off his wife and to try to make a living started wrestling in 1956. Rose said with a deep sadness felt throughout America: 'It's like seeing President Eisenhower washing dishes.'

Louis was wrestling 'Cowboy' Rocky Lee in 1956 when his 320-pound opponent sat on him and broke a rib that pierced his heart muscles. That was the end of Louis's wrestling career.

Along with Rose, Louis went on a television quiz show and over the course of six weeks they won $60,000, answering topical questions. They were just about to cash the cheque when an IRS agent snatched it, and after a long battle it was agreed that Rose, as a joint contestant, was entitled to half.

Their marriage could not stand up to the pressures put on it, and they parted in 1957, leaving Louis so lost that he blindly got himself involved with a promiscuous half-Oriental woman who started supplying him with drugs. Louis stated that she got him hooked on drugs by injecting him while he was asleep. The FBI tipped him off that the woman had Mafia connections and was a star of pornographic movies. He had the sense to get away from her, and he headed for Los Angeles, where in late 1959 he married an old lawyer friend, Martha Jefferson, who brought some order and sanity back into his messed-up life.

Louis tried to get a comedy double act going with a dancer and a comedian called

Right: Louis lost only one of twenty-seven championship fights, and the pain of defeat shows as he takes a right from Ezzard Charles in New York in 1950. Charles won on points over fifteen rounds.

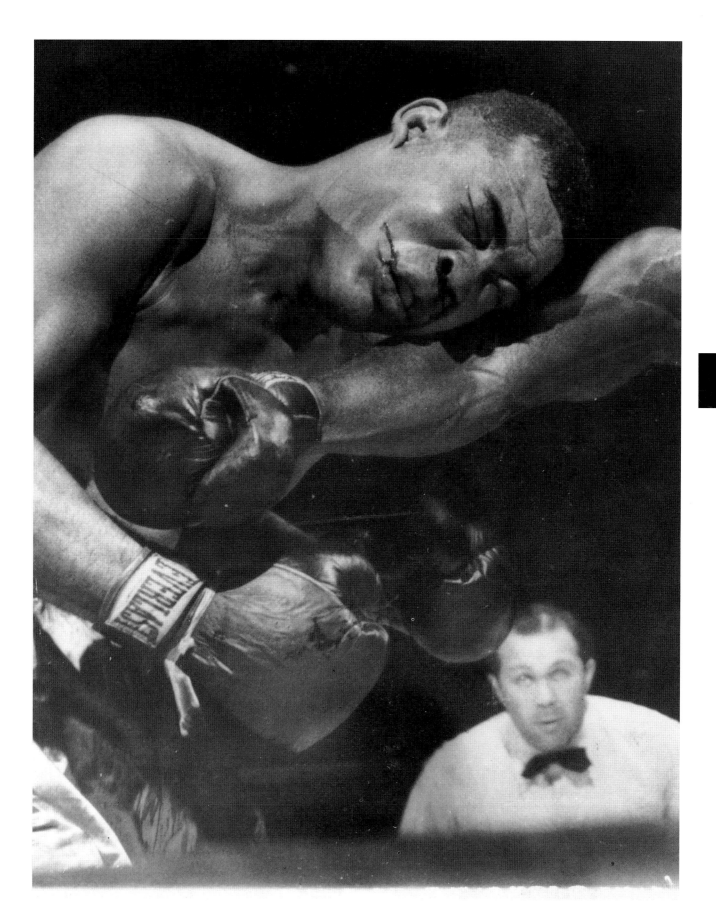

Leonard Reed, but the old champ's timing was hopeless and they bombed. Then he got involved in a public relations business, encouraging black Americans to visit Cuba where a young revolutionary called Fidel Castro had just taken over. Louis went to Havana and met Castro, and he came back saying what a great guy he was. Meanwhile, the United States Government were busy cutting off all diplomatic relations with Cuba – they considered Castro public enemy number one – which left Louis looking and feeling foolish. After this, the IRS came down even

harder on Louis until his lawyer wife went for their throats and got them to agree to tax him in future only on current earnings.

The gods were pouring boiling oil on Louis. In 1960 his eldest brother, Lonnie, was found dead in a room above his shoeshine shop. Police suspected that he had gassed himself, but a distraught Louis always argued vehemently that there was no way that his brother would take his own life.

His next major problem was self-inflicted. On a business trip to New York in 1964 he got

Louis in his final years when he was earning his daily bread as a 'greeter' at a Las Vegas hotel.

involved with yet another pretty girl who dragged him back into the world of drugs. To further complicate his life she claimed that he had made her pregnant. He finally summoned up the courage to confess all to the remarkable Martha, who went immediately to New York to confront the girl. A few days later she returned carrying a baby boy in her arms. He was the image of Louis, and they officially adopted him and gave him the name Joseph.

After recovering from gall-bladder surgery, Louis again slipped into the habit of sniffing cocaine and he had to go back into hospital in June, 1969, to have his stomach pumped after he had collapsed following a drug session. Martha stuck by him, and encouraged him to beat the habit. The New York girl who had presented Louis with a son became pregnant again – and this time Louis could prove he was not responsible. But Martha decided that little Joseph needed a brother, and they adopted the girl's second boy and called him John. It was about this time that Louis started to be convinced that Mafia 'hit men' were out to get him – a hangover from the threats he used to receive in his peak fighting days – and Martha and his eldest son, Joe Jr., who was now a law student, booked him into Colorado Psychiatric Hospital, where he had intensive treatment to cure him of his phobia.

There were a lot of friends, including singer Frank Sinatra and Louis's old opponent Max Schmeling, ready to give Louis a helping hand on his release, and even when his health deteriorated and he was confined to a wheelchair in his later years he continued to be employed as a 'greeter' in casinos and hotels in Las Vegas where he was revered by people from all walks of life. To complete their happy family, Martha – the most astonishing of the many women who entered Louis's life – adopted the New York girl's third and fourth illegitimate babies and called them Joyce and Janet Louis Barrow.

While in New York in 1974 Louis got his three wives together – Marva, Rose and Martha – to talk about old times. *New York Post* gossip columnist Earl Wilson tracked down Louis and asked him how he was doing. 'Fine, just fine,' said Louis. 'My second wife has just fixed the hair and make-up for my first and third wives. And they all look just beautiful.'

Despite all the problems that crowded in on poor old Joe, there has never been a more

respected champion in boxing history. When he died in Las Vegas on April 12, 1981, a month short of his sixty-seventh birthday, the world mourned the passing of one of the most popular sportsmen of the century.

From the moment that he was born into appalling poverty as a seventh child on that cotton plantation in Alabama he took a roller coaster ride through a life that was like no other. The 'Brown Bomber' was unique.

Louis pictured during a visit to a London casino in 1966. Perhaps he is sadly thinking of all the money he had lost – and not while at the gambling tables.

CHAPTER SIXTEEN

EZZARD CHARLES

THE CINCINNATI COBRA

Like Joe Louis, Ezzard Charles was the grandson of cotton plantation slaves and – tragically – like Louis he ended his days in a wheelchair, a penniless cripple who at one time had earned a fortune with his fists. A major difference was that Charles never enjoyed anything like the public recognition and hero worship that warmed Louis throughout his career and all the way through the turmoil and traumas of his retirement.

Charles was never the most popular of world heavyweight champions, mainly because he committed the unforgiveable sin of beating boxing legend Joe Louis. He got similar cold-shoulder treatment to that experienced by James J. Corbett after he had ended the reign of John L. Sullivan.

Opposite: A rare moment of inelegance from Charles as he misses with a left swing against his perennial opponent Jersey Joe Walcott.

UNDISPUTED CHAMPION

Born in Lawrenceville, Georgia, on July 7, 1921, Ezzard Mack Charles moved with his family to Cincinnati as a child and it was there that he became drawn to boxing. 'I used to hang around a downtown gym listening to the old pros talk about the fight game,' he said. 'There was an atmosphere about the place that really attracted me. I never forgot the first advice I was given when I started boxing. "If you want to be a fighter," I was told, "you've got to eat it, drink it and sleep it." That's just what I did throughout my career, amateur and pro. Win or lose, I was always back in the gymnasium at the first opportunity. I was just a simple, square sort of guy but I always tried to give my best.'

Charles, a high school graduate with a sharp mind, had turned professional four months before his nineteenth birthday in 1940 after an illustrious amateur career in which he won all of his forty-two contests, including the Golden Gloves final. He campaigned first of all as a middleweight and then as light-heavyweight, and his ability can be judged by the fact that he scored three victories over Archie Moore and five victories over Joey Maxim, both of whom were outstanding world light-heavyweight champions.

In the first half of his career he was known as the 'Cincinnati Cobra', and was noted for the dynamite power of his punches as well as for his skilful boxing. This all-round power and skill brought him a string of inter-services titles while he was based in Europe as a GI during the Second World War. Then, as a professional, one of his opponents, Sam Baroudi, died after a tenth-round knockout in 1948 and he switched moods in the ring, becoming a defensive boxer who seemed almost reluctant to let his heaviest punches go. Yet even with this cautious approach, he still proved too much for most of his opponents when he moved up to heavyweight.

Charles rarely weighed much more than 186 pounds, but he was so mobile in the ring that his bigger-built opponents could rarely make use of their weight advantage. When Joe Louis announced his retirement as undefeated champion in 1949, Charles was selected by Sol Strauss to fight Jersey Joe Walcott for the vacant title. Strauss, a lawyer who was acting as spokesman for the ailing promoter Mike Jacobs, was nicknamed 'Wrong-Way' Sol because he removed his glasses to read, took his teeth out to eat and would turn his hearing aid off if he was interested to hear what was being said to him. He said of Charles: 'This young man is a credit to boxing. He is well educated, wears nice clothes, has a sophisticated taste in music, is well

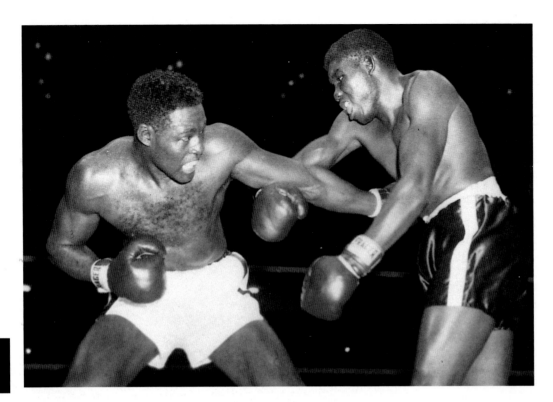

Charles (left) strengthened his claim for a shot at world champion Rocky Marciano with his fourth victory in five matches against Cleveland heavyweight Jimmy Bivins in Chicago on November 26, 1952. Ezzard won on points over ten rounds.

mannered and would represent the sport well if he were to become champion.'

Charles duly captured the championship when he outpointed Walcott over fifteen rounds in his seventy-fourth professional contest in Chicago on June 22, 1949. But he did not win worldwide recognition until the old 'Brown Bomber' unwisely decided to change his mind about retiring. They met for the undisputed title in New York on September 27, 1950, and Charles scored a clear-cut points victory over a man who was just a shambling wreck of a once-great fighter. Charles had always idolized Louis and beating his hero gave him little satisfaction. His win earned him only grudging respect from the fight fans, who, almost to a man, had wanted the 'Brown Bomber' to remain king of the ring.

THE ROCKY ROAD

Over the next two years, Charles successfully defended the title eight times before running into a classic left hook in the seventh round of a third title clash with Walcott in Pittsburgh on July 18, 1951. He was outpointed by his old adversary Jersey Joe when he tried to regain the championship 11 months later, and in 1954 lost two bruising title battles against Rocky Marciano.

Charles used every trick he knew to keep the bulldozing Marciano at bay in their first meeting in New York on June 17, 1954, and although he was clearly outpointed, he had the satisfaction of being the only challenger to take Marciano the distance. In a return three months later Charles was knocked out in the eighth round after inflicting a serious nose injury on the 'Brockton Blockbuster' that was to hurry Marciano's retirement from boxing.

'Ezzard was never given enough credit,' Marciano said following his own retirement. 'He beat Joe Louis fair and square but the treatment he got from the press and the public you would have thought he lost. I'll tell you this – he gave me the two hardest fights of my life. I had to reach down into my boots to find the strength to overcome him. He was a smart boxer and could hit much harder than people think. He was just unlucky to come to the top in an era when the fans were hungry for blood and guts. They just didn't appreciate Ezzard's finer points.'

Charles was never the same fighter after his two wars with Marciano, and lost thirteen of his last twenty-three contests. One of his final appearances came in London in 1956 when he was matched with Welshman Dick Richardson. It was clear that Charles had lost all appetite for boxing and his nerve seemed to desert him against the giant brawler from Newport. The former world champion was disqualified for the only time in his career for continually holding and was jeered and booed out of the ring after two rounds that were embarrassing to watch.

He announced his retirement just before Christmas 1956, but just eighteen months later made a half-hearted attempt at a comeback, finally quitting at the age of thirty-eight, after losing four fights against opponents who would not have been considered good enough to act as his sparring partners during his peak years as a master of ring craft.

In all Charles took part in thirteen world championship contests, yet somehow he managed to wind up without a penny to his name. He announced in 1961 that there was nothing left of the $2 million he had earned in the ring. 'I was saving for a rainy day,' he said. 'Now it's here but it's more of a flood than just rain. I always wondered what a guy does when he's got nothing to do. Now I'm finding out. He don't do nothin'!'

'Where did all your money go?' he was asked at a press conference in 1960.

'Beats me,' he said with a shrug. 'I guess I put too much into rebuilding my house, and I dropped a lot of dough in an athletic club venture that went sour on me. I could handle boxing but not money. It just kind of melted away.'

With a wife and three children to support, Charles got work as a wrestler and also as a 'greeter' in a nightclub in Newport, Kentucky. But his life became a nightmare in 1966 when he lost first the use of his legs and then the power of speech. He was diagnosed as suffering from a form of multiple sclerosis, and he was confined to a wheelchair.

The former world champion could not afford his medical bills, and Rocky Marciano, Archie Moore and Muhammad Ali turned out to raise money for him at a benefit night in 1968. He died on May 27, 1975, in the Veterans' Hospital in Chicago six days short of his fifty-fourth birthday. He is remembered warmly by true boxing lovers for having been one of the finest of all ring technicians. He was just unlucky to have lived in the shadow of Joe Louis and to have stood in the path of Rocky Marciano.

It's the beginning of the end of Charles's second championship challenge against Rocky Marciano. This crushing right set Marciano up for an eighth-round knockout victory in New York in 1954.

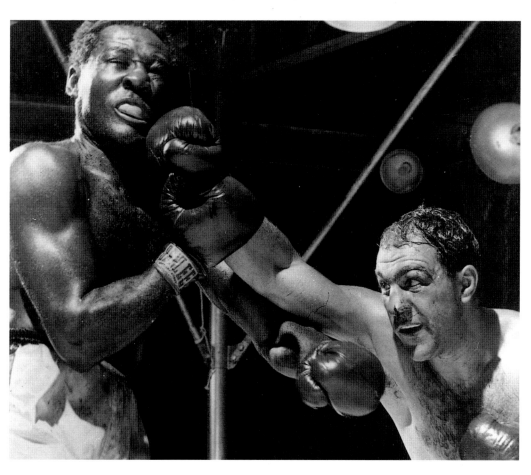

CHAPTER SEVENTEEN

JERSEY JOE WALCOTT

THE OLD MASTER

Jersey Joe Walcott became, at thirty-seven years six months, the oldest man to win the world heavyweight championship when he knocked out Ezzard Charles with a devastating left hook in the seventh round of their title fight on July 18, 1951. It was his fifth bid to win the championship, and as the count over Charles reached 'ten', Walcott dropped on his knees in the centre of the ring and offered up a prayer of thanks. The former garbage collector had reached the summit of the boxing mountain after a long, hard climb that almost broke his heart.

When interviewed for *Crown of Thorns*, forty years after his championship victory, Walcott became so emotional at the memories questions about his career evoked that he broke down in tears. His were the tears of an old master who had suffered the worst of times before enjoying the best of times at an age when most boxers are deep into retirement.

He had epic battles with Joe Louis and Rocky Marciano that guarantee him a place in boxing's Hall of Fame, but it was a long, painful climb up the boxing mountain.

A HUNGRY FIGHTER

Born in Merchantville, New Jersey, on January 31, 1914, Walcott was one of nine brothers and sisters and he started out in life as Arnold Cream. 'With a name like that I guess I had to learn to fight at an early age,' he said with a chuckle. 'I turned professional at sixteen, and decided to name myself after one of the greatest of all fighters – the old welterweight champion Joe Walcott, the 'Barbados Demon'. I then added the name of America's greatest state to make it more catchy.'

He got early advice from his cousin Jeff Clark. 'He was a class boxer who was known as the "Joplin Ghost",' said Walcott. 'He had such clever footwork that his opponents sometimes didn't know where he was in the ring and they would be thrashing away at thin air while he was off dancing around them and sticking punches in from all angles.'

Walcott had a lot of these now-you-see-me-now-you-don't tricks, and he got more good advice early in his career from Jack Blackburn until the trainer switched allegiance to Joe Louis. Fights were few and far between for Walcott in his early days and he kept quitting the ring in disillusionment because his purses were so paltry. A God-fearing man who always had a Bible with him, he held Christian principles that were continually put to the severest of tests by a procession of unscrupulous managers and promoters who swindled him right, left and centre. Walcott retired no fewer than seven times, but he forced himself into comebacks because he was – in the truest sense – a hungry fighter.

Married at nineteen to his high-school sweetheart, Lydia, Walcott had to come out fighting to help feed the six children that came along. In between fights he took any job he could get, no matter how menial. He laboured on construction sites, drove a truck, mixed cement and worked as a garbage collector. The war broke out at what should have been his peak fighting and earning years, and he worked on defence programmes in shipyards and at munition plants. Like the 'Cinderella Man' James J. Braddock, he knew the degradation of the dole queue and received $9.50 weekly relief cheques from the Camden Board in New Jersey.

He made the comeback that really counted because he literally wanted to keep the home

Ezzard Charles bows
the knee to the new
king Walcott after
Jersey Joe had connect-
ed with a perfect left
hook in the seventh
round of their world
title fight in Pittsburgh
in 1951.

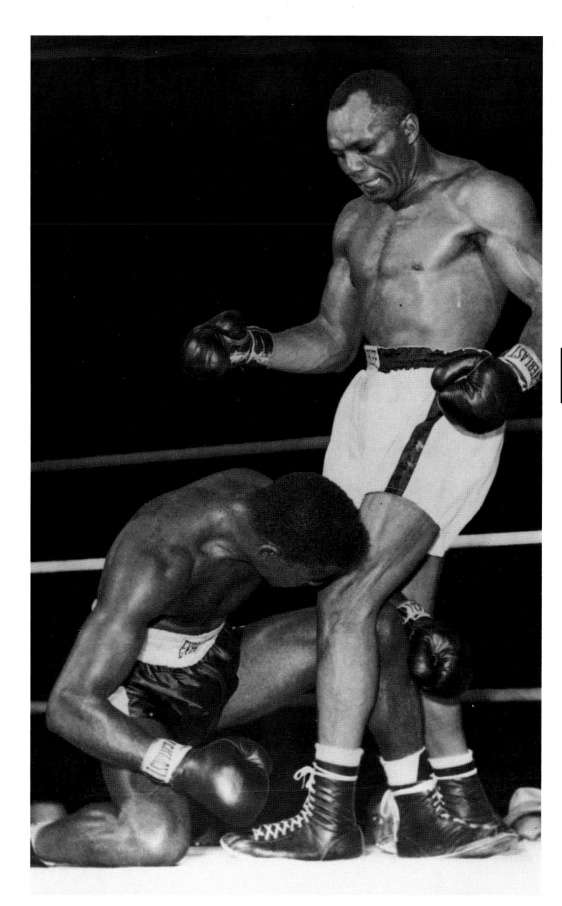

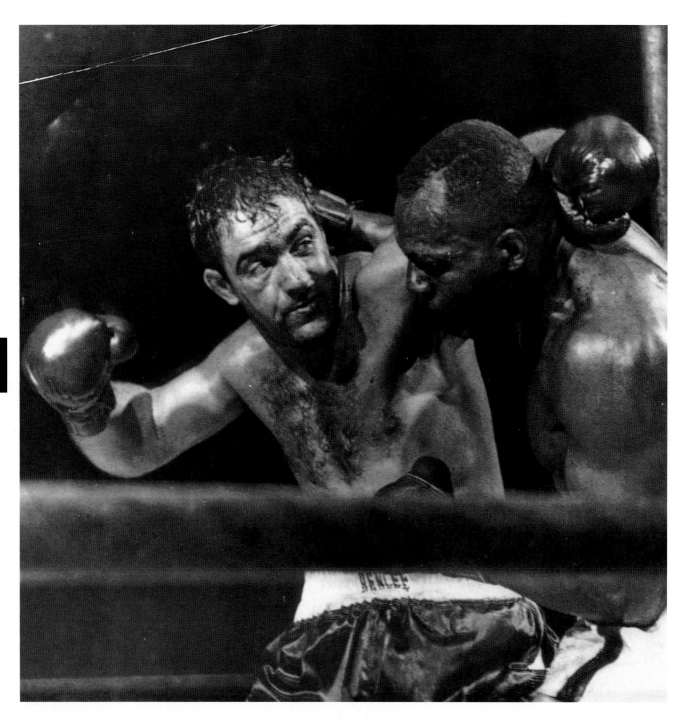

Walcott slips inside a left from Marciano, but Rocky's right is cocked for a finishing blow against the old champ in the thirteenth round of their title fight in Philadelphia in 1952.

fires burning. One freezing cold evening in the winter of 1945 he was visited at his Jersey home by a boxing manager called Felix Bocchicchio, who wanted Walcott to sign with him and his partner, Joe Webster, who ran the local Camden Athletic Club. Walcott pointed to an empty coal-bin in the corner of his living-room and said: 'Mister, if you can keep that bin full for me I will fight for you'. Over the next eight years Walcott earned enough to buy a coalmine.

Walcott's victims as he rushed up the rat-ings ladder included top-class fighters of the cal-ibre of Joe Baksi, Lee Oma and Joey Maxim. 'The victory over Baksi was the big turning point of my career,' said Walcott. 'He was the coming man, and he's well known over in Britain where he bombed out Bruce Woodcock and stopped Freddie Mills. He was a giant of a man with a chin like the bow of a destroyer. His manage-ment took me because they thought I was a washed-up old man. If he'd beaten me, I would probably have packed in the game for good. But I had a really good night and getting a clear victory over him did wonders for my confidence.'

In 1947 promoter Mike Jacobs wanted to feature Walcott in a ten-round exhibition against world champion Joe Louis for Mrs Randolph Hearst's Milk Fund charity, but the public showed little interest. But when Jacobs announced that instead they would meet over fifteen rounds for the world title, a near-capacity crowd turned out to see Jersey Joe give the 'Brown Bomber' the fight and fright of his life before Louis was awarded a split points decision.

Walcott is the most modest and mild-mannered of men, but the mention of that result can still bring a spark of anger to his eyes. 'I won that fight,' he said. 'I should have been champion four years before I finally got the title. Even one of Louis's favourite referees, Ruby Goldstein, called it for me. The two judges must have been watching a different fight.'

Louis won the return in New York on June 25, 1948, with an eleventh-round knockout. Walcott was twice outpointed in title fights by Ezzard Charles in 1949 and 1951 before finally landing the left hook that at long last brought him the championship in Pittsburgh on July 18, 1951. The cream – Arnold Cream – had finally come to the top.

THE HUMAN TANK

A counter-punching box-fighter, Walcott could bewilder opponents with clever footwork and feints, and he had the punching power to finish fights with one well-executed blow. He was particularly successful with his left hook, the punch with which he knocked out his old rival Charles to win the world title.

His brief reign as champion ended when he came up against the human destroyer Rocky Marciano in Philadelphia on September 23, 1952. He was outboxing and outfoxing Rocky and on the way to a points victory when in the thirteenth round the 'Brockton Blockbuster' caught up with him and dropped him for the full ten-second count with a shattering right cross to the jaw. In the return Walcott – understandably – did not seem to have his heart in the job and caved in under the first telling punch that he took.

At the mention of Marciano, the 'Old Master' winced. 'He was a human tank,' he said. 'Outside the ring he was a real gentleman, but when that bell rang he became a savage.'

Walcott hung up his gloves for good, and worked as a parole officer for juvenile delinquents and became a respected boxing official. He refereed the second Liston-Ali fight in 1965, and got in a terrible mix-up when Liston went down and out to what many considered was a phantom punch. What is in no doubt at all is that Jersey Joe was one of the most dignified of our century of champions. A pity that he was, in boxing terms, an old man before he reached the highest peak.

Jersey Joe Walcott, who tasted blood, sweat and tears on the way to the world title.

CHAPTER EIGHTEEN

ROCKY MARCIANO

THE BROCKTON BLOCKBUSTER

Rocky Marciano remains the only champion in this centenary roll of honour to have retired without a single defeat on his record. When he died in a plane crash the day before his forty-sixth birthday in 1969, his old foe Jersey Joe Walcott said, 'That's the only way Rocky could have been stopped. He'll go down as one of the immortals of boxing.'

Marciano, who started his working life as a ditch digger, rose to become heavyweight champion of the world on a tidal wave of legalized violence that left opponents unlucky enough to have got in his way looking as if they were the victims of a hit-and-run driver. Amazingly, he never weighed more than 186 pounds and stood barely 5 foot 11 inches tall, but he had 'Popeye-after-spinach' arms that could have belonged to a blacksmith and he used his fists as if they were sledgehammers. He launched his clubbing attacks in such a brutal, barroom brawling manner that he was called the 'Twentieth-Century Caveman'.

One of the incredible facts about Marciano is that he managed to keep secret until after his retirement that he battled through his key fights with the handicap of a slipped disc. He suffered continual problems with his back, following an injury while exercising with a medicine ball during training. Goodness knows what damage he might have inflicted on opponents had he been fully fit!

Meeting Marciano in retirement it was impossible to associate the gentle, quietly spoken, modest man with the butcher who had terrorized and tamed the world's greatest heavyweights. It was like finding out that Jack the Ripper was a pussycat. Following his tragic death, there were exaggerated stories of his meanness, which suggested that he had become a miser who hid much of his money in sealed tins buried in the ground. Yes, he did look after his hard-earned money as carefully as a nanny nursing a baby. But this comes as a heartening change after the stories of so many earlier champions who were parted from their money by crooks, swindlers and women on the make. Nobody ever managed to come between Rocky and his money or Rocky and his championship.

THE RISE OF ROCKY

Marciano's rise to fame and fortune was like something out of a Hollywood movie. Come to think of it, they could have called his life story Rocky! He was born Rocco Marchegiano on September 1, 1924, in Brockton, Massachusetts, the eldest of six children of immigrant Italian parents who lived close to the poverty line. His father, Perrino, was invalided out of the US Army during the First World War after being gassed in the trenches, and because of his poor health he was rarely able to hold down a job. Mamma Marchegiano was generously built, and it was from her side of the family that Marciano got his physical power. Poppa was only a featherweight, but he always claimed that he was the first to teach his son how to box.

At Brockton high school, Marciano had his sights set on being a professional baseball player or footballer. 'I was always squatting at centre in football and squatting behind the plate in baseball,' he said. 'This led to me developing strong, muscular legs but it took away any speed I might have had. This is why I was never exactly a twinkle toes in the ring.'

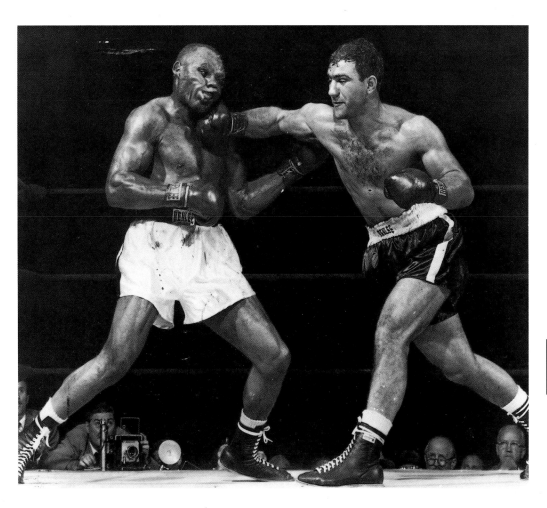

The 'Suzy-Q' right from Rocky Marciano that relieved Jersey Joe Walcott of the world title in the thirteenth round in Philadelphia in 1952.

As a baseball catcher he was good enough to get a three-week cub-farm trial at Fayetteville, North Carolina, but he strained an arm and was sent home. Then his sporting career – his life even – was threatened when a scratch on his chest from a pin became infected and poisoned his blood. He was left with a scar that looked like a war wound, but it was nothing to the scars he handed out to opponents.

Marciano's first fight did not find itself into any record book. He was briefly based in Wales while serving in the US Army in 1944 when he overheard a giant Australian soldier making insulting remarks about the United States in a Swansea pub. Eyewitnesses claimed that his right fist was just a blur as it powered into the unfortunate Australian's face and laid him flat on his back. It was to become a common sight, but in slightly more controlled circumstances.

After starting a brief amateur boxing career in the immediate post-war years, Marciano got married to a Brockton police sergeant's daughter called Barbara, and she

became an important influence on his life. He knew he needed to earn more than the 90 cents an hour he was being paid for digging ditches and decided to try his luck in the professional boxing ring. On St Patrick's Day, 1947, he launched the only unblemished record of any heavyweight champion with a third-round knockout victory over Lee Epperson at Holyoke. Marciano – who never ever learned to take it easy in sparring sessions – kept damaging his hands in training, and this delayed his progress. He was also making little headway with his first manager, Gene Caggiano, and his best pal, Allie Colombo, advised him to get a manager with connections at the top. So Marciano hitchhiked from Brockton to New York for a gymnasium trial under the all-knowing gaze of Madison Square Garden matchmaker Al Weill. Most onlookers didn't know whether to laugh or cry at Marciano's clumsy attempts at sparring. But Weill noted Marciano's raw power and had the vision to realize he could be moulded into a fearsome force. Weill put Marciano under the wing of veteran trainer Charley Goldman, an old-time bantamweight, who knew every boxing trick in the book and a few that never quite got into print.

Russian-born Goldman used to like to act the English gentleman and always wore a bowler hat, even when working in the ring. 'It was pointless trying to turn Rocky into a fancy Dan boxer,' said Goldman. 'So I decided to ignore his weaknesses such as lack of balance and reach, and concentrate on his strong points. And his strongest point was his strength. I would have backed Rocky against a lion for sheer, raw power. I got him to crouch and bob and weave to make himself more of an elusive target, and I taught him to hook short with his left and follow through with a right cross or straight right. We called that his Suzy-Q punch. And, boy, when that landed with full power you could have measured it on the Richter scale.'

Marciano had anything but an ideal build. His fists were small and his reach, at 68 inches,

124

was the shortest of any of the world heavyweight champions. But the tale of the tape doesn't give the full picture of a man who simply oozed menace. Neither does it record that Marciano had the physical strength of a weightlifter and a tough jaw and bull neck that could withstand the hardest punches. Marciano was also one of the dirtiest fighters to climb into the modern ring, and he never even managed to get a nodding acquaintance with the Marquess of Queensberry Rules. He also introduced the unheard of tactics of deliberately smashing punches into the arms of opponents until they were forced to drop them and expose their chin. When defending the title against Roland LaStarza, a college graduate, he hit his arms so hard and so often that he burst the blood vessels.

The merciless Marciano was totally dedicated to his training and there has rarely been a fitter fighting machine. With manager Weill doing the selling outside the ring and Marciano the slugging inside, they were an unbeatable

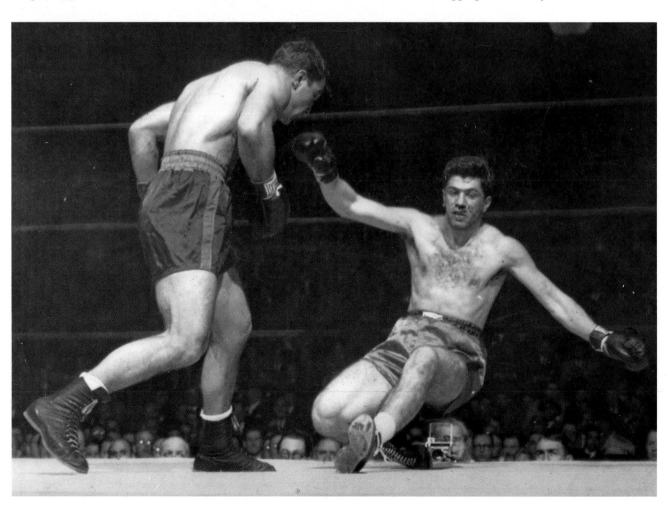

combination. Yet it was never the happiest of partnerships. To onlookers it was as if Weill was interested only in the money that Marciano could make for him. There was never any warmth between them, and Marciano revealed the resentment that was festering inside him when he said after his retirement, 'Weill would never let me forget that when I came to him I had a hole in the sole of my shoe. He'd call me 'the shoemaker' in a sneering way and tell me how he had made me the champion. Sure he did a lot for me, but I think I had something to do with it as well. He never ever gave me an ounce of credit. A pat on the back for Charley and me would have been appreciated.

'Starting out, I never questioned Weill's orders. But once I got the championship I thought he would start giving me a little respect. But he never gave it to me. Sometimes he would keep me waiting so long for my purse money that I began to wonder if it was ever going to come. It all caused a lot of resentment, which is a pity because the way things worked out we should have been as happy as sand boys.'

Wins against Roland LaStarza in 1950 and Rex Layne in 1951 were the highlights of his climb towards title contention, and when Jack 'Doc' Kearns, veteran manager of Jack Dempsey, saw him knock out the highly rated Layne in six rounds he said: 'This is the new Dempsey, and he punches even harder than Jack. Now I know why they call him the "Brockton Blockbuster".'

On the bitter-sweet night in 1951 that he battered an aged, over-the-hill Joe Louis to an eighth-round defeat Marciano learned a lesson that he kept tucked away deep in the recesses of his mind. 'I saw in Joe in particular and in several other fighters that you should never outstay your welcome in boxing,' he said. 'If you have two or three fights too many it can have terrible consequences.'

RULES OF THE JUNGLE

Marciano ripped the world crown away from Jersey Joe Walcott with a dramatic thirteenth-round knockout victory in his forty-third fight on September 23, 1952. He had problems with his eyes halfway through the fight, and there were rumours that somebody in Walcott's corner had rubbed a substance on the champion's gloves. But when questioned about it, Jersey Joe said: 'I would never have got involved in dirty tricks. I wanted to represent myself and boxing in the best light, and I was beating Rocky on sheer skill.' The referee and both judges had Walcott well ahead going into the thirteenth round when Marciano unleashed his Suzy-Q right that dropped the champion on to his knees like a subject bowing to the new king.

Marciano knocked out Walcott in the first round in a return match in Chicago on May 15, 1953, and successfully defended his crown against Ezzard Charles (twice), Roland LaStarza, Britain's Don Cockell (crudely clubbed to a ninth-round defeat) and Archie Moore in New York on September 21, 1955, before retiring as the only undefeated world heavyweight champion in history.

Critics of his crude style overlook the fact that he had a tremendous variety of finishing punches. With Louis it was a looping left. Harry 'Kid' Matthews went to an overarm right, and Walcott went out the first time to a crashing

straight right. Thanks to Charley Goldman's coaching, he also developed a solid left jab off which he could throw a wicked left hook. His body punches were devastating even if carelessly placed. Marciano claimed that he was never deliberately dirty, and said that he was astonished when watching films of his fights to see his punches continually landing on illegal territory. 'I just went in there and banged away,' he said. 'I never gave much thought to where I was landing as long as I could feel the punches hitting something. It's a jungle in that ring. It's you or him, and I just made sure I threw enough punches to dishearten which ever guy was standing in front of me.'

It was British bulldog Don Cockell who got the worst of the Marciano mean machine in a brutal battle staged in San Francisco on May 16, 1955. Marciano fouled him a dozen times on the way to a savage ninth-round victory. 'He was the bravest guy I ever fought,' said the champion. 'People were saying he was a pushover, but he took everything I could throw at him.'

In his return fight with Ezzard Charles in New York on September 15, 1954, Marciano had his nose cut so badly that it looked as if it was

Marciano stuns the boxing world by announcing his retirement as undefeated champion in New York in 1956.

hanging loose on his face. It was one of the goriest sights ever seen in a heavyweight championship fight, and anywhere but in America the fight would have been stopped. Even Al Weill, not noted for his compassion, was ready to pull his meal ticket out of the fight at about the time that Rocky unleashed the finishing punches in the eighth round. It was reported at the time that Marciano spent a fortune on plastic surgery to get his nose mended, but when meeting him he said: 'I did not go anywhere near a surgeon. I let it heal itself, and within a couple of months it was as good as new.'

Marciano staggered the boxing world in general, and Al Weill in particular, when he announced his retirement after his sixth title defence against Archie Moore. There were all sorts of rumours flying, including that he was suffering from severe headaches and also that his back problem was so bad that he was going to be crippled for life.

'It's all nonsense,' was Marciano's response to the rumours. 'The fact is that because of the way I fight I have to train harder than any fighter in history. This means I am away from home for months on end, and leading the life of a hermit has become too much of a strain. It's not fair on my wife and baby daughter, and it's not fair on my mom. I've always promised them that I would get out when I was in a strong financial position, and I think I've made enough sacrifices. I've had a great time, and now I want to try to enjoy a normal life.'

There was an offer of $1 million for Marciano to come out of retirement to fight his successor, Floyd Patterson, and later a $3 million bait was dangled to try to tempt him into the ring with Sonny Liston. But he was happy with the $4 million he had made during his career. It was said that he still had every cent. Good luck to him, if he did.

Marciano, who did a little refereeing, some managing and dabbled with business interests, did have one more fight of sorts. He and Muhammad Ali faked their way through a computerized battle in 1969 in which they simulated seven different finishes for the benefit of the film cameras. Marciano got his pasta-pumped weight down and had a special hairpiece made for the occasion to make him look years younger.

Just two weeks before the film was released – Marciano won by a thirteenth-round

knockout – he was killed when a private plane in which he was a passenger crashed in Iowa. He died on August 31 1969 – hours before his forty-sixth birthday.

'The Rock' is still held in awe by fight fans, particularly those of Italian origin. The day after Mike Tyson was knocked out by 'Buster' Douglas in 1990, London-based fight executive Denny Mancini voiced what many were thinking when he said: 'Rocky is walking six inches taller today. They still can't beat his record.'

Forty-nine fights. Forty-nine victories. The most perfect record in heavyweight boxing history. Or is it? A story surfaced in 1992 that two of his early contests were exhibition matches, slipped into his record by his notoriously crafty manager, Al Weill. The allegation, made by a relative of the late Weill, was not welcomed by true fight fans. As far as they are concerned, Marciano's record is beyond dispute.

Marciano had a brief acting career during which, of course, he played a heavy...'I guess I wasn't cut out to be a dashing hero of the screen,' he said. 'I'm glad I had no scripts to learn when I was fighting.'

CHAPTER NINETEEN

FLOYD PATTERSON

THE PEEK-A-BOO CHAMP

Floyd Patterson seemed the most mixed-up and confused of the title holders in this first century of gloved world heavyweight champions. He was cluttered with complexes that led to occasionally odd behaviour. The first Olympic gold medallist to become world heavyweight king, Patterson was a Jekyll and Hyde of a fighter. He hated violence, but he was prepared to park his pacifism outside the ring as he chased, captured, lost, historically recaptured and then tried to cling on to the richest prize in sport. Despite his puzzling personality, Patterson always represented his chosen sport with dignity, and even in defeat he was never anything less than a gentleman – but a gentleman with disturbing self-doubts.

BOYHOOD NIGHTMARES

To discover the roots of Patterson's problems we need to put him on an imaginary couch and dig back into his boyhood days, which was when he began to develop his inferiority complex. The

third of eleven children of a labourer, he has admitted to being affected by the life of poverty into which he was born in Waco, North Carolina, on January 4, 1935. When he was a year old, his family moved to the Bedford-Stuyvesant ghetto of Brooklyn, an asphalt jungle where people had to scratch, scrape and struggle to survive. Squashed with the twelve other Pattersons into a cramped, five-room apartment, his deprived childhood was plagued by terrible nightmares and he would wake up drenched in sweat and yelling at the top of his voice. Perhaps the fact that two older brothers, Frank and Billy, slept at the head of the bed while he slept at the bottom with their feet sticking into him had something to do with his restless nights.

Floyd was so ashamed at having to wear hand-me-down clothes from his brothers and father that he used to play truant from school rather than risk having the other kids taunt him. He would hide away in a cellar, where he took comfort in being alone and away from the gaze of others. His identity crisis reached new lows when he scratched his face off a family photograph. He told his mother: ' I don't like that boy.'

When he was eleven, after getting involved in a few petty crimes, Patterson was sent to the Wiltwyck School at Esopus, New York, which was a country farm for emotionally disturbed city delinquents. It was the same school that had earlier launched Rocky Graziano on an explosive boxing career as he discovered that 'somebody up there' did love him. Patterson seemed to find love harder to come by. 'D'you know something,' he once said after climbing to the top of the boxing ladder,' I can never ever remember laughing as a kid. Not once.' He was not seen laughing too often when he was champion of the world, and he went through his career with a poker face that was a mask to hide his insecurities.

After two years of strict discipline at Wiltwyck, he was sent to a school for backward children on New York's east side. The rebel had been knocked out of him, but he was still eaten up with a crippling shyness that must have felt like being handicapped by a ball and chain. He has confessed in many interviews that just walking into a crowded room was an ordeal. His life changed when he followed his two older brothers, both exceptional boxers, to the

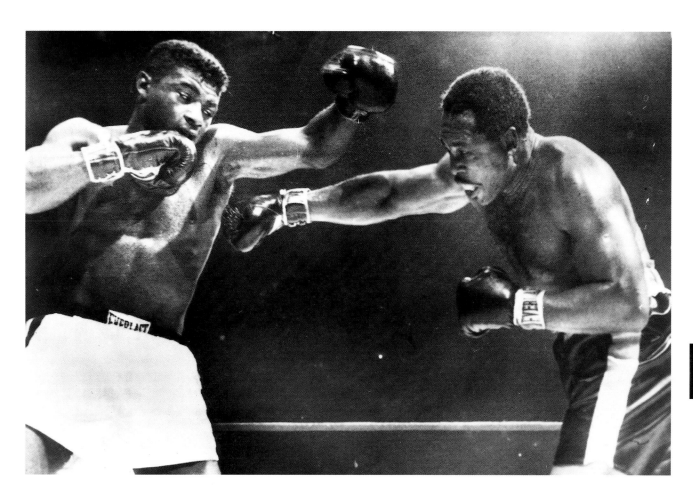

Gramercy Gym on the lower east side in Manhatten to watch them train. He was just fourteen, but convinced the man in charge – a white-haired martinet by the name of Cus D'Amato – that he was a year older so that he could be allowed to spar with the men. From the first moment he pulled on a pair of gymnasium gloves it was obvious to D'Amato that here was a kid with a special talent. Patterson had found a place where he at last had self-respect and where he could express himself without the fear of being ridiculed: the boxing ring.

Within three years of walking into the gymnasium and at the age of just seventeen he became the Olympic middleweight champion in the 1952 Helsinki Games, and he then turned professional under what was to become the almost suffocating control of D'Amato. The crusty, verbose manager, who could have stepped out of the pages of a Damon Runyon story, had even more complexes than Patterson, and was so convinced that mobsters were going to muscle in on his territory that he used to sleep in the gymnasium with a guard dog

protecting him. His suspicious, 'don't-trust-nobody' attitude rubbed off on his protegé, and it was years before Patterson could feel comfortable in the company of strangers. Many years later the Svengali-like D'Amato would discover and mould another troubled boy from Brooklyn, Mike Tyson.

Coached by D'Amato and trained by Jersey Joe Walcott's old mentor Dan Florio, Patterson developed a distinctive style, launching sudden two-handed attacks from behind a high guard that became known as his 'peek-a-boo' method. He tended to jump in like a kangaroo when delivering his hardest punches, with one or sometimes both feet off the ground, and he proved that he could take out opponents with either hand.

Matched by D'Amato with the care and caution of a man handling Dresden china, Patterson won his first thirteen professional contests before dropping a disputed eight-rounds points decision to former light-heavyweight world champion Joey Maxim in 1954. Eleven out of the twelve newspaper reporters at the ringside

Patterson on the way to winning the vacant world title with a fifth-round knockout victory over Archie Moore in Chicago in 1956.

Here comes history as Patterson knocks out Ingemar Johansson in 1960 to become the first world heavyweight champion to regain the title.

were of the opinion that Patterson had been robbed, but this was no consolation to him. He was flooded by all his self-doubts, and he went home and hid behind closed doors for a week because he felt so ashamed in defeat.

Patterson began to gain new confidence and self-belief when he married his sweetheart, Sandra Hicks, the one person who really understood him and helped him overcome his complexes. She encouraged him to convert to Roman

Catholicism, and Patterson began to find strength through religious instruction. He also began to show a new authority in the ring. In his thirty-first fight he was at last risked against a world-ranked opponent when – despite the handicap of a broken bone in his right hand – he outpointed Tommy 'Hurricane' Jackson to earn a number two rating in 1956. The only fighter ahead of him was Archie Moore, the former world light-heavyweight king who had taken

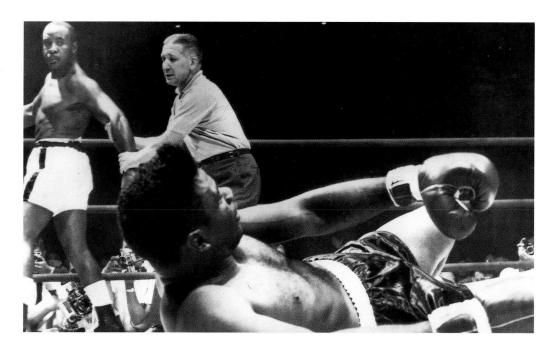

It's a repeat nightmare for Floyd Patterson as he loses the return fight with Sonny Liston in the first round in Las Vegas in 1963.

Rocky Marciano nine rounds in what proved to be 'The Rock''s final defence. He survived a brief knockdown before overpowering Moore.

YOUNGEST CHAMPION

When Marciano announced his retirement, Patterson and Moore were matched for the vacant title, and Floyd – at least twenty years younger than his opponent – knocked out 'Ageless' Archie in five rounds in Chicago on November 30, 1956. At twenty-one years, ten months and twenty-six days he was then the youngest heavyweight champion of all time, a record he later lost to Tyson. To make his day even more memorable, Sandra presented Patterson with the first of their three children – news that was given to him as he was announced as the new champion.

Everything should now have slotted into place for the introverted Patterson, but he found himself innocently caught up in the middle of a one-man war that D'Amato was waging against the International Boxing Club (IBC), that had taken over from Mike Jacobs' Twentieth-Century Club as the monopolistic force in world heavyweight boxing. D'Amato would consider challengers only if they had no connection with the IBC, and this led to four undistinguished title defences, including a monstrous mismatch against 1956 Olympic heavyweight champion Pete Rademacher, who

was making his professional debut on August 22, 1957. His other victories were against Tommy Jackson (ten rounds, 1957), Texas cowboy Roy Harris (twelve rounds, 1958) and Britain's anything-but-daring Brian London (eleven rounds, 1959).

D'Amato then imported what he thought was another pushover challenger in the shape of Swedish playboy Ingemar Johansson for a title defence in New York on June 26, 1959. Patterson was sucked into thinking that he had nothing to beat, and his world was turned upside down when he was stopped in three rounds after walking into Johansson's thunderous right-hand punch that became known as 'Ingo's Bingo'. Perhaps even worse for Patterson than the humiliation of defeat was the discovery that he could no longer give his complete trust to his puppeteer D'Amato, who without Patterson's knowledge had allowed notorious gangster 'Fat Tony' Salerno to have part of the promotion. After an investigation by the boxing authorities D'Amato had his licence revoked, and although he still held Patterson's reins, he and Patterson lost the close father-son relationship that had developed between them over the years.

Patterson was consumed with shame over his defeat by Johansson, but gradually he managed to turn his despair into a fanatical desire for revenge. On June 20, 1960, in New York's Polo Grounds he created history by becoming the first heavyweight champion to regain the title.

Patterson knocked Johansson flat out in the fifth round with a wicked left hook that carried every ounce of his frustration and longing for recognition and respect.

At last Patterson was able to walk round with his head held high, and he confirmed his superiority over Johansson with a sixth-round knockout in Miami on March 16, 1961. But after another pushover defence against Tom McNeeley in Toronto on December 4, 1961, he found his 'bogeyman' waiting around the corner for him in the menacing form of Sonny Liston. When they first met in Chicago on September 25, 1962, Liston bludgeoned him to defeat in two minutes six seconds. Patterson, who had taken the fight against the advice of D'Amato, was so ridden by guilt over his performance that he left the stadium by a back exit wearing a false beard and glasses so that nobody would recognize him. He really looked the part of 'Freud' Patterson. There was a bizarre incident as he drove towards home at high speed, still wearing his disguise. He was pulled up by a traffic cop, who asked for his driving licence. Patterson could not find it, and then sheepishly pulled down the beard to identify himself. The policeman scratched his head, and then – almost as embarrassed as Patterson – waved him on to continue his lonely, tortured journey home.

Ten months later in Las Vegas, Liston gave an action replay of the first fight, this time stopping the powerless Patterson in two minutes ten seconds. Patterson did not don a disguise when leaving the dressing-room after his second humiliation. He knew he had to learn to live with himself, and he regained his self-respect with a fourth-round knockout victory over British heavyweight Henry Cooper in London in 1966 and two brave shows against Muhammad Ali. He made unsuccessful bids to regain the title for a second time, against Ali in 1965 and then against Jimmy Ellis in a WBA version of the championship in Sweden on September 14, 1968, when he was considered by most observers to have been robbed of a points victory.

CONQUERING THE COMPLEXES

Patterson had been a top-quality fighter, but never an outstanding champion because he simply wasn't big enough and he had a suspect chin. His leaping-in style of attack too often left him open to counter blows and in seven of his thirteen title bouts he was knocked down sixteen times. But there was no doubting his bravery, and no matter how hard he was hit he kept trying to get up. He lost just eight of his sixty-four fights, and only Johansson, Liston and Ali stopped him; and of all his opponents, only the powerhouse Sonny Liston completely outclassed him.

His two battles with Ali had the added unpleasant ingredient of differences over religious outlooks. 'I did not feel any hatred for Ali,' said Patterson, 'but I detested the Black Muslims. They were a hate group at the time that I was fighting Ali and I considered that he was doing a terrible disservice to boxing and the heavyweight title by being associated with them.' Patterson had himself been a victim of segregation on many occasions, but he preferred Dr Martin Luther King's softly-softly approach to the problem. He was lambasted by Ali as being 'just a frightened rabbit'.

Ali stopped Patterson in twelve rounds in their title fight in Las Vegas on November 22, 1965, when Patterson was handicapped by a back injury. Patterson suffered a cut eye and was stopped in seven rounds in their return non-title fight in New York on September 20, 1972, after which he announced his retirement.

By the early 1990s Patterson had matured into a composed and confident man who had completely conquered the complexes that had gnawed at him for so much of his career. He was happily settled into a new marriage, his adopted son, Tracy, was a world-class featherweight and Patterson had managed to put a lot back into the sport that had made him prosperous by serving as a New York boxing commissioner. His major regret was not having adopted different tactics against Liston in their second fight. ' I should have fought him with caution,' he said. 'But I was overpowered by my pride, and tried to become aggressive with him. I paid the price.' Patterson will not be remembered as having been one of the greatest champions, but everyone who comes into contact with him finds him to be a fine, decent, likeable man who has always been a good advertisement for his sport – for somebody who spent so long doubting himself, he could not ask for a more satisfying tribute.

Right: Patterson is on the receiving end of a left uppercut from Muhammad Ali in Las Vegas in 1965. Ali won in the twelfth round.

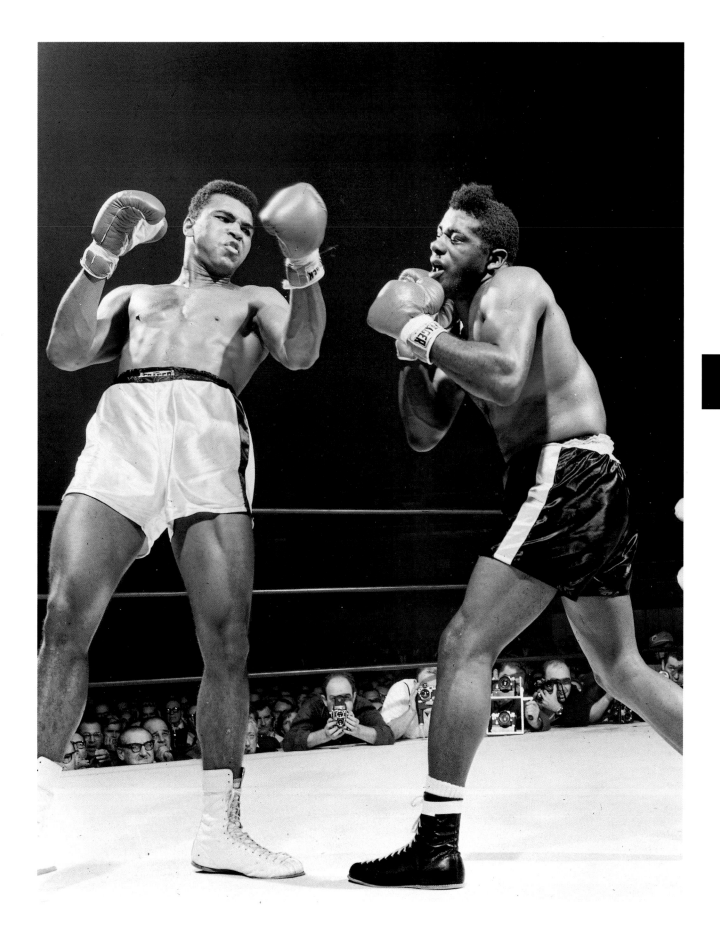

CHAPTER TWENTY

INGEMAR JOHANSSON

THE HAMMER OF THOR

For seven long years Ingemar Johansson had to live with the humiliation of having been publicly denounced as a coward, but eventually he was able to make those who had levelled the accusation at him grovel with apologies for one of the most insulting misjudgements in the history of boxing. Yet in some ways it can be argued that the slur did him a favour because it lit the fuse to a burning desire and determination to conquer the world. He did exactly that, and in a style that was nothing short of sensational.

The moment that brought scorn showering down on Johansson's wide shoulders came in the 1952 Olympic heavyweight final in Helsinki. Johansson was boxing a giant American called Ed Sanders. As the United States champion plodded forward swinging and missing, Johansson retreated around the ring not throwing a single punch. After two rounds of this non-violence, French referee Roger Vaisberg announced that he was disqualifying Johansson for 'not trying'.

As if that was not bad enough, at home Swedish journalists tore him apart rather than take his side for what appeared to be a harsh – heartless even – decision. The headlines in his home newspapers included such vicious dismissals as 'The fleeing rat ... the cup of shame ... Johansson's cowardly show ... Johansson makes me ashamed to be Swedish'. He was advised in vitriolic articles to 'get out of the sport you have disgraced' ... 'forget about becoming a professional because your career is kaput' ... 'at nineteen, Johansson is washed up in boxing where there is no room for cowardice.'

There was even worse degradation to follow for the young Swede. He was barred from receiving his silver medal, and the Swedish flag stayed furled at the medal ceremony. Officals stopped him from attending the official banquet and he was treated like an outcast. Nobody would believe his story that he had been waiting for the opportunity to land his speciality, a right-hand counter punch. 'I was going to give it everything I had in the third round,' he said. Nobody listened. And it was seven long years before it was accepted that he must have been telling the truth.

THE VICTORY ROAD

Johansson, the son of a road builder, was born in Gothenburg on October 16, 1932, and was a bright scholar who preferred to follow the boxing road rather than join his father's business. The highlight of his 71-bout amateur career before the Olympics came in 1951 when, representing Europe against America in Chicago, he knocked out Golden Gloves champion Ernest Fann in two rounds.

Swedish promoter Eddie Alhquist, a wealthy publisher, stayed loyal to Johansson after his undignified exit from the Olympics, and he guided him throughout a professional career that started with a fourth-round knockout win against Robert Masson in Gothenburg on December 5, 1952. He won the Scandinavian heavyweight title before doing his national service in the Swedish Navy in 1954, and then started to defeat all the best heavyweights in Europe.

On September 30, 1956, Johansson travelled to Italy to take the European crown from Franco Cavicchi with a thirteenth-round knockout victory, and successfully defended it with wins against such highly regarded British heavyweights as Henry Cooper (fifth-round knockout, 1957) and Joe Erskine (stopped in the thirteenth round, 1958).

Johansson was matched in a final eliminator for Floyd Patterson's world heavyweight title against American contender Eddie Machen in Gothenburg on September 14, 1958, and knocked Machen cold in the first round with the right-hand punch that been the main weapon in his rise up the boxing ladder.

When he arrived in the United States to challenge Patterson for the world heavyweight title in New York on June 26, 1959, he talked about his right as if it was something separate from the rest of his body. 'It is a gift from the Gods,' he said. 'It is mystic and moves faster than the eye can see. I do not tell it when to go. Suddenly, boom! It lands like toonder.' Hard-bitten American sportswriters thought they were being given ticket-selling spiel, but they – along with Patterson – found it was not just sales talk when the right exploded on the champion's jaw, making Johansson the first Swede to win the heavyweight crown and the first European holder of the title since Primo Carnera twenty-five years earlier.

The title fight had been postponed for twenty-four hours because of a rain storm, and there was still a stormy atmosphere in the stadium when, just before Patterson and Johansson made their entries into the ring, a bat flew eerily among the ringside fans, and became tangled in promoter Bill Rosensohn's hair. It was going to prove a completely batty night.

For the first two rounds Johansson hardly threw a punch apart from an off-target right and some novice-like, pawing left jabs, and Swedish reporters anxiously exchanged glances. Surely not another Helsinki? But this time Johansson was allowed to come out for the third round – which was bad news for Patterson. Suddenly twenty-seven seconds into the round the right – the 'Hammer of Thor' – exploded on the champion's jaw, and he went down as if he has been hit across the face by a baseball bat. As he got up with referee Ruby Goldstein's count at nine, he walked unsteadily like a drunk out on the town to his own corner as if he thought the round was over. Later he revealed that he thought that he must have knocked Johansson down and that he was instinctively going to a neutral corner.

Patterson made six more trips to meet the canvas as the Swede clubbed him with wild but stunning punches, and referee Goldstein finally rescued the champion – the ex-champion – from his nightmare with fifty-seven seconds of the round still to go.

Johansson did not have to say a word. His fists had done the talking and the question powerfully tatooed across Patterson's face was: 'So who's a coward now?' Swedish newspapers fell over themselves to right the wrong of 1952 and to bury the ghost that had haunted Johansson, and the International Olympic Association eventually admitted that they were wrong to have deprived him of his silver medal and eventually a special presentation was made to him. Sadly, Ed Sanders was not around to see Johansson vindicated. He had died of brain damage after his eighth professional fight in 1954.

Ingemar Johansson, the last European to hold the world heavyweight championship title.

135

THE PLAYBOY PUNCHER

Johansson was a one-off as a world heavy-weight champion. He was a handsome man with a big dimple in his chin, a winning smile and an almighty thump in his right hand.

Nothing was ever allowed to stop him enjoying the good life, and he led a playboy existence even when training for major fights. It was the norm for him to go nightclubbing and dancing into the early hours during the build-up to his fights, and his beautiful 'secretary' Birgit – later

The 'Hammer of Thor' drops Patterson in the first round of their third contest in Miami in 1961. Patterson got up to win by a knockout in the sixth round.

his second wife – used to stay with him at his training camps, along with his mother and father, two brothers, a sister and his astute managerial adviser, Eddie Alhquist.

The American press, like Patterson and his manager Cus D'Amato, were completely taken in by Johansson. The reporters wrote him off as a no-hoper after watching him in lethargic training sessions when the crafty Swede kept his right hand under wraps. Johansson cleverly exaggerated his playboy image while in the United States preparing for his title shot against Patterson, and he duped the press and the unsuspecting Patterson into thinking he was more interested in fun than fighting.

Johansson and Patterson tied up the championship for the next two years. They met in a return at the Polo Grounds in New York a year later, and this time a fanatically determined Patterson created history by becoming the first world heavyweight champion to regain the title. He stretched Johansson out on his back with a crashing left hook in the fifth round after the Swede had been floored for a count of nine. The back of his head thudded against the canvas as he landed, and a trapped nerve sent his right leg twitching as he was counted out. There was concern, particularly from Patterson, that he had been seriously injured, but he was released after an overnight stay in hospital suffering from concussion.

The 'decider' was staged in Miami on March 13, 1961. Patterson settled it once and for all by getting off the canvas to knock out Johansson in the sixth round. Johansson returned to Sweden nearly £2 million richer from the three battles with Patterson, but he was still hungry for another crack at the title. He got back on the championship trail by beating British-based Jamaican Joe Bygraves in Gothenburg on February 9, 1962, and then detonating the old 'Hammer of Thor' (also known as 'Ingo's Bingo') on Welshman Dick Richardson's jaw on June 17, 1962, to regain the European crown that he had given up after winning the world championship.

He was being manoeuvred into a world title showdown with Sonny Liston when he took what he thought would be a routine fight with former British champion Brian London in Stockholm on April 21, 1963. But it didn't work out as planned. Johansson won on points over twelve rounds but he was the last person to

know it. London landed a volley of punches in the dying moments of the fight, and Johansson was flat on his back when the bell saved him from a knockout defeat. It was too close for Johansson's comfort and he wisely decided to call it a day at the age of thirty-one after a career during which he caused some earthquaking shocks with his 'toonder' and lightning 'Hammer of Thor' right.

Johansson had always been a keen businessman throughout his career, and on his retirement increased his interests in haulage, construction and fishing-boat companies. After parting from his wife Birgit he moved to Florida where he and his son owned a successful motel.

In 1982, aged fifty, he ran and completed the New York marathon. Just ahead of him at the finish line was his old foe Floyd Patterson. They have become good friends, and together present the best face of boxing.

'Ingo's Bingo' lands on Welshman Dick Richardson. Johansson won by an eighth-round knockout to regain the European title in Gothenburg in 1962.

CHAPTER TWENTY-ONE

SONNY LISTON

OLD STONEFACE

Sad Sonny Liston, who rose from convict to champion, took all his dark secrets to the grave with him, and no one will ever be able to unravel the truth from the rumours and gossip that enveloped him and made him the most mysterious of this first century of world heavyweight kings. If all of the scandal-spreading stories written about him were placed end to end there would be enough reams of paper to lay a path right round the largest of mazes – and that is what Liston's life was, one big maze in which he often became lost and confused.

Liston spent so many years in the company of law-breakers that he seemed to have difficulty telling right from wrong, and throughout his career he was a constant companion of controversy. Even his death in a Las Vegas apartment six months after a winning fight against Chuck Wepner was shrouded in mystery, and stories persist to this day that he was murdered by a contract killer after allegedly trying to muscle in on a drug-dealing racket. Nobody will ever know the truth, but Liston's entire life was stranger than fiction.

THE POVERTY TRAP

We're all of us shaped by the environment in which we grow up and Charles 'Sonny' Liston got dealt just about the worst hand of any of this parade of champions. He was one of twenty-five children fathered during two marriages by Tobe Liston, a poverty-belt Arkansas cotton farmer for whom Liston had only contempt. The sort of deprived childhood Liston had can be glimpsed from this snatch of evidence he gave in 1960 to a Senate committee headed by Senator Estes Kefauver of Tennessee, who was investigating underworld control of boxing:

Senator Kefauver: 'How much education did you get?'

Liston: 'I didn't get any.'

'You didn't go to school at all?'

'No, sir. My father said if you can go to the dinner table you can go to the cotton fields to work and help pay for the food going into your belly.'

'Could you write the address where you lived?'

'No, sir. Can't read or write properly.'

'Suppose your share of a fight purse was $25,000 and they handed you a cheque for it. Could you tell whether the amount on the cheque showed $25,000?'

'Not exactly.'

'How long did you stay helping on the farm?'

''Til I was thirteen. We hardly had enough food to keep from starving, no shoes and only a few clothes. My father whipped me hard. If he missed a day, I'd feel like saying, 'How come you didn't whip me today?' I ran away and followed my mother to St Louis ...'

Liston might have done better staying down on the farm. In St Louis he fell among thieves, and for the rest of his life he was never able to shake free of the influence of hoodlums and underworld figures, who, it was believed, had control of him throughout his ring career.

He was continually in trouble with the police in St Louis, and one of the early rumours about him was that, because they could not pin a murder charge on him after a wealthy local businessman had been killed for molesting Liston's sister, they hit him with a trumped-up burglary charge for which he was sentenced to five years in jail. It was while serving his time that he was

directed towards boxing by a Roman Catholic chaplain. He was paroled in 1952 on the understanding that he concentrated on his new-found sport, and after winning a Golden Gloves title he turned professional in 1953.

Standing 6 foot 1 inch and weighing around 200 pounds, Liston was a fearsome sight in the ring. He could knock opponents out with a left ('death') or right ('and destruction'), and would intimidate them before the bell with a baleful, mean-eyed stare that often turned them to jelly before a punch had been thrown. His ramrod left jab was likened by one opponent to 'having an iron bar pushed into your face'.For such a big man he was surprisingly light on his feet, and his rope-skipping to his favourite 'Night Train' record was always a much-applauded feature on his exhibition tours when he became world champion.

Liston won fourteen of his first fifteen fights, seven of his victories coming by the knockout route. His one setback was an eight-rounds points defeat by Marty Marshall, who broke his jaw in the second round. In two re-matches he knocked out Marshall in six rounds and then outpointed him in March, 1956. He was just beginning to punch his way into championship contention when he got involved in an argument with a policeman over a parking ticket. The policeman finished up in hospital with a broken leg. Liston finished up back in prison for nine months. When he came out of jail he found his opponents were not only in the ring. He was stopped and questioned by police more than a hundred times and was arrested nineteen times on charges that never led to anything but aggravation. Liston was not the most popular person in St Louis as far as the police were concerned,

The 1962 championship fight: Liston crosses with a right and Patterson starts to fold like a puppet that has had its strings cut away. The world is about to have a new world heavyweight champion.

and he moved to Philadelphia in a bid to make a new life for himself, but many of the suspect acquaintances that he had mixed with during his law-breaking days continued to cling to him.

He made his comeback after twenty months out of the ring on January 29, 1958, with a two-round knockout victory over Billy Hunter in Chicago. He took his winning streak to thirty-three out of thirty-four fights, including top-flight fighters Zora Folley, Nino Valdes, Cleveland Williams, Howard King, Mike DeJohn and Eddie Machen among his victims.

There were several investigations into Liston's gangster connections and it was with some reluctance that he was given the go-ahead to challenge Floyd Patterson for the world title in Chicago on September 25, 1962. It was with even greater reluctance that Patterson's manager, Cus D'Amato, agreed to the match.

AN AWESOME REPUTATION

A bull-shouldered powerhouse of a fighter with huge 13-inch fists that he used like clubs, Liston flattened Floyd in two minutes six seconds of the first round. He gave a repeat performance when they met again the following year in Las Vegas, actually taking four seconds longer. Liston looked just about unbeatable, and Jim Wicks – manager of British champion Henry Cooper – summed up his awesome reputation when he said: 'I will not let 'Enry in the same room as him, let alone the same ring.'

It took Liston ten hard years to slog his way to the championship, but only seventeen months to be parted from it. He tamely surrendered the title to chatter-boxer Cassius Clay, retiring at the end of six rounds with a mysterious shoulder injury in Miami Beach on February 25, 1964. It was the most startling abdication since Edward VIII. There was an even bigger stink fifteen months later when Clay knocked him out with a phantom punch in the first round at Lewiston, Maine, on May 25, 1965. Jersey Joe Walcott was the referee, and he lost control as Liston went down to a right-hand punch that did not seem damaging enough to keep Liston on the canvas. Twenty-two seconds passed before a muddled Walcott finally completed the count, and as he turned to check with the timekeeper, Liston got

unsteadily to his feet to be met by another barrage of blows from Clay, who had screamed at him as he lay on his back: 'Get up you big ugly bear. We're on television.'

The rumour-mongers had a ball. Theories about his defeats ranged from betting coups to stories that he had been told by gangsters that he would be shot if he did not lie down. Another tale that had a long run was that Liston was under the influence of Black Muslims he had met in jail, and that they wanted Clay (or Ali, as he was eventually to become) as champion to further their cause. Perhaps the truth was that age had caught up with Liston, and that Clay was simply too quick and too clever for him. Just how old Liston was when he won the title has never been satisfactorily established. He and his mother could not agree on his date of birth, but the favourite seems to be May 8, 1932.

We have painted a picture of 'big, bad' Liston, whose scowling countenance earned him the nickname 'Old Stoneface'. But he was

Liston gets a tongue lashing from the 'Louisville Lip' Cassius Clay – as he was known then – in the publicity build-up to their first fight in 1964. 'I don't want to get charged with murder,' growled Sonny when Clay challenged him to put his title on the line.

'They'll look up at the sun and ask if it's shining. Then they will throw in an insulting question about something that might or might not have happened to me years ago. Why can't they just accept me for what I am – a boxer earning his living at what he does best?'

After his second fight with the champion now known as Ali, Liston had four winning comeback contests in Sweden and he won fourteen out of fifteen fights over the next five years. His one defeat was a ninth-round knockout by Leotis Martin in Las Vegas on December 6, 1969. Seven months later he stopped Chuck Wepner in ten rounds in Jersey City. It was his last fight. On

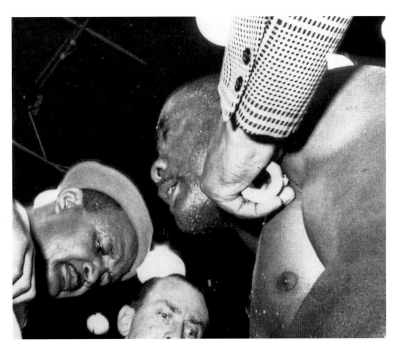

not all bad. He put in a lot of time with children's and old peoples' charities, and he had quite a sense of humour. This is captured by the story of when, in front of some pressmen, he had a mock row with a colleague over a $50 loan. Suddenly Liston pulled a revolver and 'shot' his friend, who collapsed with 'blood' seeping from his chest. The bullet was a blank and the blood was red sauce, but it was realistic enough to cause a watching television executive to faint.

Willie Reddish, his faithful trainer, was closer to Liston than most and he said: 'All the time I was with him I never knew him do a mean thing. He used to get angry when reporters asked him damn fool questions, but who wouldn't?'

On the whole Liston disliked and distrusted the media and he was always suspicious of reporters, convinced they were out to rake up easy-to-find dirt about his past. He thought they were more interested in his prison record than his ring record. And he was probably right. 'I'm always being asked dumb questions,' he said.

January 5, 1971, his wife, Geraldine – who had been one of the few reliable cornerstones in his turbulent life – returned to their Las Vegas apartment from a family visit to find her husband lying dead on the floor. Newspapers dating from December 29 were stacked on the front porch, and the coroner estimated that he had been dead for about a week.

Drugs were found in the apartment, and there were traces of drug substances in his blood, but the coroner ruled after an autopsy that death was due to lung congestion. But strong rumours persist to this day that mystery man Liston had been 'eliminated' by gangster associates. Sad Sonny Liston took his secrets with him to the grave.

Liston receives treatment to the shoulder he is alleged to have damaged, forcing his retirement at the end of the sixth round of his first title fight against Clay in 1964.

CHAPTER TWENTY-TWO

MUHAMMAD ALI

THE GREATEST

How best to tell the story of Muhammad Ali, the most famous, the most controversial, the most loved, just occasionally the most hated, arguably the most gifted and always the most entertaining heavyweight champion of the century? He transcended boxing and his face – and voice – became just about the best known in the world, even more recognized and revered than those of many presidents and kings. His remarkable life and career is best captured by quoting what the man with the golden tongue himself was saying as he passed the most important milestones on the journey that carried him into sporting legend.

He was at various times a poet, a prophet, a political pawn and a preacher, but it is as a punching perfectionist that he has won a lasting place in the history of boxing.

The descendant of slaves and the son of a Kentucky signwriter, he has five faces that must be portrayed to paint an accurate picture of the man who compiled impressive evidence to support his continually repeated claims that he was 'The Greatest'.

MAN OF DESTINY

The first face belonged to the brash, flash gaseous Cassius Marcellus Clay – his given name following his birth in Louisville on January 17, 1942. He started boxing at the age of twelve after he had sworn revenge on whoever it was who stole his pride and joy, a bicycle. He never did find the culprit, but developed such exceptional skills that by the time he was eighteen he was the Olympic light-heavyweight champion and headed for immortality.

After winning his gold medal in the 1960 Rome Games, he told everybody and anybody who would listen: 'I am a Man of Destiny. I'm gonna win the heavyweight championship of the world, earn a million dollars and get me a chauffeur-driven, tomato-red Cadillac with built-in hi-fi, television and telephones. I'm gonna make the world sit up and take notice and say, "Wow, this kid is The Greatest".'

He achieved all of this within three years of being launched as a professional by a syndicate of white millionaire businessmen and while sharpening his skills under the expert eye of his Miami-based trainer, Angelo Dundee. Standing a beautifully chiselled 6 foot 3 inches and weighing around 224 pounds at his peak, he was dubbed the 'Louisville Lip' as he drummed up box-office business with a tongue that was even quicker than his fast fists. He was a prophet and a poet in those early razzle-dazzle days, winning fights with unprecedented speed and style in the rounds he predicted. This is how he correctly predicted the fall of former light-heavyweight champion and two-times challenger for the world heavyweight crown, 'Ageless' Archie Moore, in his sixteenth fight in Los Angeles on November 15, 1962:

> Archie's been living off the fat of the land;
> I'm here to give him his pension plan.
> When you come to the fight
> Don't block the aisle,
> Don't block the door.
> For y'all all go home after round four.

It would not win any poetry prizes, but it did win the attention of the fans and in no time at all he managed to make himself the most talked-about boxer in the world. On the way to challenging Sonny Liston for the world title, in only

The start of the legend: Clay on the winners' rostrum at the 1960 Rome Olympics. Poland's Zbigniew Pietrzykowski, the three-times European champion whom he beat in the light-heavyweight final, is on the right. Australian Tony Madigan, outpointed by Clay in the semi-finals, is second from left; the other bronze medallist is Italian Giulio Saraudi.

his twentieth contest on February 25, 1964, he survived the shock of being dumped on his backside by the famous left-hook hammer of British heavyweight hero Henry Cooper at Wembley. The bell saved him, and in the predicted fifth round he stopped Cooper with a cut eye.

In his next fight Clay went in with the fearsome Liston despite being warned by his syndicate managers that he was trying to go too far too soon. He mounted a headline-hitting publicity campaign, organizing a 'bear hunt' to Liston's home where he taunted the champion by chanting through a megaphone: 'You're a tramp, I'm the champ ... you big ugly bear.'

In inimitable style, he spouted to television viewers this poetic prophecy of how the fight would end:

Clay comes out to meet Liston, and Liston starts to retreat
If Liston goes back any further he'll end up in a ringside seat.
Clay swings with a left, Clay swings with a right
Look at young Cassius carry the fight.
Liston keeps backing, but there's not enough room
It's a matter of time, and there – Clay lowers the boom.
Now Clay swings with a right, what a beautiful swing
And the punch raises the bear clear out of the ring.
Liston is still rising, and the ref wears a frown

For he can't start counting 'til Sonny comes down.

Now Liston disappears from view, the crowd's getting frantic

But our radar station's picked him up over the Atlantic.

Who would have thought when they came to the fight

That they'd witness the launching of a human satellite.

Clay – a seven-to-one underdog – danced rings round a lethargic-looking Liston, who quit on his stool at the end of the sixth round with a mysterious shoulder injury. Clay's tongue went into overdrive as he raced around the ring yelling at the ringside reporters who, almost to a man, had tipped defeat for the spring-heeled youngster: 'Now watcha gonna say, you hypocrites? He's gonna go in one? He's gonna go in two? Well, I've just whipped that big old ugly bear so bad that he's going off to hospital. And just look at Cassius. Why, he's still the prettiest.

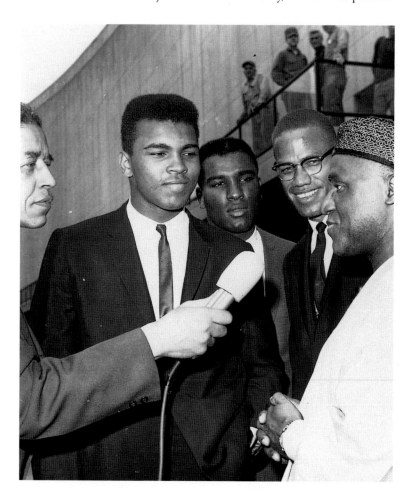

Cassius Clay announces that in future he will answer only to the name of Muhammad Ali, and among his companions is the bespectacled black extremist Malcolm X.

Not a mark on him. You saw it with your own eyes. I've shook up the world, just like I said I would. C'm on, watcha gonna say? Huh? Let's hear it: Who's the greatest?'

And hard-bitten reporters took time off from filing their reports to chant back: 'You are Cassius. You are the greatest.'

GOODBYE CASSIUS

On the way to a highly controversial first-round knockout victory over Liston in their return fight in Lewiston, Maine, on May 25, 1965, he dropped his slave name of Clay and his white managers and started the next phase of his career with the Muslim name Muhammad Ali. This was his second face. His new advisors were Muslim leader Elijah Muhammad and his son, Herbert, and among his regular companions was controversial Black Muslim activist Malcolm X.

Pressed about his Black Muslim connections he revealed: 'I believe in the religion of Allah and peace. What's wrong with that? I don't try to move into white neighbourhoods. I don't want to marry a white woman. I don't want to hurt no one like the Ku Klux Klan. I was baptised when I was twelve, but I didn't know what I was doing. I'm not a Christian any more. I am a black man who has adopted Islam. I want peace and I do not find peace in an integrated world. I love to be black, and I love to be with my people ... Why do I want to live in the white man's way? Why do I want to get bit by dogs, washed down a sewer by fire hoses? Why does everybody attack me for being righteous? Let me tell you that I've got this feeling that I was born for a special purpose. I don't know what I'm here for. I just feel abnormal, a different sort of man. I've always had this feeling since I was a little boy. Perhaps I was born to fulfil biblical prophecy. I just feel as if I might be part of something – a Divine thing. I believe Allah has a purpose for me. Being the world champion is just a part of it.'

After defending the title with a twelfth-round victory against Floyd Patterson in Las Vegas, Ali made seven more successful defences before being stripped of the championship in 1967 for refusing to join the US Army on religious grounds. The war in Vietnam was at its peak, and he caused uproar in the United States with the comment: 'I ain't got no quarrel with them Viet Cong. No Viet Cong ever called me nigger. We Muslims don't bear weapons. We don't fight wars unless it's a war declared by Allah himself.'

THE ALI SHUFFLE

The third face of Ali came after his three-and-a half-year politically forced lay-off which robbed him of his peak boxing years. He was no longer the twinkle-toed stylist, but he still entertained spectators with his Ali shuffle, and quick wit.

In Ali's third comeback fight he attempted to regain the world heavyweight title from the new champion, Joe Frazier, in New York on March 8, 1971. A left hook dropped Ali in the last round to clinch a narrow points victory for 'Smokin'' Joe in one of the classic contests of the century. Ali, talking through a jaw swollen like a balloon, said to his main motivator, Bundini Brown, in the dressing-room immediately after the fight: 'Set the traps, man. We're goin' huntin' for that championship ... Float like a butterfly ... sting like a bee ... Rumble, young man, rumble ...'

Liston has quit in his corner and in 1964 Clay is the new champion. 'I told you, I told you,' he yells at the press. 'I AM the Greatest!'

Liston is on his back in the first round of his second title fight with Ali in 1965. Ali is saying, 'Get up you big ugly bear. We're on television.'

He floated and stung his way to victory in thirteen of his next fourteen fights, avenging the one defeat against Ken Norton, who broke Ali's jaw in their first meeting. Ali then outpointed Joe Frazier to set up a championship showdown with the new king, George Foreman, in a 'Rumble in the Jungle' in Zaire on October 30, 1974. Ali introduced his rope-a-dope tactics, allowing Foreman to punch himself to the edge of exhaustion while he rested on the ropes behind a gloved defence. In the eighth round he catapulted himself forward from the ropes to land a volley of punches that knocked out the previously unbeaten Foreman. Ali said later: 'First I concentrated on breaking George's concentration and then his heart. I was deliberately conserving energy while lying on the ropes, and as George kept whamming in those big punches of his I was saying, "That the best you can do, George? Surely you can hit harder than that. Show me somethin'. You're not a champ, you're a chump." He slowly got dispirited and then very tired, and I was fresh when I came off the ropes and finished him off in the eighth round.'

Ali defended the title ten times, including winning a 'Thriller in Manila' against Joe Frazier on October 1, 1975, in which both fighters took heavy punishment before trainer Eddie Futch stopped Frazier from going out for the fifteenth round. As he was announced as the winner, Ali dropped flat to the canvas in a state of complete exhaustion. He said later, after recovering in the dressing-room: 'Joe and I went close to death out there. That's three times we've had wars. He's the toughest man I've ever met, but it's time we stopped beating up on each other. I don't think any men in boxing history have fought fights like me and Joe.'

The authors had the privilege of getting really close to Ali in Munich while working in a public relations capacity on his championship defence against British lionheart Richard Dunn on May 24, 1976. Suddenly, it became apparent why he had to keep on fighting while his best was clearly behind him. He flew into Munich with a vulturous party of fifty-four hangers-on feeding off him, many of them charging all hotel expenses to his room. All his boasting and bragging was just an act. Away from the cameras and the reporters he was quietly spoken and a joy to be with, but he was blind to the fact that a lot of people were taking advantage of

his sweet nature and exploiting him. 'I just don't like to say no to nobody in need,' he explained. 'If I've got it they can have it. They'd be a lot less misery in this world if everybody would share.'

THE SAD SHADOW

Face number four was the saddest of all. Ali was now just a shadow of the fleet-footed youngster who had thrilled millions with his clever footwork and lightning-fast fists. Dr Ferdie Pacheco, his personal physician, tried to tell him that he was putting his health at risk by continuing to box. But Ali – in need of ego-massaging public acclaim and money – would not listen, and on February 15, 1978, he lost his title to Leon Spinks, who was having only his eighth professional fight after winning the light-heavyweight Olympic title in Montreal in 1976. It provided Ali with a dream scenario: 'Just think, I can now become the first fighter in all history to win the heavyweight championship for a third time.'

He duly outpointed Spinks in their return match in New Orleans on September 15, 1978,

Ali explains to a National Selective Service committee in 1967 why he does not wish to join the US Army. 'I ain't got no quarrel with them Vietcong,' he said, causing uproar. Following his refusal to be inducted on religious grounds, he was stripped of the world title and went into exile for three and a half years.

An aggressive Ali throws a right lead against Joe Frazier. Their three-fight series was one of the most exciting serials in ring history, with Ali winning two-one.

and then – to the relief of all his devoted followers – he announced his retirement. But Ali, his funds depleted by heavy alimony payments to three ex-wives and much of his money fleeced from him by his army of hangers-on, was persuaded to challenge the new lion of the heavyweight division, Larry Holmes, in Las Vegas on October 2, 1980. Ringsiders were in tears as he plodded through the motions, trying to fight from memory. He was stopped for the only time in his career when Angelo Dundee retired him at the end of the tenth round. It was later revealed that he could hardly hold up his hands during the fight because of a serious thyroid condition.

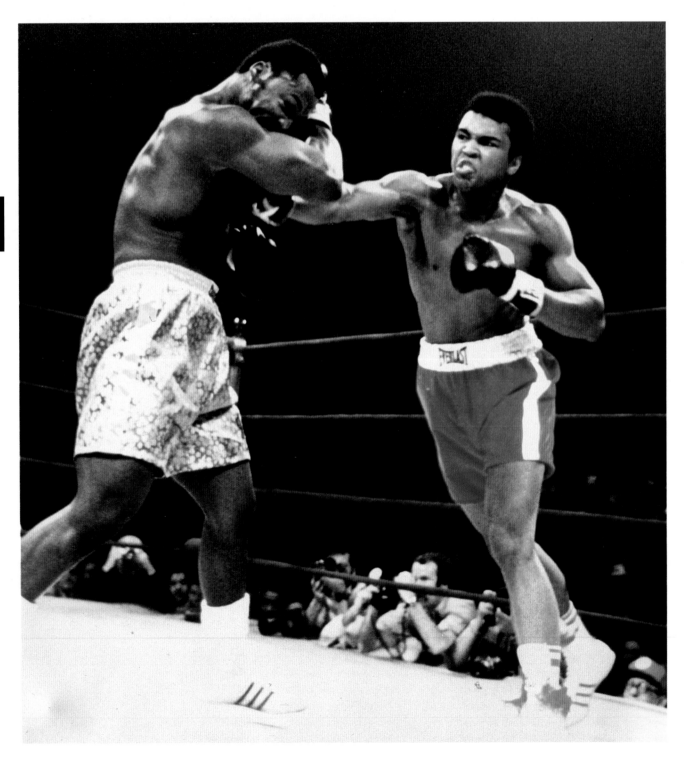

Those who knew of his problem and allowed him to go through with the fight should never forgive themselves. They allowed one of the gods of the ring to be used as a punchbag by one of his former sparring partners, and all for a fistful of dollars bound for pockets other than Ali's. It was believed that a major reason for Ali's later health problems was that he had gone on a crash diet to get his weight down for a Holmes fight that should never have been allowed to take place.

He foolishly decided to have one more fling in a meaningless affair against Jamaican-born Trevor Berbick in the Bahamas on December 11, 1981. His timing and reflexes were like those of a man punching his way through heavy treacle, and he lost on points over ten rounds against an opponent who would not have laid a glove on him at his peak. At last he saw himself as others who cared had seen him for several years. 'Father Time has caught up with me. I'm coming up forty years of age, and for the first time I really feel it. When Holmes beat me I had excuses 'cos I wasn't feeling right. No excuses this time, but at least I didn't go down and I didn't get cut up. I'm still the prettiest. I didn't do bad for an old man.'

When at his best, Ali was an absolute master of long-range boxing, nearly always shooting for the head with a powerful left jab followed by overarm rights that had a jarring rather than a concussive effect. He avenged three of the five defeats in his 21-year, 61-fight career (by Joe Frazier, Ken Norton and Leon Spinks) and his setbacks against Larry Holmes and Trevor Berbick came long after he should have dropped the curtain on what was arguably the greatest heavyweight boxing career of them all.

NO COMPLAINTS

And so to his fifth and final face, the Ali of the nineties. It could be painted as a sad face, because the old champ is not at all well. He stayed in boxing at least two years longer than was good for him, and he is suffering from a form of Parkinson's Disease and has to take heavy medication. Catch him at the right time and he can still be witty and entertaining, and he will treat you to a show of magic tricks that he has perfected. But on a bad day his speech is slurred, and his memory poor.

Yet he never complains, and devotes every spare moment to Islam and the religion he has followed faithfully now for more than a quarter of a century. His fourth wife, Lonnie, is a source of tremendous strength to him, and he sees a lot of his seven daughters and one son, Muhammad Ali Jr., from previous marriages. He also has his life-long friend, photographer Howard Bingham, close by as somebody he can trust and rely on. The hangers-on have all disappeared.

No one has to feel sorry for Ali, because he is happy with his life, but there are those who should feel ashamed for having played a part in letting him go to the well too often. The last word goes to the 'Louisville Lip':

'Muhammad Ali is still fighting. I'm fighting injustice and fighting for the downtrodden, the poor, the hungry, the illiterate and all those who don't get a fair crack. It's no longer boxing that interests me. That was all part of Allah's purpose to get me recognized so that I could help to spread his word. I enjoyed boxing, but I'm just as happy now trying to do my best to make it a better world to live in.'

MUHAMMAD ALI, THE GREATEST.

Leon Spinks forces the pace against Muhammad Ali in their first fight in Las Vegas in 1978. Spinks scored an upset points victory.

CHAPTER TWENTY-THREE

JOE FRAZIER

SMOKIN' JOE

Joe Frazier started out in life like Joe Louis, fought like a black Rocky Marciano and had established himself as a star in his own right until running into a heavyweight hurricane by the name of George Foreman. His defeat by Foreman was so crushing that it put a permanent dent in his reputation, but for a brief span he looked as mighty as any previous champion.

Frazier became champion after Ali had been stripped of the title for refusing to join the US Army. Those who dismissed him as a pretender to the throne were given a rude shock when he outpointed Ali in New York in 1971 in a never-to-be-forgotten battle. The victory underlined Frazier's right to the title, and he was accepted as a worthy champion. Then Foreman fell on him like a ton of bricks.

PERPETUAL MOTION

Like so many of the champions in this centenary parade, Frazier used the boxing ring to escape the poverty trap. Born in Beaufort, South Carolina, on January 12, 1944, he was the seventh son in a family of thirteen and worked on his father's run-down vegetable plantation from the age of eight. In those early days he was known as Billy-Joe, and he used to listen to stories about how Joe Louis had made a similar start in life before becoming the world's best-loved heavyweight boxing champion. By the time he was ten he had made up his mind that he would become another Louis. Frazier fed his dreams by stuffing old turnip sacks with moss and then hanging them from trees as makeshift punchbags. His could be labelled a bags-to-riches story.

Frazier married his schoolgirl sweetheart, Florence Smith, and then followed his elder brothers to Philadelphia, where he got himself a $75-a-week job, perhaps fittingly, in a slaughterhouse. He took up boxing as much to control his ballooning weight as anything, and while sparring at the Philadelphia Police Athletic Club he was spotted by ring-wise trainer Yancey 'Yank' Durham. He recognized Frazier's potential and helped him develop some style and technique to go with his raw power.

Frazier won thirty-eight of his forty amateur contests, his two defeats both being at the massive hands of Grand Rapids giant Buster Mathis. The second setback came in the 1964 United States Olympic trials, but the victory cost the luckless Mathis a broken thumb and it was Frazier who went in his place to the Tokyo Games. Frazier won the gold medal in impressive style, pounding his way to a points victory over West German bus driver Hans Huber in the final. Frazier then revealed that he had battled from the quarter-final with a broken left hand, which stopped him letting his favourite left hook go with full weight.

He had to pick up his own medical bills when he returned home to the United States for surgery. The Olympic hero had his hand placed in a plaster cast and found himself out of work with a wife and three children – Marvis, Jacqueline and Weatta – to feed. When his plight was publicized in the Philadelphia press the public rallied round and sent him food parcels and donations to keep him going. Frazier finally turned professional in the summer of 1965 with a syndicate of millionaire businessmen – Cloverlay Inc – backing him, and with his mentor, Yank Durham, as his manager. Later, the renowned Eddie Futch joined the camp as trainer.

Frazier fought with a Marciano-style perpetual motion two-fisted fury that earned him the nickname 'Smokin" Joe. His physique was also similar to Marciano's. At half an inch under 6 foot, he was short by modern standards, and his reach was 9 inches shorter than Ali's telescopic 82 inches. His legs were strong, his shoulders wide and – like 'The Rock' – he was boiling with mischief and menace in the ring. A rock-band singer when not boxing, he had an in-built rhythm to his punches.

In his first twenty-eight months as a professional he hurried through nineteen straight victories, all but two of his opponents hammered out of his path inside the distance. Only the Argentinian bull, Oscar Bonavena, gave him real trouble in 1966, and Frazier proved he had courage among his qualities as he hauled himself off the canvas twice before winning on points over ten bruising rounds.

On March 4, 1968, he was matched with his old rival and bogeyman Buster Mathis in a fight that was billed by the New York Boxing Commission as being for the heavyweight title taken away from Ali. He gave the 293-pound Mathis quite a mauling before the referee stopped the fight in the eleventh round. He successfully defended his title against Manuel Ramos (stopped second round, 1962), Bonavena (a clear-cut points win, 1968), Dave Zyglewicz (first-round knockout, 1969) and Jerry Quarry (stopped seventh, 1969) before being paired with WBA-recognized champion Jimmy Ellis for the undisputed title in New York on February 16, 1970.

Ellis, Muhammad Ali's former chief sparring partner and close friend, was stopped in the fourth round. Then, on November 18, 1970, he landed with his speciality left hook to flatten world light-heavyweight champion Bob Foster in two rounds. This set up the showdown with Ali, who had just launched a comeback campaign with victories over Jerry Quarry and Oscar Bonavena. For once the fight publicists did not have to bang their drums and make exaggerated claims about the contestants to attract an audience for the fight on March 8, 1971 in New York.

The proudest moment of Frazier's amateur career as he is named winner of the 1964 Olympic heavyweight gold medal. He boxed from the quarter-finals with a broken bone in his left hand.

Frazier against Ali was a 'natural'. It was the Irresistible Force against the Immoveable Object – and something had to give. For the first time in ring history two undefeated heavyweights had been matched for the world title.

It was a contest that ushered in a new era in financial as well as fighting terms. This wasn't an old-fashioned million-dollar fight. It was a Billion-Dollar Bonanza and both Frazier and Ali picked up an unprecedented $2.5 million each.

Frazier's non-stop aggression had him slightly ahead on most scorecards going into the fifteenth and final round of a seesawing struggle, and he clinched victory by dropping Ali for a nine count with the left hook that served him so well throughout his career. Both boxers finished up in hospital, Ali for treatment to a damaged jaw and Frazier to recover from total exhaustion.

A DEVASTATING DEFEAT

In 1972 Frazier had easy-pickings fights against Terry Daniels and Ron Stander before agreeing to take on the unheralded George Foreman in Kingston, Jamaica, on January 23, 1973. It was one of the matchmaking mistakes of the century. Frazier's handlers considered it no more than a warm-up fight for a megabucks return with Ali, but it proved not so much a warm-up as a roasting. Foreman had him up and down like a yo-yo before the referee stopped what had become a slaughter in the second round.

Frazier was never again quite the same force after this first heartbreaking defeat of his career, but he motivated himself for two more storming fights with Ali. He was outpointed in a twelve-round battle for the North American championship in New York on January 28, 1974, and then – in the 'Thriller in Manila' on October 1, 1975 – he was forced to retire on his stool after fourteen viciously fought rounds that completely drained both fighters.

Tortured Frazier could never get the humiliation against Foreman out of his system. Two and a half years after his nightmare in Jamaica he got his chance to try to avenge that terrible defeat. By then he had lost two punishing fights to Ali, and Foreman was an ex-champion with – so it seemed – little appetite left for the game. Frazier went to extraordinary lengths to try to get a pyschological advantage over Foreman. He

A study in concentration. Frazier listens to instructions during the first memorable fifteen-round battle with Muhammad Ali in New York on March 8, 1971.

152

climbed into the ring at Uniondale on June 15, 1976, with a dressing-gown hood covering his head. When he removed the hood just moments before the first bell it was revealed that he had shaved all his hair off his head in Marvin Hagler style. It certainly made him look more menacing, but Foreman was unmoved and gave poor old Joe another shellacking before the referee stopped the fight in the fifth round.

Frazier tried forgetting about boxing and gave more time to singing appearances with his group, The Knockouts, but the call of the ring was too strong and in 1981 he fought ex-convict Floyd 'Jumbo' Cummings over ten rounds. It

was clear that 'Smokin' Joe''s fire had gone out, and after he had struggled to a ten-round draw he hung up his gloves for good. Frazier then switched to management, and under his guidance his son Marvis looked promising until he was rushed too quickly to title contention, suffering one-round batterings against both Larry Holmes and Mike Tyson. Marvis had inherited his father's energy but not his chin.

Frazier will go down as a good rather than great member of our century of champions. He was unlucky to have to live in the shadow of the charismatic Ali and even unluckier to have run into the mighty fists of George Foreman.

Manager Joe Frazier with his son, Marvis, who was hurried too quickly into a fight against Larry Holmes.

CHAPTER TWENTY-FOUR

GEORGE FOREMAN

THE PUNCHIN' PREACHER

Whether the reign of George I or George II is taken into consideration, the astonishing George Foreman is well worthy of his place in this centenary roll of honour. He stirred up the world punchbowl with his 'second coming' after a ten-year retirement, but he had achieved enough the first time around to earn himself a rating in the 'great' category.

Boxing followers were first alerted to the power of Foreman when he won the gold medal in the 1968 Olympics in Mexico. They were the Games in which several American athletes staged 'black power' demonstrations at the victory ceremonies. Foreman got himself noticed with a patriotic waving of the Stars and Stripes on the winner's rostrum. It was the way he waved his fists, however, that really caught the eye.

ON THE WILD SIDE

Born in Marshall, Texas, on January 22, 1948, Foreman was the fifth of seven children of a railroad construction worker and his wife, Nancy.

Foreman frankly admits that he lived on the wild side in his early years. 'I was always in trouble when I was a kid,' he said. 'You name it, I did it. I grew up in the tough Fifth Ward in Houston where I became well known to the juvenile authorities and the cops. One week I broke two hundred windows just for the hell of it, and I didn't get caught. Went back the next week to break me some more glass when a cop caught me as I was about to throw my first rock.'

Foreman went on: 'Our district was heaving with bad guys – dope addicts, ex-cons, thieves and criminals of every description. I was going down that path but fast until the day I saw one of my pro-football heroes Jim Brown on television talking about the Jobs Corp. It was a scheme for educating lost youngsters like myself and for keeping them out of trouble. I got myself a qualification as an electronics assembler and, even more important, got an introduction to boxing by Doc Broadus, who was vocational guidance director at one of the Corps' camps. Boxing saved me from a wasted life of crime.'

After his triumph in the Olympic final in which he bombed out Russian champion Ionas Chepulis in two rounds, Foreman turned professional under the management of Dick Sadler, a former vaudeville song-and-dance man who brought in Archie Moore as one of Foreman's trainers. Old Archie watched Foreman work out and said: 'God bless the puncher! There's a lot to be smoothed out, but with his power he can go all the way to the stars ... and stars are what his opponents will be seeing!'

In his first four years as a professional Foreman knocked out all but three of his thirty-seven opponents, clubbing them to defeat in a brutal fashion that owed little to the boxing textbook. There was an almost novice-like rawness about his style that persuaded world champion Joe Frazier that he could handle him in what was intended as a warm-up fight in Kingston, Jamaica on January 22, 1973 – Foreman's twenty-fifth birthday – for a rematch with Muhammad Ali. It is now history that Frazier's handlers made what is considered the biggest misjudgement in modern boxing history, and he was parted from his championship and a promised fortune in two rounds of unbridled savagery. Frazier was blitzed to the canvas six times before the referee, Arthur Mercante, saved him from the ignominy of a count out.

Of all the scores of reporters at the ring-side, only Walter Bartleman of the London *Evening Standard* boldly tipped Foreman to win. The next morning as he walked in the grounds of his hotel he was so busy reading a hero-gram from his Editor that he failed to see the swimming pool in front of him and went in with a great splash. His friendly Fleet Street rival Reg Gutteridge, now the voice of boxing on Britain's Independent Television, shouted: 'You might be some prophet, Bart, but you're not yet able to walk on water!'

In almost any other era Foreman – magnificently sculptured at 6 foot 4 inches and weighing around 224 pounds – could have looked forward to a long reign, but the one and only Muhammad Ali was waiting in the wings for *his* 'second coming'. After destroying Joe Roman in 1973 and Ken Norton in 1974, Foreman was talked into putting his title on the line against Ali in the 'Rumble in the Jungle' in Zaire on October 30, 1974. It was Don King's first world heavyweight championship promotion. Ali psyched Foreman out of the fight and his championship (see page 147). The eighth-round knockout defeat ended Foreman's unbeaten run of forty fights.

Foreman was so shattered by the defeat that he confesses that he lost his way in life, going back to his bad old ways as the fortune he had made in the ring ran away from him like water through a gold prospector's fingers. He returned to the ring for a gimmick night in Toronto when, in exhibition contests, he took on five different fighters one after the other and knocked them all out. Then victories over Ron Lyle and Joe Frazier put him back in the title picture before a points defeat by Jimmy Young in San Juan on March 17, 1977, was followed by the shock announcement that he was quitting the ring to become a preacher. He claimed that he had a religious experience in the dressing-room after the loss to Young.

'I found God,' explained Foreman. 'There I was floundering back into a life of sin when I

Foreman is seconds away from the world championship as Joe Frazier is literally lifted into the air by the power of his punches in Jamaica in 1973.

Right: Foreman flattens
Gerry Cooney in two
rounds in Atlantic City
in 1990.

157

was given the sense and the strength to save myself. I decided there and then to devote the rest of my life to the word of the Lord, and I have since used my God-given gifts as a boxer to help spread my belief. The answers for all of us are right there in the good ol' Bible.'

A STUNNING COMEBACK

For ten years Foreman pounded the Bible and set up a charity to help wayward youngsters in Texas where he had often been tempted to cross the wrong line of the law. Then, after ten years out of the ring and shortly before his fortieth birthday, he stunned the boxing world again by announcing his comeback. Few took him seriously at first as he thumped his way to slow-motion victories over a procession of cruiser-weights and unrated heavies, but there was no doubting that all his old power was still packed into his fists.

He was more than 30 pounds heavier than in his championship days, and his shaven head gave him a menacing appearance that was totally alien to the image he had fashioned outside the ring as a preacher spreading the word of God. As he entered the 1990s he looked capable of overtaking Jersey Joe Walcott's record of being the oldest world heavyweight champion, and at the age of forty-three he got a shot at new champion Evander Holyfield, who was just a schoolboy when Foreman won the title the first time around.

The fight was staged in Atlantic City's Convention Centre on April 19, 1991, and Foreman – a winner of all his twenty-four comeback contests – gave Holyfield all the trouble he could handle before going down to a twelve-rounds points defeat. Foreman was never once off his feet, not even bothering to sit down between rounds. His evening's work brought him a massive $12.5 million purse, much of which he sank into his church charity in the small town of Humble in Texas where he is the pastor of the Church of the Lord Jesus Christ. Five times married, Foreman also needed a lot of money to pay his alimony and feed and clothe his nine children, four of whom are called George! He was back in the ring in Las Vegas on April 11, 1992, when he scored a ten-rounds split points decision over British-born Alex Stewart.

Foreman took a fearful hiding from Stewart in the last third of the fight and at the final bell was almost unrecognizeable because of the lumps and bumps on his face, but he insisted that he was not through punching. 'I've still got a lot of the Lord's work to do,' he said, 'and the boxing ring is as good a place as any to get my message across.'

George I and George II – both of them regal, both of them remarkable.

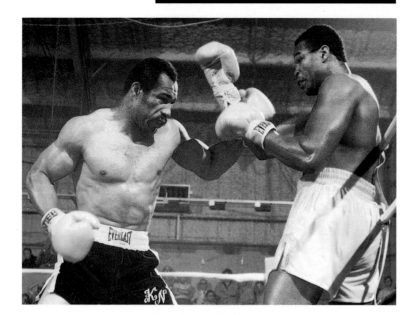

CHAPTER TWENTY-FIVE

KEN NORTON

AND THE ALPHABET BOYS

A s the first century of gloved championships approached the 1980s a cloud of confusion gathered over the world heavyweight scene when rival associations started recognizing a queue of different title holders. There was the World Boxing Association (WBA), the World Boxing Council (WBC), the International Boxing Federation (IBF) and, later, the World Boxing Organization (WBO), all of whom were dishing out championships to a parade of boxers who became known as the Alphabet Boys. This, in processional order, is how they won and lost their paper crowns.

Above: Holmes is in control on the ropes as Ken Norton launches a two-fisted attack during their classic contest in Las Vegas in 1978. Holmes won narrowly on points over fifteen rounds.

ERNIE TERRELL, WBA TITLE-HOLDER
1965-1967

Ernie Terrell, born on April 4, 1939, was the first of the pretenders to the heavyweight throne. The WBA stripped Ali of his championship because he entered into a return-match agreement with Sonny Liston. Terrell, a 6-foot 6-inch giant from Chicago via Mississippi, was

nominated to fight veteran Eddie Machen and outpointed him on March 5, 1965. He outpointed George Chuvalo and Doug Jones in title defences before a summit showdown with Ali in Houston on February 6, 1967. Ali handed out a humiliating hiding over fifteen rounds, during which he repeatedly demanded that Terrell should call him by his new name instead of Cassius Clay. Terrell, the human skyscraper, was never the same force after his hammering by Ali.

JIMMY ELLIS, WBA TITLE-HOLDER
1968-1970

Jimmy Ellis, born on February 24, 1940, came from the same Louisville background as Muhammad Ali, and was one of Ali's best friends as well as his chief sparring partner. He outpointed Jerry Quarry on April 27, 1968, to win the WBA version of the title after Ali had been stripped of the crown because of his refusal to join the US Army. Ellis successfully defended the title with a controversial points win against Floyd Patterson in Sweden on September 14, 1968, before being matched with Joe Frazier for the undisputed championship in New York on February 16, 1970. 'Smokin" Joe floored Ellis at the end of the fourth round with a devastating left hook. He was saved by the bell, but was in no condition to come out for the fifth round. A stylish, upright boxer, Ellis continued to tour with his pal Ali, who beat him in 1971, but he then dropped out of championship contention because of eye problems.

Muhammad Ali jolts Ken Norton with a straight right on his way to avenging the defeat that left him with a broken jaw.

159

Michael Spinks goes
'walkabout' on his way
to a disputed points vic-
tory over Larry Holmes
in Las Vegas in 1986.

LEON SPINKS, UNDISPUTED TITLE-HOLDER 1978

Leon and Michael Spinks created ring history by becoming the first brothers to win Olympic titles in the 1976 Games in Montreal. Leon, the light-heavyweight champion, was then rushed with indecent haste into a title fight with Muhammad Ali after only seven professional fights, six of which he won with one drawn. Born in St Louis on July 11, 1953, Leon caused one of the boxing shocks of the century by outpointing Ali at Las Vegas on February 15 1978, but he had the title only on loan. Ali outpointed him in the return in New Orleans seven months later to win the crown for a record third time. These were peak performances by ex-Marine Spinks, who was never able to cope with the pressures and fame

that come hand in hand with the world title. He had problems with drugs and seemed doomed to disappear back into the ghetto from which boxing had briefly released him.

KEN NORTON, WBC TITLE-HOLDER 1978

Ken Norton, born in Jacksonville, Illinois, on August 9, 1945, was a 'paper' champion, the title being handed to him by the WBC after Leon Spinks had refused to defend against him because of Spinks' return match with Ali. Norton was named champion after a title eliminator victory over Jimmy Young in Las Vegas on November 25, 1977, but he more than any of the other Alphabet Boys deserves his places in this centenary parade because of his three marvellous battles with Ali. He broke Ali's jaw and outpointed him in their first contest in San Diego on March 31, 1973, and many spectators considered him unlucky to be judged a points loser in their two other meetings on September 10, 1973, and September 28, 1976. Norton had a magnificent physique and good boxing skills, but his reign was brief. Larry Holmes edged him out in a battle in Las Vegas on June 9, 1978. His promising Hollywood acting career was finished by a car crash from which he has only recently recovered.

JOHN TATE, WBA TITLE-HOLDER
1979-1980

John Tate, born in Marion City, Arkansas, on January 29, 1955, became one of the biggest of all heavyweight champions when he outpointed South African Gerrie Coetzee for the vacant WBA title in Pretoria on October 20, 1979. Standing 6 foot 4 inches and weighing around 240 pounds, he captured the championship in his twentieth contest. He lost the title in dramatic fashion in his first defence on March 31, 1980, when Mike Weaver produced an explosive punch to knock his man-mountain opponent down and out in the last minute of their fifteen-round battle. Tate had turned professional after being hammered to a first-round defeat by the Cuban Teofilo Stevenson in the 1976 Olympic semi-finals. Following his knockout by Weaver, his hopes of getting back into the title reckoning were shattered when Trevor Berbick beat him in nine rounds in Montreal on June 20, 1980.

MIKE WEAVER, WBA TITLE-HOLDER
1980-1982

Mike Weaver, born in Gatesville, Texas, on June 14, 1952, has always been a dangerous opponent provided he can get past the first round! A mighty muscled black Adonis of a fighter, he has had a string of first-round knockout defeats in a seesawing career. His greatest moments were knocking out John Tate in the final minute to win the WBA title in Knoxville on March 31, 1980, and then defending it with a knockout win over Gerrie Coetzee in Bophuthatswana on October 25, 1980, and a points victory over James 'Quick'

Tillis on October 3, 1981. But then his world came apart when Mike Dokes stopped him in sixty-three seconds of his third defence in Las Vegas on December 10, 1982. Weaver claimed he could have continued and screamed for a return. He came within a whisker of regaining the title, drawing with Dokes over fifteen gruelling rounds. His career continued late into his thirties, but he was never able to recapture the form of his peak years.

MIKE DOKES, WBA TITLE-HOLDER
1982-1983

Mike Dokes, born in Akron, Ohio, on August 10, 1958, messed up what could have been one of the great careers in heavyweight boxing by getting involved in a drugs scandal. He was undefeated when he grabbed the WBA version of the world title from Mike Weaver in 1982 with a sensational sixty-three seconds victory that caused an uproar of controversy. 'Dynamite' Dokes had rocked Weaver with a big left hook, but most spectators thought the referee was too hasty in stopping the fight. Dokes clung on to the title by drawing with Weaver, but then suffered the first defeat of his career when he was clubbed to a tenth-round defeat by Gerrie Coetzee at Richfield on September 23, 1983. His arrest on a drugs charge suddenly wrecked his comeback campaign. After rehabilitation treatment, he returned to the ring, but stoppages by Razor Ruddock and Evander Holyfield, followed by a return to his drugs habit, seemed to have pushed him out of the title picture.

GERRIE COETZEE, WBA TITLE-
HOLDER 1983-84

Gerrie Coetzee, born in Boksburg, South Africa, on August 4, 1955, was known as the 'Bionic Man' because of surgery on his feared right hand, which prolonged his career. He was a devastating puncher, as he proved when stopping Leon Spinks in one round in Monte Carlo in 1979. Because of the politics of his country, Coetzee found it difficult to get top contenders into the ring with him, but when he finally got his title chance in 1983, he proved too powerful for Mike Dokes, stopping him in the tenth round to become the first South African to win the world heavyweight crown. He lost the WBA title in controversial circumstances, getting stopped by Greg Page in an eighth round that ran into overtime in Sun City on December 1, 1984. Coetzee's chances of getting back on to the title bandwagon ended with a first-round knockout defeat by British heavyweight hope Frank Bruno at Wembley in 1986.

TIM WITHERSPOON, WBC TITLE-HOLDER 1984 AND WBA TITLE-HOLDER 1985-1986

Tim Witherspoon, born on December 27, 1957, was nicknamed 'Terrible Tim' by Muhammad Ali in the days when he hired the young Philadelphian to be his sparring partner. Witherspoon thought he had won the WBC title in his sixteenth professional fight, but a disputed points decision went to Larry Holmes. When

Holmes switched to the newly founded International Boxing Federation (IBF), Witherspoon outpointed Greg Page for the vacant WBC crown on March 9, 1984. His reign was brief; Pinklon Thomas took the title from him with a points win five months later. Witherspoon became only the third champion to regain the title when he outpointed Tony Tubbs in 1985, this time for the WBA version of the championship. He beat a drugs habit and after a successful title defence against Frank Bruno at Wembley Stadium on July 19, 1986, he looked set for a big-money showdown with Mike Tyson. But then he was bombed to a stunning first-round defeat by 'Bonecrusher' Smith in New York on December 12, 1986, after which he became frozen out of the title scene, following a bitter legal battle with promoter Don King. Dennis Rappaport took over as Witherspoon's promoter, and he started to move back up the championship ladder with a sequence of impressive victories.

'Bonecrusher' Smith celebrates his first-round victory over Tim Witherspoon in 1986.

GREG PAGE, WBA TITLE-HOLDER 1984-1985

Greg Page, born on October 25, 1958, is out of the same Louisville, Kentucky, territory as Muhammad Ali and Jimmy Ellis. He was a brilliant amateur, and he chalked up twenty-three successive wins as a professional to earn a fight with Tim Witherspoon for the vacant WBC title on March 9, 1984. Witherspoon outpointed him, but within nine months Page had helped himself to a title by stopping Gerrie Coetzee in the eighth round of an eventful WBA championship contest in Sun City. A timekeeping error meant the round ran into extra time and it was in the closing moments that Page pounded Coetzee to defeat when by rights the South African should have been sitting on his stool. But the musical chairs with the title continued when Page was outpointed by Tony Tubbs at Buffalo, New York, on April 29, 1985. Page never really lived up to his early potential, and drifted out of championship contention.

PINKLON THOMAS, WBC TITLE-HOLDER 1985-1986

Pinklon Thomas, born in Pontiac, Michigan, on February 10, 1957, appeared to be the best of the new crop of 'dreadnought' heavyweights and realized his potential when outpointing Tim Witherspoon to win the WBC championship in Las Vegas on August 31, 1984. He looked set for a long reign and an eighth-round knockout defeat of Mike Weaver on June 15, 1985, seemed to confirm that he was a class above most other contenders. It was one of the biggest shocks of the decade when he lost his unbeaten record and his title to Trevor Berbick at Las Vegas on March 22, 1986. He started a comeback seven months later with a victory over Narciso Maldonado, but he went on the slide after taking a hammering from Mike Tyson in a world championship contest at Las Vegas on May 30, 1987. Like so many of the other Alphabet Boys, he got mixed up with drugs but he managed to beat the habit, and then became a trial horse opponent for up-and-coming prospects with much less talent than he showed in the early stages of his career.

TONY TUBBS, WBA TITLE-HOLDER 1985-1986

Tony Tubbs, born in Cincinnati, Ohio, on February 15, 1959, was nicknamed 'T.N.T.', but he was not an explosive puncher, and relied on skill to emerge as a title challenger. Tubbs is surprisingly light on his feet and a slick boxer considering his enormous 230-pounds bulk. He won the WBA title by smartly outpointing Greg Page in what was tagged as the 'Buffalo Blockbuster' on April 29, 1985, but was then outmauled by Tim Witherspoon in his first defence on January 17, 1986. It was announced after the fight that Witherspoon had failed a drugs test and he was ordered to give Tubbs a return, but he took step-aside money so that Tim could defend against Frank Bruno – a fight that Witherspoon won in the eleventh round. After being blasted to a second-round defeat by Mike Tyson in Tokyo on March 21, 1988, Tubbs admitted to being hooked on cocaine. When he hit the comeback trail in 1991, he dropped a disputed points decision to the rising young prospect Riddick Bowe. In March 1992 he was tested positive for cocaine in Las Vegas, and was ordered to do 100 hours community service after being suspended by the Nevada Boxing Commission.

'Terrible' Tim Witherspoon in confident mood before his world title defence against Britain's Frank Bruno in London in 1986. He won in the eleventh round.

MICHAEL SPINKS, IBF TITLE-HOLDER 1985-1988

Michael Spinks, born in St Louis on July 13, 1956, was the 1976 Olympic middleweight gold medallist and after an unbeaten four-year reign as world professional light-heavyweight champion, he challenged Larry Holmes for the IBF heavyweight crown at Las Vegas on September 21, 1985. Inspired by the wonderfully eccentric and dynamic manager-promoter Butch Lewis, he put on more than 20 pounds and the performance of a lifetime to outpoint the previously undefeated Holmes and to follow his brother, Leon, as heavyweight king. Just to show it was no fluke, he outpointed Holmes in the return match. Both decisions were angrily disputed by Holmes. An easy victory by Spinks over Norway's European champion Steffan Tangstad on September 6, 1986, set him up for a championship showdown with Mike Tyson in Atlantic City on June 27, 1988. Spinks folded in just ninety-one seconds against 'Iron' Mike, and cried all the way to the bank as he announced his retirement after his first defeat as a professional. In 1992 he prepared himself for a comeback at the age of thirty-six. He was attracted by the phenomenal success of the pay-per-view television system that was promising to put millions of dollars into the pockets of even mediocre heavyweights. Like so many of his predecessors, Spinks was finding the call of the ring too strong to ignore.

TREVOR BERBICK, WBC TITLE-HOLDER 1986

Trevor 'The Preacher' Berbick, born in Port Anthony, Jamaica, on August 1, 1953, caused a major upset when he outpointed Pinklon Thomas to win the WBC version of the title in Las Vegas on March 22, 1986. It was his second bid for the championship, having been outpointed by Larry Holmes five years earlier. He was Muhammad Ali's last opponent and scored a ten-rounds points victory in 1981 that at last convinced the great old champ that he should hang up his gloves. It was Berbick who stood between Mike Tyson and history in Las Vegas on November 22, 1986. But he did not stand for long, getting knocked down and stopped in two

explosive rounds as Tyson became the youngest champion of them all. Berbick has since run into difficulties both inside and outside the ring. He looked a shadow of himself against a run of ordinary opponents, and – for a man respected for his religious preachings – he managed to get himself involved in some extraordinary scrapes. In 1992 he had charges ranging against him that included theft, mortgage fraud, rape and assault, and – like his old rival Tyson – he was bound for prison.

JAMES SMITH, WBA TITLE-HOLDER 1986

James 'Bonecrusher' Smith, born in Magnolia, North Carolina, on April 3, 1955, came in as a late substitute for the allegedly injured Tony Tubbs against Tim Witherspoon in New York on December 12, 1986, and snatched the WBA title away with a sensational smash-and-grab first-round victory. Witherspoon, who held a points decision over Smith, was battered to the canvas three times and stopped on the three-knock-down rule. The victory made 'Bonecrusher' the 'Cinderella Man' of the 1980s. He had not started boxing until twenty-three while serving as a sergeant in the US Army. After coming from behind to hand Frank Bruno his first defeat at Wembley on May 13, 1984, he failed in a bid for the IBF title held by Larry Holmes, who stopped him in twelve rounds on November 9, 1984. Smith was outpointed by Mike Tyson in an uninspiring fight for the undisputed title on March 7, 1987, and during a comeback campaign was beaten by Razor Ruddock and then, after a long sequence of victories, surprisingly dropped a points decision to Levi Billups on November 4, 1991.

TONY TUCKER, IBF TITLE-HOLDER 1987

Tony Tucker, born in Grand Rapids, Michigan, on December 28, 1958, was shaping up as the best of the Alphabet Boys until he ran into the fists of Mike Tyson. He won the IBF title on May 30, 1987, by stopping James 'Buster' Douglas in ten rounds. Three months later he took a pounding from Tyson, but managed to survive the full twelve rounds. He was never the same force after his points defeat and he got involved in the drugs scene. He looked to the disciplines demanded of boxing to help him beat the habit, and started to shape up well in a comeback campaign in the 1990s.

FRANCESCO DAMIANI, WBO TITLE-HOLDER 1989-1991

Francesco Damiani, born in Ravenna, Italy, on October 4, 1958, had an impressive amateur career, the highlight of which was a victory over triple Olympic champion Teofilio Stevenson. He was the silver medallist at the 1984 Olympics. After winning the European title as a professional, Damiani became the first holder of yet another confusing version of the world heavyweight championship as the title became further devalued. He knocked out South African Johnny Duplooy in three rounds on May 6, 1989, to win the WBO crown. He successfully defended the title against Daniel Netto in 1990 before being knocked out by Ray Mercer in the ninth round in Atlantic City on January 11, 1991.

RAY MERCER, WBO TITLE-HOLDER 1991

Ray Mercer was a US Army sergeant when he won the 1988 Olympic heavyweight gold medal. He made rapid progress as a professional, and after outpointing highly rated Bert Cooper in a war in 1990, he challenged Damiani in 1991. After blasting out 'white hope' Tommy Morrison – the star of the 1990 film *Rocky V* – in five rounds, he was stripped of the WBO title for agreeing to a match against the veteran Larry Holmes at Atlantic City on February 7, 1992. He was soundly outpointed and his world championship value suddenly dropped several points. Michael Moorer, a product of the Detroit Kronk Gym, became the first southpaw heavyweight champion of the century when he twice got off the canvas to stop Bert Cooper in the fifth round of a fight for the vacant WBO title in Atlantic City on May 15, 1992.

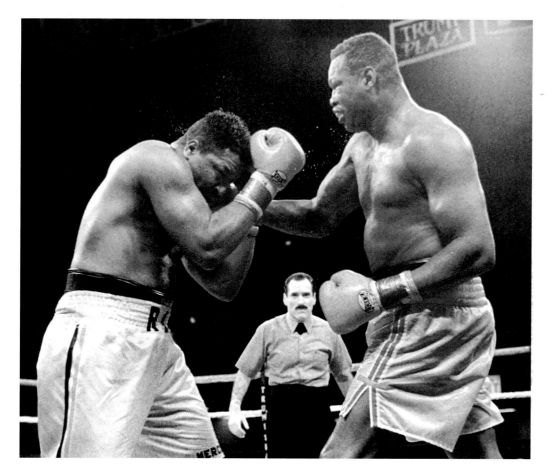

Larry Holmes lands with a right on his way to taming Ray Mercer, one of the modern pretenders to the heavyweight throne. The veteran Holmes scored a convincing points victory at Atlantic City on February 7, 1992.

CHAPTER TWENTY-SIX

LARRY HOLMES

THE EASTON ASSASSIN

Larry Holmes found himself haunted by a living legend, Muhammad Ali, and a dead hero, Rocky Marciano, during a three-tier career in which he made a not-quite-accepted bid to be recognized as the greatest of all in this century of champions. Like George Foreman, he decided to make a comeback as a forty-something fighting grandfather out to prove that the modern young contenders were just pretenders. He was convinced they were not in the same class as he had been when he ruled the world heavyweights for seven years while a fleet of Alphabet Boys sank out of sight like torpedoed ships in the night.

THE SHOESHINE BOY

One of a family of nine brothers and three sisters, Holmes was born into a humble home in Cuthbert, Georgia, on November 3, 1949. The family moved to Easton, Pennsylvania, and into an immediate crisis when the father walked out on them, leaving mother Flossie to bring up her huge flock. Holmes left school at thirteen to start earning his daily bread as a shoeshine boy. 'I was a real hell raiser,' he admitted. 'I had the choice of quitting school or getting thrown out.'

He swept floors in a foundry, worked in a car wash, a wool mill and a steel factory, and during this time he lived with a woman seven years older than him. Before he was nineteen, Holmes became the father of two baby girls, and he continued to support his daughters after the relationship broke up. To boost his income he used to sit in on all-night card games, and he became a master poker player.

Somehow he found the time and energy to start an amateur boxing career at an Easton youth club, and he reached the finals of the United States Olympic boxing trials in 1972, only to be disqualified for holding against Duane Bobick.

The following year he made his professional debut, earning $63 in the fight that launched him on a career that was to net him more than $30 million. He overcame the problem of a broken right hand, which kept him out of action for eight months in 1976, and heralded his arrival as a world title contender in 1978 by comfortably outpointing the fearsome-hitting Earnie Shavers, who used to employ him as a sparring partner.

In the first phase of his career Holmes was never able to exorcise the ghost of his phenomenally popular predecessor Muhammad Ali, whose performances and personality continually cast a giant shadow over just about every move that Holmes made. Even Holmes idolized Ali, for whom Holmes used to work as a young sparring partner. It was one of the saddest days of his life when he forced Ali – dangerously weakened by shedding too much weight too quickly – to retire at the end of ten rounds in a championship contest at Las Vegas in 1980. 'I love that man and didn't want to see him getting hurt,' said Holmes.

The only way Holmes might have closed the gap on Ali in the never-ending 'Who's the greatest?' debate was to equal or beat Rocky Marciano's record of forty-nine unbeaten fights. He was one away from drawing level when he dropped a disputed points decision to light-heavyweight champion Michael Spinks in Las Vegas on September 21, 1985. He also lost the return match in Las Vegas seven months later. It was then that Rocky came back to haunt him. After losing to Spinks he made the throwaway remark: 'Rocky Marciano couldn't have carried my jockstrap.' He had not only shot off his mouth but had also managed to shoot himself in the foot, trampling on the memory of a revered old champion like Marciano. The media were unmerciful in the scorn that they poured on Holmes. He immediately apologized for his remark, even personally contacting leading boxing writers to explain that it was something said in the heat of the moment and instantly regretted. But the damage had been done, and – certainly with white American boxing fans – Holmes was never again held in quite the same esteem.

DISPUTED VERDICTS

Holmes hinted that he was the victim of a Las Vegas plot against Spinks, and he bitterly disputed both verdicts. It was in this mood of resentment that he announced his retirement in 1986 with a record of forty-eight victories in fifty fights. Two years later he was made an offer he could not refuse to stage a comeback at the age of thirty-eight for a crack at Mike Tyson's world crown. Even his $5 million purse seemed small consolation for the humiliation and pain he suffered at the hands of a peak-power Tyson, who knocked him out in four rounds.

Holmes had ascended to the WBC heavyweight throne on June 10, 1978, by narrowly outpointing Ken Norton in an absolute classic of a fifteen-round contest. This time the Las Vegas judges were kind to him because many witnesses of one of the greatest of all modern championship

Holmes swings and Mike Weaver sways out of range. He stopped 'Muscle Man' Weaver in the twelfth round of this 1979 title fight.

Holmes (right) is on his way to taming 'Alphabet Boy' Ray Mercer during his comeback campaign in 1992.

fights thought that Norton had just edged a points decision. Holmes – more Larry the Lion than Larry the Lamb – later revealed that he had been handicapped during the most important fight of his life by a torn muscle in his left arm. His victory over Norton was the start of an ideal Holmes reign that helped erase the memory and the misery of his early struggling days.

He always suffered in comparisons with quick-on-the-jaw Ali (who wouldn't have done?), but he was an outstanding fighter in his own right. He had an exceptional left jab, and made the most of his 81-inch reach. Holmes was not an explosive knockout specialist, but evidence of the cumulative effect of his punches is that in the first phase of his career he stopped thirty-four opponents and equalled Tommy Burns' championship record of eight successive stoppages in title defences from 1978 to 1981. Standing 6 foot 4 inches tall and with wide, powerful shoulders, he had a strong chin and proved it by getting off the floor to win in title fights against both Earnie Shavers and Renaldo Snipes. His best performance in twenty-one championship contests came against 'white hope' Gerry Cooney. In a fight weighed down with racial tension, Holmes hammered the giant Cooney into

submission in thirteen rounds in Las Vegas on June 11, 1982. This was a quality performance that at last brought him grudging respect as a champion worthy to follow in the footsteps of the idolized Ali.

SURRENDERS CROWN

Holmes surrendered the WBC heavyweight crown in 1983 and accepted recognition from the infant IBF as champion. It was more a business deal than a boxing deal for Holmes, who had a stormy up-and-down relationship with dominating promoter Don King. Holmes became self managed and also part promoter of his fights. 'Now that I'm with the IBF I don't have to give money to Don King or anybody else,' he said. 'Every dime I earn is mine. You hear a lot of talk coming from the young guys who want my title, but while they're yapping away I'm up here on top of the mountain with the money I've got in the bank earning me $400,000 in interest. These guys don't get that to fight. I'm a businessman first, and a boxer second.'

Back home in Easton with his wife, Diane, and growing family he owned a mansion, a fleet of limousines, a hotel, a parking lot, a restaurant, a garage, a gymnasium ... they were thinking of calling it Holmesville until the recession started to gnaw away at his vast fortune. He saw only one way to restore the riches, and that was to return to the ring for a second comeback. Once he had got the humiliation of the Tyson defeat out of his system, he started the third phase of his career as a fighting grandad in 1991. He gave Ray Mercer a boxing lesson over twelve rounds **and stubbornly went the distance with Evander Holyfield on his way to setting up** a possible championship of the forty-somethings with the redoubtable George Foreman. The golden oldies were rolling back the years.

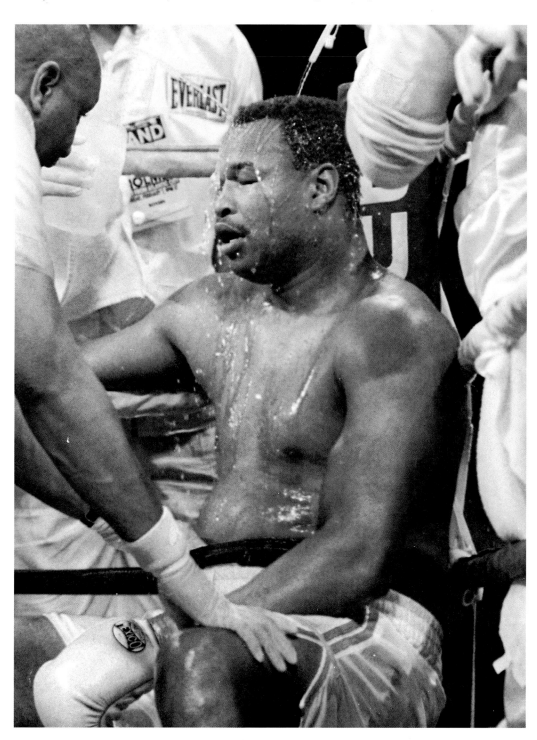

Holmes freshens up, ready for the last round of his winning fight against Ray Mercer in 1992.

169

CHAPTER TWENTY-SEVEN

MIKE TYSON

IRON MIKE

It took the fists of James 'Buster' Douglas and the fury of a sensational rape trial to first dent and then destroy the image of Mike Tyson, who until these shocking interruptions had been giving the distinct impression of having arrived from another planet. Or perhaps you prefer the New York-inspired legend that in the mid-Sixties a slab of concrete was pneumatically drilled out of a Brooklyn sidewalk, was sprayed with black paint and then left to dry before becoming the ox-necked Mike Tyson. Looking at the rock face that Tyson's opponents found so intimidating, it would be easy to believe the legend, but in time he was revealed as having the sort of boxing weaknesses that proved he was merely mortal, while outside the ring he got his private life into a nightmare of a mess.

A guilty verdict by the jury after Tyson had been accused of raping a contestant in the Miss Black America beauty pageant seemed almost certain to have delivered a knockout blow to one of the most explosive boxing careers in ring history. He was sentenced to a six-year jail sentence pending appeal, and while prisoner

number 92335 will be young enough to pick up his career when he is released, it is difficult to believe that he will still have the motivation and the menace necessary to regain his place as the world's most feared heavyweight.

CONTROLLED VIOLENCE

For Tyson, life had seemed to be one long fight almost from the day he was born on June 30, 1966, in the tough Bedford-Stuyvesant section of Brooklyn. The youngest of three children, he never knew his father and the biggest influence on him in his formative years was his mother, Lorna, who had always been totally opposed to violence. Lorna died in 1982 without seeing her son proving that, in the ring, he could control violence and turn it into a legitimate and accepted way of making himself one of the richest and most famous sportsmen of the twentieth century. Thankfully, she also missed him hitting the headlines for a lot of the wrong reasons as he rode a non-stop roller coaster of controversies.

In his earliest years Tyson was fed messages of pacifism by his mother, who preached a love-thy-neighbour code. Taught right from wrong, rather than left hook from right cross, the young Tyson struggled to grow up in a district where rob-thy-neighbour was too often the rule.

'My mother detested violence,' a lisping Tyson recalled in an after-fight interview, while not a dozen yards away one of his early opponents was being repaired after suffering grievious bodily harm. 'She was a very gentle and timid person. I had only my sister to play with because my brother was five years older, and so I guess I picked up a lot of gentle, sort-of effeminate habits. In fact when I was a kid they used to call me a little fairy boy.' Only a fool would have dared call him that to his face when he was knocking over opponents right, left and centre as the most feared and fearsome fighter in the world.

The toughening up process for Tyson started when his mother moved house to another district of Brooklyn: Brownsville, where the streets are so mean they say even the birds are armed. Tyson was ten when he arrived in Brownsville and was pitched unsuspectingly into a world where the strongest ruled and the weakest were walked on. 'I was always getting set on,' he recalled. 'You'd be walking along a street when a couple of big guys would jump you and steal anything you had – your money, your rings, your necklace, your sneakers, your clothes. They'd take everything you'd got and then give you a whipping just for laughs.'

Tyson remembers his first fight like most of us would remember our first kiss. 'I was into raising pigeons,' he said. 'Still am. I love those birds. I'm really at peace when I'm with them. Anyways, this particular day an older boy tried to steal one of my birds. No, to tell you the truth he ripped its head off. I was eleven at the time and had never given any thought to using

violence. But I just blew. I threw everything at the guy – fists, feet, head. I became an animal and beat the living crap out of him. And d'you know somethin'? I found I loved every second of it. I had discovered a way of letting all my frustration out.'

This first fight launched Tyson the wild boy, and instead of crossing the street when the muggers came his way he joined them. He became a member of The Jolly Stompers. No, not a traditional jazz band, but a notorious street gang committed to stomping on anybody who got in the way. Tyson was the youngest member of the gang, but he had the respect of the older

One of Mike Tyson's most prized photographs, autographed for him by 'The Greatest'.

Tyson rocks
'Bonecrusher' Smith
with a right cross dur-
ing their title fight in
Las Vegas in 1987.
Tyson won on points
over twelve rounds.

Stewart, a former fighter, who, after sparring sessions with the fourteen-year-old Tyson, recommended him to Cus D'Amato.

It was D'Amato, Floyd Patterson's former
manager, who shaped Tyson into the fighting
machine that would cause earthquaking shocks
throughout the boxing world. He took him out
of reform school and adopted him, teaching him
about life as well as about boxing. Tyson moved
in with D'Amato at his home in the Catskills
where they were looked after by Camille
Edward, who had been married to one of
D'Amato's brothers and who, following the
death of Tyson's mother in 1982, became a surro-
gate mother to the young rebel from Brooklyn.

D'Amato, whose hobby was reading
biographies of all the world's great leaders, filled
young Tyson with tales of what could be
achieved with the right attitude and discipline.
Tyson listened and learned. After failing to make
it into the United States team for the 1984
Olympics in Los Angeles, he made a hurricane
start to his professional career by winning his
first ten fights in a total of only sixteen rounds.

His almost barbaric approach to fighting
was captured in a quote that he later tried to dis-
miss as a joke: 'I like to punch the bone in the
other guy's nose right the way through to his
brain.' Those closest to him later admitted that
Tyson was not joking. He really meant it.

THE HISTORY MAKER

In his twenty-eighth fight and at the age of just
twenty years, four months and two days he
knocked out Trevor Berbick in two rounds to
take over from Floyd Patterson as the youngest
world heavyweight champion in history. (It is a
chilling fact that Berbick was arrested and jailed
on a rape charge at almost the same time as
Tyson). In nine title fights after defeating
Berbick, Tyson beat 'Bonecrusher' Smith (points
twelve rounds, 1987), Pinklon Thomas (stopped
six rounds, 1987), Tony Tucker (points twelve
rounds, 1987), Tyrell Biggs (stopped seven
rounds, 1987), Larry Holmes (knocked out
fourth round, 1988), Tony Tubbs (stopped second round, 1988), Michael Spinks (knockout
first round, 1988), Frank Bruno (stopped five
rounds, 1989) and Carl Williams (stopped first
round, 1989).

boys because of the way he could hold his own
in fights. Included among his catalogue of crime
was pickpocketing, housebreaking, mugging
and even armed robbery. 'The older kids had the
guns,' he said. 'We'd go into the stores and while
they did the sticking up I would fill the bags
from the shelves.'

Tyson was now beyond the control of his
distraught mother, and after a succession of sen-
tences at detention centres, he was finally sent to
the Tryon School, a correction centre for juvenile
delinquents in upstate New York noted for its
harsh discipline. It was here that his fighting
ability was noted by school counsellor Bobby

Mike Tyson, belted in the most acceptable way as the undisputed champion.

By the time he fought Bruno in Las Vegas on February 25, 1989, Tyson's life outside the ring was in such turmoil that it was a wonder he could concentrate on his boxing career. Tyson seemed to lose his way when the two mentors who guided him away from a criminal existence, Cus D'Amato and wealthy boxing *aficionado* Jim Jacobs, both died within three years of each other. His stormy marriage to actress Robin Givens lasted just six months; he got involved in an early-hours street fight with a former opponent, Mitch Green; he wrote off a car in what was reported as a suicide attempt, and he parted with trainer Kevin Rooney and teamed up with boxing 'overlord' Don King rather than his official manager, Bill Cayton. There were court cases, further street fights and car smashes, assault charges, angry clashes with reporters – a whole catalogue of incidents that suggested Tyson had his finger on the self-destruct button.

Tyson appeared to be cracking under all the self-afflicted pressure, but the boxing world was still astonished when he lost his title to James 'Buster' Douglas in Tokyo on February 11, 1990, in what was expected to be just a routine defence. Frank Bruno had showed that Tyson could be hit and hurt by staggering him in the first round of their world title fight, and that should have sounded alarm bells. Too many of his opponents had frozen with fear because of the hype that surrounded 'Iron' Mike, but Douglas realized that Tyson was only human and thoroughly deserved his startling victory. Boxing politicians, interested only in the money they could make with Tyson, tried to take the glory away from Douglas because of a slow count by the referee after he had been dropped in the eighth round. Douglas was clearly listening to the count, and it was not his fault that the referee was tolling one second behind the official timekeeper.

DYNAMIC ACTION

Tyson licked his wounds and was back in dynamic action four months later, winning in one round against Henry Tillman, the opponent who had beaten him in the 1984 United States Olympic trials. On December 8, 1990, he knocked out Alex Stewart in one round in Atlantic City.

175

Then in 1991 he had two wars with Razor Ruddock in Las Vegas, winning both of them, but with performances that made critics wonder if his best was far behind him.

His biggest battles were coming outside the ring. He was involved in a paternity case, faced allegations of being 'a serial buttocks fondler' after complaints from a succession of women, and then – as he was preparing for a mega-bucks showdown with Evander Holyfield – came the rape trial during which he was painted as some sort of sexual beast.

When the jury arrived at their guilty verdict, the boxing world wondered whether it would ever again see a mighty force quite like Tyson. The unanswered question is whether there is still a lot of 'bad intentions' left in those iron fists of his. Or has he by his own behaviour rung the final bell on his wild, and at times, wonderful career? Only prison inmate number 92335 can answer these questions.

Above: The decline and fall of Mike Tyson is complete as he is finger-printed before the start of his prison sentence after being found guilty on a rape charge.

Opposite: Tyson connects with a mighty right and Pinklon Thomas is about to take a final trip to the canvas in the sixth round of their world heavyweight title fight at Las Vegas on May 30, 1987.

CHAPTER TWENTY-EIGHT

A FORMIDABLE FORCE

Born in Columbus, Ohio – Jack Nicklaus territory – on April 7, 1960, Douglas was taught to box at an early age by his father, Billy Douglas, who had been a highly rated middleweight. Douglas Senior had the last fight of his long career only ten months before his son turned professional. Nicknamed 'Buster', Douglas Junior preferred basketball to boxing and won a two-year scholarship to a college in Kansas where his 6-foot 4-inch height and his 84-inch reach made him a formidable force on the basketball court.

JAMES BUSTER DOUGLAS

THE TOKYO TYPHOON

James 'Buster' Douglas had two universally recognized world title fights during which he managed to cause first the biggest shock and then one of the biggest stinks in boxing history. His knockout defeat of Mike Tyson in 1990 could not have caused a greater sensation had he mugged the President. Eight months later he surrendered the crown so tamely to Evander Holyfield that it was almost impossible to believe that this was the same fighter who had vanquished the 'unbeatable' Tyson.

Douglas was carefully selected as a pushover opponent for Tyson because a $30 million defence had been arranged against number-one challenger Holyfield, and nobody believed that Douglas could throw a spanner – or rather, a sledgehammer – into the works. He had won twenty-nine of his thirty-five fights since turning professional in 1981, and defeats by David Bey, Mike White, Jesse Ferguson and Tony Tucker lured the Tyson camp into thinking that here was an easy defence. They were about to make the same expensive mistake that Joe Frazier made against George Foreman.

Right: The last seconds of Tyson's reign. Douglas is the new heavyweight champion of the world.

It was after winning a junior Olympics boxing title that he decided to follow in his father's footsteps, but the way his weight seesawed between 220 pounds and a massive 245 pounds suggested he was not totally dedicated to his chosen profession. Despite his great bulk, he had rarely looked a devastating puncher and had stopped only eighteen of his opponents. He fought Tony Tucker for the paper IBF crown on May 30, 1987, and suddenly ran out of steam and ambition on his way to a painful tenth-round defeat.

Tyson took all these facts on board, and made the fatal mistake of completely underestimating his challenger at the Tokyo Dome in the early hours of Sunday, February 11, 1990. Douglas came in at a trim 231.5 pounds and had obviously got himself in good shape. There were doubts whether he was mentally right for the contest, because his mother had died suddenly during his early training preparation, and the mother of his son Lamar, who was at the ringside, was seriously ill at home in Ohio.

But from the first moments of the fight it was clear that Douglas was in the mood to go all out for a mind-blowing victory, while Tyson was struggling to get into anything like his usual rhythm. The champion's head was continually rocked back on his 20-inch neck by jolting left jabs, and the following rights kept sitting him back on his heels. Tyson was not throwing his usual explosive combinations with 'bad intentions', and was thrashing away with single punches that lacked their customary timing and deadly accuracy.

Douglas had one moment of real crisis. Tyson was under heavy attack in the eighth round when he produced a crushing right

The right hand that tamed Tyson and earned Douglas a fortune.

177

Above: Home is the hero. Douglas parades his world championship belt on his return to Columbus, Ohio, in 1990.

Opposite: Evander Holyfield steps inside a jab and prepares to unleash the punching power that proved too much for James 'Buster' Douglas in Las Vegas on October 25, 1991. Holyfield won by a knockout in the third round, to become the twenty-ninth undisputed world heavyweight title-holder of the first century of gloved champions, not counting Marvin Hart and the Alphabet Boys.

uppercut that screwed Douglas's head around on his broad shoulders and dropped him like a sack of potatoes. The referee struggled to pick up the timekeeper's count and was out of synch with him by one second as the challenger pulled himself up on to one knee and listened to the count. When he heard 'nine' he rose and braced himself to meet the following attack from Tyson as the bell rang.

It was a final fling by Tyson. He took a terrible tanking in the ninth round, and in the tenth was forced to retreat under assault from a procession of left jabs before a furious flurry of lefts and rights sent him crashing backwards. His mind clearly in a mist, he was scrabbling around on the canvas for his gumshield as the referee counted him out for the first time in his career. Douglas, who, at the age of twenty-nine, was six years older than Tyson, wept as he was named as the new heavyweight champion of the world.

LEGAL WRANGLES

The championship should have brought Douglas great joy, but there were months of aggravation waiting for him. The authorities tried, shamefully, to take the title away from him because of the long count, which was no fault of his. All he could do was listen to the seconds being tolled by the referee, and when he called 'nine' Douglas was not to know that it was in fact ten seconds since he had been knocked down. Don King and his associates quickly climbed down when they saw the outraged public reaction to their 'strip the champion' suggestion, and Douglas was allowed to keep his world heavyweight crown. Then he got involved in a legal wrangle with promoter King over the hold King had over him for future defences, and he demoted his manager, John Johnson, and restored his father – ditched before the Tyson fight – as one of his trainers.

By the time Douglas climbed into the ring for his first defence against Evander Holyfield at the Mirage Hotel in Las Vegas on October 25, 1990, he had clearly lost his appetite for carrying the championship on his wide shoulders. He had given hours of his time to charity causes, and the joke going the rounds was that Elvis Presley had been sighted in gymnasiums more times than the new champion. But it was no laughing matter when he weighed in at a huge 245 pounds, clear evidence that he was not in the same super condition as when he faced Tyson.

It was also obvious that his determination was nothing like the same. He managed only one worthwhile punch before going down and out in the third round to a right counter to the head from Holyfield that did not seem heavy enough to unhinge a man of his size and strength. Douglas slumped heavily on his left side, brushed at his face with his gloves and then, as if tucking himself up for the night, slowly rolled over while appearing to listen to the count by the referee, Mills Lane, who later voiced the opinion of most ringsiders: 'I thought he could have got up.' The 'Tokyo Typhoon' could not raise even a light breeze in Las Vegas.

Douglas had managed in just seven minutes to tarnish the glory of his victory over Tyson, and to follow the shame of his performance came the real body blow. He had expected a $20 million payday, but – after taxes, expenses and legal costs – finished up with 'only' $3 million. Many of the 16,000 fans who had paid to watch the fight no doubt considered that Douglas had been overpaid.

He will always be remembered as the man who knocked out Mike Tyson. That alone guarantees him a lasting place in boxing history.

CHAPTER TWENTY-NINE

EVANDER HOLYFIELD

THE REAL DEAL

Above: Holyfield holds his arms aloft as the new heavyweight title-holder, and the world has its first computer champion.

As this first century of gloved champions approached its end the world heavyweight crown was in the powerful hands of Evander Holyfield. James J. Corbett had started it all in 1892 as a pioneer of 'scientific' boxing. When Holyfield came to the throne ninety-eight years later, he took boxing into the age of computer science.

After Holyfield had ripped the title away from 'Buster' Douglas with a third-round knockout in Las Vegas on October 25, 1990, his manager, a colourful character called Lou Duva, revealed that computer scientists had been called in to help plan the coronation of the new king.

'This has been the best planned championship campaign in boxing history,' crowed Duva, who then provided the facts to prove his claim was no idle boast. 'We employed specialist coaches to improve Evander's strength and fitness and to help him put on necessary weight in a sensible way. Then we brought in a ballet teacher to work on his balance and flexibility. Finally we turned to computer experts, who used modern technology to analyse each of his opponents. We showed him how it could be done, then he did

the important part of climbing into the ring and executing the plans to perfection.'

No computer could have prepared boxing followers in general and Holyfield in particular for the shock of seeing Mike Tyson knocked out by Douglas in Tokyo. Then the number-one challenger for the title, Holyfield must have felt like crying with frustration as he sat at the ringside watching $12 million being snatched from under his nose. This sum was Holyfield's guarantee for a summer showdown with Tyson, but 'Iron' Mike's defeat – followed by his rape trial – put an end to plans for the mega-bucks match.

MAJOR HONOURS

Trained by former middleweight master George Benton, Holyfield had risen to the top like cream with a procession of impressive victories, winning his fights with style and precision in contrast to Tyson's bludgeoning ferocity. It was obvious that the thoroughbred Holyfield – nicknamed the 'Real Deal' – was destined for major honours from his earliest amateur days. Born in Atmore, Alabama, on October 9, 1962, he made his home in Atlanta, Georgia, where he was such an exceptional prospect that he was persuaded to give up his ambitions of a military career to concentrate on boxing. He captured a coveted Golden Gloves title at light-heavyweight and was a roasting-hot favourite to collect an Olympic gold medal in the 1984 Games in Los Angeles. He was overpowering New Zealander Kevin Barry in the light-heavyweight semi-final, but was then disqualified in controversial circumstances, following a punch that unintentionally landed after the bell. A distraught Holyfield had to settle for a bronze medal, and he then started prospecting for gold in the professional ring after winning 160 out of 174 amateur contests.

The only thing that seemed to stand between him and an eventual shot at the world heavyweight crown was a lack of bulk in an age of super heavyweights. He launched his professional career as a cruiserweight – the 190-pounds division in which the likes of 182-pounders Rocky Marciano, Gene Tunney and Ezzard Charles would have had to campaign if launching their careers today.

Holyfield made his paid debut against Lionel Byam in New York on November 15,

1984, and won on points over six rounds. He swept to victories in his next ten fights, but many people in the fight game thought the Duva brothers were pushing him along too quickly when he was matched with the ring wise Dwight Muhammad Qawi for the world WBA title in only his twelfth contest in Atlanta on July 12, 1986. Fears that he had taken too short a route to the top seemed well founded when Qawi bossed

and bullied him in the early rounds, but Holyfield proved he had a big heart and a strong chin to go with his skill and he came from behind to steal a split points decision over fifteen gruelling rounds.

He defended the title three times, including a seventh-round victory over his Olympic team-mate Henry Tillman, before accepting a rematch with Qawi in Atlantic City on

Holyfield's right detonates on Douglas's jaw. A new king is about to be crowned.

George Foreman is off target with a huge left uppercut. Holyfield survived this pressure to win on points over twelve rounds.

December 5, 1987. As evidence of his improved power and confidence, he knocked out Qwawi in four rounds.

After adding the IBF and WBC cruiser-weight titles to his collection, Holyfield concentrated on pumping pounds on to his frame with a special diet and fitness programme, and he made his debut in the heavyweight ranks as a solid, 210-pounds force in 1988 with a fifth-round victory over James 'Quick' Tillis. Remarkably, as well as building up his muscles and bodyweight, he also managed to increase his height by an inch and a half from the 6 foot 1 inch he had been when campaigning as a cruiserweight, or so his publicists claimed.

BREAKING THE MONOPOLY

Holyfield hammered out spectacular victories over Pinklon Thomas, Michael Dokes, Adilson Rodrigues and Alex Stewart to set up what he thought would be a get-rich-quick confrontation with Mike Tyson. He had the consolation of taking the title from Tyson's conqueror, 'Buster' Douglas, with an easier-than-expected third-round knockout victory, and then joined the queue of boxers battling in the law courts with Don King, the man with the electric shock of hair and fingers in so many heavyweight pies.

With the Duva family and their partner, Shelly Finkel, determined to break King's monopoly, they decided that Holyfield's first defence would be against the veteran George Foreman rather than Tyson. They won their case in court to go ahead with the fight after the WBC had threatened to take away the title. Holyfield won the fight in the ring with the remarkable Foreman in 1991. The new champion had to dig deep down into his boots before pounding out a points victory over the old champion, and after millions of dollars had been laid in his path, he agreed to go through with the on-off-on-off showdown with Tyson.

The fight with Tyson was scheduled for Caesars Palace in Las Vegas on November 8, 1991, but was called off when Tyson damaged his ribs in training. Tyson then concentrated on preparing for his rape trial, and the Holyfield camp arranged what everybody expected would be a take-the-money-and-run defence against Bert Cooper in the champion's home town of Atlanta on November 23, 1991.

Cooper – once handled by Joe Frazier, nicknamed 'Smokin'' Bert and a rehabilitated drug user – came in as a late substitute for Italian Francesco Damiani. Holyfield did not seem able to get himself motivated for the fight, and Cooper had him rocking and reeling before Holyfield finally produced his champion's form in the seventh round to force the referee to save the gallant challenger from further punishment.

It seemed that the crown of thorns curse had already invaded Holyfield's life when his elder brother, Willie, was found shot dead in his Atlanta home in April, 1992. A brother-in-law was charged with his murder.

Suddenly there were doubts whether Holyfield – the computer champion – had the staying power to carry the title into the second century of gloved champions. Cooper had made him look distinctly vulnerable, and he would never have complete acceptance while memories of Mike Tyson were still fresh in the minds of fight fans. **A laboured points victory over Larry Holmes on June 18, 1992, did little to boost his reputation.**

Holmes was haunted by Ali. Holyfield will always be stalked by the awesome reputation of Tyson.

FOR THE RECORD

WORLD HEAVYWEIGHT TITLE FIGHTS 1892-1992

(NOTE: *In the dates given below, the day appears first, followed by the month, then the year.*)

James J. Corbett wko21 John L. Sullivan, New Orleans 7.9.1892
  wko3 Charlie Mitchell, Jacksonville 25.1.1894
Bob Fitzsimmons wko14 James J. Corbett, Carson City 17.3.1897
James J. Jeffries wko11 Bob Fitzsimmons, Coney Island 9.6.1899
  wpts25 Tom Sharkey, Coney Island 3.11.1899
wko23 James J. Corbett, Coney Island 11.5.1900
  wret5 Gus Ruhlin, San Francisco 15.11.01
wko8 Bob Fitzsimmons, San Francisco 25.7.02
  wko10 James J. Corbett, San Francisco 14.8.03
  wko2 Jack Munroe, San Francisco 26.8.04
Jeffries announced his retirement as undefeated champion
Marvin Hart wrsf12 Jack Root, Reno 3.7.05
Tommy Burns wpts20 Marvin Hart, Los Angeles 23.2.06
  wko15 Jim Flynn, Los Angeles 2.10.06
  drew 20 Jack O'Brien, Los Angeles 28.11.06
  wpts20 Jack O'Brien, Los Angeles 8.5.07
  wko1 Bill Squires, California 4.7.07
  wko10 Gunner Moir, London 2.12.07
  wko4 Jack Palmer, London 10.2.08
  wko1 Jem Roche, Dublin 17.3.08
  wko5 Jewey Smith, Paris 18.4.08
  wko13 Bill Squires, Paris 13.6.08
  wko13 Bill Squires, Sydney 24.8.04
  wko6 Bill Lang, Melbourne 2.9.08

Jack Johnson wrsf14 Tommy Burns, Sydney 26.12.08
  wko12 Stanley Ketchel, California 16.10.09
  wrsf15 James J. Jeffries, Reno 4.7.10
  wrsf9 Jim Flynn, Las Vegas 4.7.12
  wko2 Andre Spoul, Paris 28.11.13
  drew10 Jim Johnson, Paris 19.12.13
  wpts20 Frank Moran, Paris 27.6.14
Jess Willard wko26 Jack Johnson, Havana 5.4.15
  no dec10 Frank Moran, New York 25.3.16
Jack Dempsey wret3 Jess Willard, Toledo 4.7.19
  wko3 Billy Miske, Benton Harbour 6.9.20
  wko12 Bill Brennan, New York 14.12.20
  wko4 Georges Carpentier, Jersey City 2.7.21
  wpts15 Tom Gibbons, Montana 4.7.23
  wko2 Luis Angel Firpo, New York 14.9.23
Gene Tunney wpts10 Jack Dempsey, Philadelphia 23.9.26
  wpts10 Jack Dempsey, Chicago 22.9.27
  wrsf11 Tom Heeney, New York 23.7.28
Tunney announced his retirement as undefeated champion
Max Schmeling wdis4 Jack Sharkey, New York 12.6.30
  wrsf15 Young Stribling, Cleveland 3.7.31
Jack Sharkey wpts15 Max Schmeling, Long Island NY 21.6.32
Primo Carnera wko6 Jack Sharkey, Long Island N.Y. 29.6.33
  wpts15 Paolino Uzcudun, Rome 22.10.33
  wpts15 Tommy Loughran, Miami 1.3.34
Max Baer wrsf11 Primo Carnera, Long Island N.Y. 14.6.34
James J. Braddock wpts15 Max Baer, Long Island N.Y. 13.6.35

Joe Louis wko8 James J. Braddock, Chicago 22.6.37
 wpts15 Tommy Farr, New York 30.8.37
 wko3 Nathan Mann, New York 23.2.38
 wko5 Harry Thomas, Chicago 1.4.38
Joe Louis wko1 Max Schmeling, New York 22.6.38
 wrsf1 John Henry Lewis, New York 25.1.39
 wko1 Jack Roper, Los Angeles 17.4.39
 wrsf4 Tony Galento, New York 28.6.39
 wko11 Bob Pastor, Detroit 20.9.39
 wpts15 Arturo Godoy, New York 9.2.40
 wrsf2 Johnny Paychek, New York 29.3.40
 wrsf8 Arturo Godoy, New York 20.6.40
 wret6 Al McCoy, Boston 16.12.40
 wko5 Red Burman New York, 31.1.41
 wko2 Gus Dorazio, Philadelphia 17.2.41
 wrsf13 Abe Simon, Detroit 21.3.41
 wrsf9 Tony Musto, St Louis 8.4.41
 wdis7 Buddy Baer, Washington 23.5.41
 wko13 Billy Conn, New York 18.6.41
 wrsf6 Lou Nova, New York 29.9.41
 wko1 Buddy Baer, New York 9.1.42
 wko6 Abe Simon, New York 27.3.42
 wko8 Billy Conn, New York 19.6.46
 wko1 Tami Mauriello, New York 18.9.46
 wpts15 Jersey Joe Walcott, New York 5.12.47
 wko11 Jersey Joe Walcott, New York 25.6.48
Louis announced his retirement as undefeated champion
Ezzard Charles wpts15 Jersey Joe Walcott, Chicago
 22.6.4 *(NBA title)*
 wrsf7 Gus Lesnevich, New York 10.8.49
 wko8 Pat Valentino, San Francisco 14.10.49
 wrsf14 Freddy Beshore, Buffalo 15.8.50
 wpts15 Joe Louis, New York 27.9.50 *(undisputed title)*
 wko11 Nick Barone, Cincinnati 5.12.50
 wrsf10 Lee Oma, New York 12.1.51
 wpts15 Jersey Joe Walcott, Detroit 7.3.51
 wpts15 Joey Maxim, Chicago 30.5.51
Jersey Joe Walcott wko7 Ezzard Charles, Pittsburgh
 18.7.51
 wpts15 Ezzard Charles, Philadelphia 5.6.52
Rocky Marciano wko13 Jersey Joe Walcott, Philadelphia
 23.9.52
 wko1 Jersey Joe Walcott, Chcago 15.5.53
 wrsf11 Roland LaStarza, New York 24.9.53
 wpts15 Ezzard Charles, New York 17.6.54
 wko8 Ezzard Charles, New York 17.9.54
 wrsf9 Don Cockell, San Francisco 16.5.55
 wko9 Archie Moore, New York 21.9.55
Marciano announced his retirement as undefeated champion
Floyd Patterson wko5 Archie Moore, Chicago 30.11.56
 wrsf10 Tommy Jackson, New York 29.7.57
 wko6 Pete Rademacher, Seattle 22.8.57
 wret12 Roy Harris, Los Angeles 18.8.58
 wko11 Brian London, Indianapolis 1.5.59
Ingemar Johansson wrsf3 Floyd Patterson, New York
 26.6.59
Floyd Patterson wko5 Ingemar Johansson, New York
 20.6.60
 wko6 Ingemar Johansson, Miami 13.3.61
 wko4 Tom McNeeley, Toronto 4.12.61
Sonny Liston wko1 Floyd Patterson, Chicago 25.9.62
 wko1 Floyd Patterson, Las Vegas 22.7.63
Cassius Clay wret6 Sonny Liston, Miami 25.2.64
Clay changed his name to Muhammad Ali. He was stripped of

*WBA title because he signed for return bout with Liston,
14.9.64*
Ernie Terrell wpts15 Eddie Machen, Chicago 5.3.65
 (vacant WBA title)
Muhammad Ali wko1 Sonny Liston, Maine 25.5.65
Ernie Terrell wpts15 George Chulavo, Toronto 1.11.65
 (WBA title)
Muhammad Ali wrsf12 Floyd Patterson, Las Vegas
 22.11.65
Muhammad Ali wpts15 George Chuvalo, Toronto 29.3.66
Muhammad Ali wrsf6 Henry Cooper, Highbury Stadium
 21.5.66
Ernie Terrell wpts15 Doug Jones, Houston 28.6.66
 (WBA title)
Muhammad Ali wko3 Brian London, London 6.8.66
Muhammad Ali wrsf12 Karl Mildenberger, Frankfurt
 10.9.66
Muhammad Ali wrsf3 Cleveland Williams, Houston
 14.11.66
Muhammad Ali wpts15 Ernie Terrell, Houston 6.2.67
 (undisputed title)
 wko7 Zora Folley, New York 22.3.67
Ali stripped of both titles for refusing to join US Army, 28.4.67
Joe Frazier wrsf11 Buster Matthis, New York 4.3.68
 (New York State version of vacant title)
Jimmy Ellis wpts15 Jerry Quarry, Oakland 27.4.68
 (WBA version of vacant title)
Joe Frazier wret2 Manuel Ramos, New York 24.6.68
 (New York State title)
Jimmy Ellis wpts15 Floyd Patterson, Stockholm 14.9.68
 (WBA title)
Joe Frazier wpts15 Oscar Bonavena, Philadelphia 10.12.68
 (New York State title)
Joe Frazier wko1 Dave Zyglewicz, Houston 22.4.69
 (New York State title)
Joe Frazier wrsf7 Jerry Quarry, New York 23.6.69
 (New York State title)
Joe Frazier wret4 Jimmy Ellis, New York 16.2.70
 (undisputed title)
 wko2 Bob Foster, Detroit 18.11.70
 wpts15 Muhammad Ali, New York 8.3.71
 wrsf4 Terry Daniels, New Orleans 15.1.72
 wrsf4 Ron Stander, Omaha 26.5.72
George Foreman wrsf2 Joe Frazier, Kingston Jamaica
 22.1.73
 wko1 Joe Roman, Tokyo 1.9.73
 wrfs2 Ken Norton, Caracas 26.3.74
Muhammad Ali wko8 George Foreman, Kinshasa
 30.10.74
 wrsf15 Chuck Wepner, Cleveland 24.3.75
 wrsf11 Ron Lyle, Las Vegas 16.5.75
 wpts15 Joe Bugner, Kuala Lumpur 1.7.75
 wret14 Joe Frazier, Manila 1.10.75
 wko5 Jean-Pierre Coopman, Puerto Rico 20.2.76
 wpts15 Jimmy Young, Maryland 30.4.76
 wrsf5 Richard Dunn, Munich 25.5.76
 wpts15 Ken Norton, New York 28.9.76
 wpts15 Alfredo Evangelista, Maryland 16.5.77
 wpts15 Earnie Shavers, New York 29.9.77
Leon Spinks wpts15 Muhammad Ali, Las Vegas 15.2.78
*Spinks was stripped of the WBC version for failure to defend
against **Ken Norton**., who was proclaimed WBC champion*
Larry Holmes wpts15 Ken Norton, Las Vegas 10.6.78
 (WBC title)

Muhammad Ali wpts15 Leon Spinks, New Orleans
15.9.78 *(WBA title)*
Larry Holmes wko7 Alfredo Evangelista, Las Vegas
10.11.7 *(WBC title)*
Larry Holmes wrsf7 Osvaldo Ocasio, Las Vegas 24.3.79
wrsf12 Mike Weaver, New York 22.6.79
wrsf11 Earnie Shavers, Las Vegas 28.9.79
*Ali announced his retirement as WBA champion, September
1979*
John Tate wpts15 Gerrie Coetzee, Johannesburg 20.10.79
(vacant WBA title)
Larry Holmes wko6 Lorenzo Zanon, Las Vegas 3.2.80
wrsf8 Leroy Jones, Las Vegas 31.3.80
Mike Weaver wko15 John Tate, Knoxville 31.3.80
(WBA title)
Larry Holmes wrsf7 Scott Le Doux, Bloomington 7.7.80
wret10 Muhammad Ali, Las Vegas 2.10.80
Mike Weaver wko13 Gerrie Coetzee, Sun City 25.10.80
(WBA title)
Larry Holmes wpts15 Trevor Berbick, Las Vegas 11.4.81
wrsf3 Leon Spinks, Detroit 12.6.81
Mike Weaver wpts15 James Tillis, Rosemount 3.10.81
(WBA title)
Larry Holmes wrsf11 Renaldo Snipes, Pittsburgh 6.11.81
wdis13 Gerry Cooney, Las Vegas 11.6.82
wpts15 Randy Cobb, Houston 26.11.82
Michael Dokes wrsf1 Mike Weaver, Las Vegas 10.12.82
(WBA title)
Larry Holmes wpts12 Lucien Rodriguez, Scranton 27.3.83
wpts12 Tim Witherspoon, Las Vegas 20.5.83
Michael Dokes drew15 Mike Weaver, Las Vegas 20.5.83
(WBA title)
Larry Holmes wrsf5 Scott Frank, Atlantic City 10.9.83
Gerrie Coetzee wko10 Michael Dokes, Richfield 23.9.8
(WBA title)
*Holmes relinquished WBC title and accepted recognition by
the newly formed International Boxing Federation*
Tim Witherspoon wpts12 Greg Page, Las Vegas 9.3.84
(vacant WBC title)
Pinklon Thomas wpts12 Tim Witherspoon, Las Vegas
31.8.84 *(WBC title)*
Larry Holmes wrsf12 James 'Bonecrusher' Smith, Las
Vegas 9.11.84
(IBF title)
Greg Page wko8 Gerrie Coetzee, Sun City 1.12.84
(WBA title)
Larry Holmes wrsf10 David Bey, Las Vegas 15.3.85
(IBF title)

Tony Tubbs wpts15 Greg Page, Buffalo, NY 29.4.85
(WBA title)
Larry Holmes wpts15 Carl Williams, Reno 20.5.85
(IBF title)
Pinklon Thomas wko8 Mike Weaver, Las Vegas 15.6.85
(WBC title)
Michael Spinks wpts15 Larry Holmes, Las Vegas 21.9.85
(IBF title)
Tim Witherspoon wpts15 Tony Tubbs, Atlanta 17.1.86
(WBA title)
Trevor Berbick wpts12 Pinklon Thomas, Las Vegas
22.3.86 *(WBC title)*
Michael Spinks wpts15 Larry Holmes, Las Vegas 19.4.86
(IBF title)
Tim Witherspoon wrsf11 Frank Bruno, London 19.7.86
(WBA title)
Michael Spinks wrsf4 Steffen Tangstad, Las Vegas 6.9.86
(IBF title)
*Spinks relinquished the IBF title for refusing to defend
against Tony Tucker*
Mike Tyson wrsf2 Trevor Berbick, Las Vegas 22.11.86
(WBC title)
James Smith wrsf1 Tim Witherspoon, New York 12.12.86
(WBA title)
Mike Tyson wpts12 James 'Bonecrusher' Smith, Las
Vegas 7.3.87
(WBA/WBC titles)
Mike Tyson wrsf6 Pinklon Thomas, Las Vegas 30.5.87
(WBA/WBC titles)
Tony Tucker wrsf10 James Douglas, Las Vegas 30.5.87
(vacant IBF title)
Mike Tyson wpts12 Tony Tucker, Las Vegas 1.8.87
(undisputed title)
wrsf7 Tyrell Biggs, Atlantic City 16.10.87
wrsf4 Larry Holmes, Atlantic City 22.1.88
wrsf2 Tony Tubbs, Tokyo 21.3.88
wko1 Michael Spinks, Atlantic City 27.6.88
wrsf5 Frank Bruno, Las Vegas 25.2.89
Francesco Damiani wko3 Johnny Duplooy, Syracuse
6.5.89 *(vacant WBO title)*
Mike Tyson wrsf1 Carl Williams, Atlantic City 21.7.89
Francesco Damiani wrtd2 Daniel Netto, Cesena 16.12.89
(WBO title)
James Douglas wko10 Mike Tyson, Tokyo 11.2.90
Evander Holyfield wko3 James Douglas 25.10.90
Ray Mercer wko9 Francesco Damiani, Atlantic City
11.1.91 *(WBO title)*
Evander Holyfield wpts12 George Foreman, Atlantic City
9.4.91
Ray Mercer wrsf5 Tommy Morrison, Atlantic City
18.10.91 *(WBO title)*
*Mercer was stripped of the WBO title because he signed to fight
Larry Holmes, 7.2.92. Holmes won on points.*
Evander Holyfield wrsf7 Bert Cooper, Atlanta 23.11.91
Michael Moorer wrsf5 Bert Cooper, Atlantic City 15.2.92
(WBO title)

COMPUTER RATINGS

THE FIRST 50 YEARS

These computer ratings for the first 50 years of gloved world title fights cover the champions from John L. Sullivan to James J. Braddock. Among the factors taken into account when feeding the computer program were skill, power, strength, stamina, title defences, bodyweight, complete ring records and the calibre of opponents. The authors also added personal feelings to go with the facts.

1. JACK JOHNSON (1908-1919)
Born Galveston, Texas, 31 March 1878. Died N. Carolina, 10 June 1946
Ht.: 6ft., Wt: 13st. 10lb (192lbs). Reach: 74in. Chest: 38-43in. Fist: 14in.
Nicknames: Li'l Artha and The Galveston Giant
Career span: 1897-1928
Record: 113 fights, 79 wins (45 KOs*), 12 draws, 8 losses (KO'd 5)
14 no decisions. Total rounds boxed: 977.
Age at which title was won: 30, in his 79th fight.
*KOs as in stoppages as well as count-outs

2. GENE TUNNEY (1926-1928)
Born New York City, 25 May 1898
Died Greenwich, Connecticut, 7 November 1978
Ht.: 6ft.1in Wt.: 13st. 5lb (187lbs)
Reach: 77in. Chest: 42-45in. Fist: 11.25in.
Nickname: The Fighting Marine
Career span: 1915-1928
Record: 77 fights, 57 wins (42 KOs), 1 draw, 1 loss.

17 no decisions, 1 dnc. Total rounds boxed: 535.
Age at which title was won: 28, in his 75th fight.

3. JACK DEMPSEY (1919-1926)
Born Manassaa, Colorado, 24 June 1895
Died New York, 31 May 1983
Ht.: 6ft.1in Wt.: 13st. 4lb (186lbs)
Reach: 77in. Chest: 42-46in. Fist: 11.25in.
Nickname: Manassa Mauler
Career span: 1914-1940
Record: 81 fights, 60 wins (49 KOs), 8 draws, 7 losses (KO'd 1)
6 no decisions. Total rounds boxed: 450.
Age at which title was won: 24, in his 73rd fight

4. JAMES J. JEFFRIES (1899-1905)
Born Caroll, Ohio, 15 April 1875
Died Burbank, California, 3 March 1953
Ht.: 6ft. 2.5in Wt.: 15st. 7lb (217lbs)
Reach: 76.5in. Chest: 43-48.5in. Fist: 13.5in.
Nickname: The Boilermaker and The Californian Grizzly Bear
Career span: 1896-1910
Record: 21 fights, 18 wins (15 KOs), 1 loss (KO'd 1), 2 draws.
Total rounds boxed: 209.
Age at which title was won: 24, in his 13th fight.

5. BOB FITZSIMMONS (1897-1899)
Born Helston, Cornwall, 4 June 1862. Died Chicago, 22 October 1917
Ht.: 5ft. 11.75in Wt.: 11st. 8lb (162lbs)
Reach: 71.75in. Chest: 41-44in. Fist: 12.5in.
Nickname: Freckled Bob and Ruby Robert.
Career span: 1880-1914
Record: 62 fights, 40 wins (32 KOs), 11 losses (KO'd 8)
10 no decisions, 1 dnc. Total rounds boxed: 290.
Age at which title was won: 35, in his 45th fight.

6. JAMES J. CORBETT (1892-1897)
Born San Francisco, 1 September 1866
Died Bayside, Long Island, 18 February 1933
Ht.: 6ft.1in Wt.: 13st (182lbs)
Reach: 73in. Chest: 38-42in. Fist: 12.75in.
Nickname: Gentleman Jim
Career span: 1884-1903
Record: 19 fights, 11 wins (7 KOs), 2 draws, 4 losses (KO'd 3), 2 dnc.
Total rounds boxed: 215.
Age at which title was won: 26, in his 13th fight.

7. JOHN L. SULLIVAN (1882-1892)
Born Roxbury, Mass., 15 October 1858
Died Abington, Mass., 2 February 1918
Ht.: 5ft.10in Wt.: 13st. 6lb (188lbs)
Reach: 74in. Chest: 43-48in. Fist: 14in.
Nickname: The Boston Strong Boy
Career span: 1878-1905
Record: 42 fights, 38 wins (33 KOs*), 3 draws, 1 loss (KO'd 1)
Total rounds boxed: 258.
Age at which title was won: 26, in his 35th fight.

8. TOMMY BURNS (1906-1908)
Born Chesley, Ontario, 17 June 1881
Died Vancouver, 10 May 1955
Ht.: 5ft. 7in Wt.: 12st. 5lb (173lbs)
Reach: 74.5in. Chest: 40-44in. Fist: 12in.
Career span: 1900-1920

Record: 60 fights, 46 wins (36 KOs), 8 draws, 5 losses (KO'd 1), 1ND
Total rounds boxed: 516.
Age at which title was won: 25, in his 42nd fight.

9. MAX SCHMELING (1930-1932)
Born Klein Luckaw, Brandenburg, Germany, 28 September 1905
Ht.: 6ft. 1in. Wt.: 13st. 4lb (186lbs)
Reach: 76in. Chest: 43-47in. Fist: 12in.
Nickname: The Black Uhlan
Career span: 1924-1948
Record: 70 fights, 56 wins (38 KOs), 4 draws, 10 losses (KO'd 5)
Total rounds boxed: 475.
Age at which title was won: 24, in his 50th fight.

10. MAX BAER (1934-1935)
Born Omaha, Nebraska, 11 February 1909
Died Hollywood, 21 November 1959
Ht.: 6ft. 2.5in. Wt.: 15st (210lbs)
Reach: 81in. Chest: 44-47in. Fist: 12in.
Nickname: The Livermore Larruper and Madcap Maxie
Career span: 1929-1941
Record: 83 fights, 70 wins (52 KOs), 13 losses (KO'd 3
Total rounds boxed: 406.
Age at which title was won: 25, in his 47th fight.

11. JESS WILLARD (1915-1919)
Born Pottawatomie County, Kansas, 29 December 1881
Died Los Angeles, 15 December 1968
Ht.: 6ft. 5.25in. Wt.: 17st. 8lb (246lbs)
Reach: 83in. Chest: 46-49.5in. Fist: 14in.
Nickname: The Pottawatomie Giant.
Career span: 1911-1923
Record: 35 fights, 24 wins (21 KOs), 1 draw, 6 losses (KO'd 3)
4 no decisions. Total rounds boxed: 273.
Age at which title was won: 33, in his 31st fight.

12. PRIMO CARNERA (1933-1934)
Born Sequals, Italy, 26 October 1906
Died Sequals, 29 June 1967
Ht.: 6ft. 5.75in. Wt.: 18st. 6lb (258lbs)
Reach: 85.5in. Chest: 48-54in. Fist: 14.75in.
Nickname: The Ambling Alp
Career span: 1928-1945
Record: 103 fights, 88 wins (69 KOs), 14 losses (KO'd 5), 1 dnc.
Total rounds boxed: 406.
Age at which title was won: 26, in his 82nd fight.

13. JACK SHARKEY (1932-1933)
Born Binghampton, New York, 6 October 1902
Ht.: 6ft. Wt.: 14st. 6lb.
Reach: 74.5in. Chest: 40.5 - 45.5in. Fist: 12.75in.
Nicknames: The Boston Gob and The Weeping Warrior
Career span: 1924-1936
Record: 55 fights, 38 wins (14 KOs), 3 draws, 13 losses (KO'd 4)
1 no decision. Total rounds boxed: 462.
Age at which title was won: 29, in his 47th fight.

14. JAMES J. BRADDOCK (19251937)
Born New York City, 6 December 1905
Died New Jersey, 29 November 1974
Ht.: 6ft. 2in. Wt.: 13st. 8lb (192lbs)
Reach: 75in. Chest: 41-44in. Fist: 11.5in.
Nickname: Cinderella Man
Career span: 1926-1938
Record: 86 fights, 46 wins (27 KOs), 4 draws, 23 losses

(KO'd 2)
11 no decisions, 2 dnc. Total rounds boxed: 695.
Age at which title was won: 29, in his 84th fight.

15. MARVIN HART (1905-1906)
Born Jefferson County, Kentucky, 16 September 1876
Died Fern Creek, Kentucky, 17 September 1931
Ht: 5ft 11.25in, Wt: 13st 6lbs (190lbs)
Reach: 74in. Chest: 42-45in. Fist: 12in.
Nickname: The Kentucky Plumber
Career span: 1899-1910
Record: 48 fights, 29 wins (20 KOs), 4 draws, 7 losses (KO'd 4), 8 no decisions.
11 no decisions, 2 dnc. Total rounds boxed: 695.
Age at which title was won: 28, in his 36th fight.

THE SECOND 50 YEARS

These computer ratings for the second 50 years of gloved world heavyweight title fights cover the champions from Joe Louis to Evander Holyfield. Of the 'Alphabet Boys', only Ken Norton and Tim Witherspoon were considered. Michael Spinks was not included because the vast majority of his fights were in the light-heavyweight division.

1. JOE LOUIS (1937-1948)
Born Lafayette, Alabama, 13 May 1914
Died Las Vegas, 12 April 1981
Ht.: 6ft. 1.5in. Wt.: 14st. 2lb (198lbs).
Reach: 76in. Chest: 42 - 45in. Fist: 11.75in.
Nicknames: The Brown Bomber
Career span: 1934-1951
Record: 70 fights, 67 wins (53 KOs), 3 losses (KO'd 2).
Total rounds boxed: 452.
Age at which title was won: 23, in his 36th fight.

2. MUHAMMAD ALI (1964-1967, 1974-1978)
Born Louisville, Kentucky, 17 January 1942
Ht.: 6ft. 3in. Wt.: 15st. 10lb (220lbs)
Reach: 82in. Chest: 43-45.5in. Fist: 12.5in.
Nicknames: The Louisville Lip and The Greatest.
Career span: 1960-1981
Record: 61 fights, 56 wins (37 KOs), 5 losses (stopped once).
Total rounds boxed: 551.
Age at which title was first won: 22, in his 20th fight.

3. ROCKY MARCIANO (1952-1955)
Born Brockton, Mass., 1 September 1923
Died in an air crash Newton, Iowa, 31 August 1969
Ht.: 5ft. 10.25in. Wt.: 13st. 2lb (184lbs)
Reach: 68in. Chest: 39-42in. Fist: 11.5in.
Nickname: The Brockton Blockbuster.
Career span: 1947-1955
Record: 49 fights, 49 wins (43 KOs). Total rounds boxed: 240.
Age at which title was won: 29, in his 43rd fight

4. MIKE TYSON (1986-1990)
Born Brooklyn, New York, 30 June 1966
Ht.: 5ft. 11in. Wt.: 15st 6lbs (219lbs).
Reach: 71in. Chest: 43-45in. Fist: 13in.
Career span: 1985-1991

Nicknames: Iron Mike, Mighty Mike
Record: 42 fights, 41 wins (36 KOs), 1 loss (ko'd).
Total rounds boxed: 157
Age at which title was won: 20, in his 28th fight.

5. GEORGE FOREMAN (1973-1974)
Born Marshall, Texas, 22 January 1948
Ht.: 6ft. 4in. Wt.: 16st 6lbs (230lbs)
Reach: 82in. Chest: 42-44.5in. Fist: 12in.
Nickname: The Punchin' Preacher
Career span: 1969-1977. He announced a comeback in 1987.
Record: 74 fights, 71 wins (66KOs), 3 losses (KO'd 1).
Total rounds boxed: 272
Age at which title was won: 25, in his 38th fight.

6. LARRY HOLMES (1978-1985)
Born Cuthbert, Georgia, 3 November 1949
Ht.: 6ft. 4in. Wt.: 15st 3lbs (215lbs)
Reach: 81in. Chest: 45-48in. Fist: 13.5in.
Nicknames: The Easton Assasin and The Black Cloud
Career span: 1973-1988. He announced a comeback in 1991.
Record: 57 fights, 54 wins (37 KOs), 3 losses (ko'd 1).
Total rounds boxed: 413
Age at which title was won: 28, in his 28th fight.

7. SONNY LISTON (1962-1964)
Born Arkansas, 8 May 1932.
Died Las Vegas, 30 December 1970
Ht.: 6ft. 1in. Wt.: 15st. 3lb (213lbs)
Reach: 84in. Chest: 44-46.5in. Fist: 15in.
Nickname: Old Stoneface.
Career span: 1953-1970
Record: 54 fights, 50 wins (39 KOs), 4 losses (KO'd 3).
Total rounds boxed: 270.
Age at which title was won: 30, in his 35th fight.8.

8. EVANDER HOLYFIELD (1990-)
Born Atmore, Alabama, 19 October 1962
Ht.: 6ft. 2in. Wt.: 15st. 1lb (211lbs)
Reach: 77in. Chest: 43-46in. Fist: 13in.
Nickname: The Real Deal.
Career span: 1984-
Record: 27 fights, 27 wins (24 KOs)
Total rounds boxed: 153
Age at which title was won: 28, in his 25th fight.

9. JOE FRAZIER (1968-1973)
Born Beaufort, South Carolina, 12 January 1944
Ht.: 5ft. 11.5in. Wt.: 14st. 7lb (203lbs)
Reach: 73.5in. Chest: 42-44in. Fist: 13in.
Nickname: Smokin' Joe
Career span: 1965-1981
Record: 37 fights, 32 wins (27 KOs), 1 draw, 4 losses (KO'd 3).
Total rounds boxed: 214.
Age at which title was won: 24, in his 20th fight.

10. JERSEY JOE WALCOTT (1951-1952)
Born Merchantville, New Jersey, 31 January 1914
Ht.: 6ft. Wt.: 13st. 8lb (190lbs)
Reach: 74in. Chest: 40-43in. Fist: 12in.
Nickname: Jersey Joe
Career span: 1930-1953
Record: 69 fights, 50 wins (30 KOs), 1 draw, 18 losses (KO'd 6).

Total rounds boxed: 475.
Age at which title was won: 37, in his 66th fight.

11. EZZARD CHARLES (1949-1951)
Born Lawrenceville, Georgia, 7 July 1921.
Died Chicago, 27 May 1970
Ht.: 6ft. Wt.: 13st (182lbs). Reach: 74in. Chest: 39-42in. Fist: 12in.
Nickname: The Cincinnati Cobra
Career span: 1940-1959
Record: 122 fights, 96 wins (58 KOs), 1 draw, 17 losses (KO'd 7). Total rounds boxed: 968.
Age at which title was won: 29, in his 74th fight.

12. FLOYD PATTERSON (1956-1959-1961)
Born Waco, North Carolina, 4 January 1935
Ht.: 5ft. 11in. Wt.: 13st. 2lb (184lbs)
Reach: 71in. Chest: 40-42in. Fist: 12.75in.
Nickname: The Peek-a-Boo Champ
Career span: 1952-1972
Record: 64 fights, 55 wins (KOs 40), 1 draw, 8 losses (KO'd 5).
Total rounds boxed: 418.
Age at which title was first won: 21, in his 32nd fight.

13. INGEMAR JOHANSSON (1959-1960)
Born Gothenburg, Sweden, 22 September 1932
Ht.: 6ft. 0.5in. Wt.: 14st (196lbs)
Reach: 72.5in. Chest: 43-45in. Fist: 13.5in.
Nickname: The Hammer of Thor
Career span: 1952-1963
Record: 28 fights, 26 wins (KOs 17), 2 losses (KO'd 2).
Total rounds boxed: 173.
Age at which title was won: 26, in his 22nd fight.

14. KEN NORTON (1978)
Born Jacksonville, Illinois, 9 August 1945
Ht.: 6ft. 3in. Wt.: 15st. 6lb (216lbs)
Reach: 80in. Chest: 45-48in. Fist: 13in.
Career span: 1967-1981
Record: 50 fights, 42 wins (33 KOs), 1 draw, 7 losses (KO'd 4).
Total rounds boxed: 319. Age at which title was won: 32 (44th fight).

15. TIM WITHERSPOON (1984, 1985-1986)
Born Philadelphia, 27 December 1957
Ht.: 6ft. 3in. Wt.: 15st 10lb (220lbs).
Reach: 77in. Chest: 43-45in. Fist: 12in.
Nickname: Terrible Tim.
Career span: 1979-
Record: 40 fights, 37 wins (24 KOs), 3 losses (KO'd 1)
Total rounds: 262.
Age at which title was first won: 26, (19th fight).

ACKNOWLEDGEMENTS

Authors Neil Duncanson and Norman Giller wish to place on record their thanks to their New York City friend Bill Cayton for allowing them the run of his incomparable Big Fights Inc film collection, and also full access to his impressive picture library. The publishers and authors would also like to thank the following for their cooperation in loaning photographs for use in this publication. Full effort has been made to locate the copyright owners of every photograph; we apologize for any omissions, which will be rectified in future editions. Allsport Photographic: pages 153, 156, 157, 160, 162, 163, 165, 168, 169, 176, 177, 178, 179, 180, 181, 182; Allsport USA: pages 165, 168, 169; Associated Press: page 175.

Their thanks, too, to the champions who willingly gave of their time to share their memories, and particularly to Max Schmeling, Jersey Joe Walcott, Floyd Patterson, Ingemar Johansson, Joe Frazier, Archie Moore and George Foreman for being so hospitable. No authors can produce a boxing book without bowing the knee to the bibles of the sport, *The Ring* magazine, *The Ring Record Book and Boxing Encyclopedia* and *Boxing News*. Thanks, also, to Jennifer Jones for her diligent editing, Bill Mason for his design work, the computer expertise and record book knowledge of Michael Giller, the seconding work of Derek O'Dell, and the refereeing of Boxtree motivators Elaine Collins and Stephanie Walsh.

Thanks also to the following for their valued help: Al Braverman, Howard Bingham, *Boxing Illustrated*, British Museum, British Newspaper Library, Frank Bruno, Barbara Piatelli Dempsey, Mickey Duff, Federal Bureau of Investigation, German Press Agency, Reg Gutteridge, Peter Heller, Alan Hurndall, International Boxing Hall of Fame, Marcia Kapustin, Terry Lawless, Library of Congress, Joe Louis Barrow Jr, Louisville Public Libraries, Peter Marciano, Missouri State Penitentiary, Graham Miller, Ron Olver, Professor Randy Roberts of Indiana State University, *Sports Illustrated*, John Tunney, Wisconsin Centre for Film and Theatre Research, Professor Alan Woods, of Ohio State University, and also to Yale University.

Thanks, too, to Mike Tyson for helping to provide information, and we wish him a happy end to his personal nightmare. And a final thanks to the one and only Muhammad Ali for showing us what dignity is all about.

The authors dedicate this book to all the heavyweight boxing champions, who have made the world a more exciting place ... and, in particular, to Muhammad Ali, The Greatest.